A DICTIONARY OF
CRIMINOLOGY

edited by
Dermot Walsh and Adrian Poole

Routledge & Kegan Paul
London, Boston, Melbourne and Henley

First published in 1983
by Routledge & Kegan Paul plc
39 Store Street, London WC1E 7DD,
9 Park Street, Boston, Mass. 02108, USA,
296 Beaconsfield Parade, Middle Park,
Melbourne, 3206, Australia, and
Broadway House, Newtown Road,
Henley-on-Thames, Oxon RG9 1EN
Set in 10pt Times
Printed in Great Britain by
Billing & Sons Ltd
Worcester

Library of Congress Cataloging in Publication Data

A Dictionary of criminology.
1. Criminal justice, Administration of—England—Dictionaries.
2. Criminal justice, Administration of—Wales—Dictionaries. I. Walsh,
Dermot. II. Poole, Adrian, 1934–
HV6949.E5D5 1983   364'.03'21   83–4611

ISBN 0–7100–9549–X
ISBN 0–7100–9556–2 (pbk.)

A DICTIONARY OF
CRIMINOLOGY

Introduction

Now that Criminology has been established for some years in academic institutions, and particularly in view of developments in theory and empirical knowledge, we feel that there is a strong need for a dictionary for students of the subject to function as a guide to concepts and terminology.

Our principles of selection involved choosing terms currently in use in criminology (chiefly in psychology, psychiatry, penology, sociology, social work and in the law of England and Wales), together with some limited historical information.

This has not been an easy task and we have had much heart-searching over what to include or exclude to keep within out compass and inevitably final decisions represent both a compromise and an act of editorial authoritarianism. (Regrettably for reasons of space nearly all biographical information had to be excluded, with one notable exception.) Our thanks are due to the many contributors who have co-operated so willingly and painstakingly. The errors remain ours alone.

Abbreviations

Sources frequently referred to are abbreviated as follows:

AJS	*American Journal of Sociology*
ASR	*American Sociological Review*
BJC (BJD)	*British Journal of Criminology* (formerly *Delinquency*)
BJS	*British Journal of Sociology*
CLR	*Criminal Law Review*
HJ	*Howard Journal of Penology & Crime Prevention*
HORS	*Home Office Research Study*
JCLC	*Journal of Criminal Law & Criminology*
JCLCPS	*Journal of Criminal Law, Criminology & Police Science* (from 1973 becomes *JCLC*)
PSJ	*Prison Service Journal*

Contributors

John C. Alderson	Formerly Chief Constable, Devon & Cornwall Constabulary
Peter Archard	Research Fellow, Department of Social Science, Polytechnic of the South Bank
John Baldwin	Lecturer in Law, Institute of Judicial Administration, University of Birmingham
Mervyn Bennun	Lecturer in Law, University of Exeter
Deryck Beyleveld	Lecturer in Criminology, Centre for Criminological & Socio-Legal Studies, University of Sheffield
Anthony E. Bottoms	Professor of Criminology, Centre for Criminological & Socio-Legal Studies, University of Sheffield
Roy A. Carr-Hill	Social Statistician, MRC Medical Sociology Unit, University of Aberdeen
Jason Ditton	Lecturer in Sociology, University of Glasgow
William M. Donovan	Consultant Forensic Psychiatrist, Langdon Hospital
David P. Farrington	Lecturer in Criminology, Institute of Criminology, University of Cambridge
M. Philip Feldman	Senior Lecturer in Psychology, University of Birmingham
William J. Forsythe	Lecturer in Social Work, University of Exeter
Henri Giller	Lecturer in Law, University of Keele

CONTRIBUTORS

Robin Griffiths	Barrister at Law, Gray's Inn
Stuart Henry	Senior Lecturer in Sociology, Trent Polytechnic
J. Michael Hepworth	Senior Lecturer in Sociology, University of Aberdeen
William J. O. Jordan	Lecturer in Social Work, University of Exeter
Nigel Lemon	Head of Department of Social Studies, Sunderland Polytechnic
Sarah McCabe	Formerly Senior Research Officer, Centre for Criminological Research, University of Oxford
Michael Maguire	Senior Research Officer, Centre for Criminological Research, University of Oxford
Patricia Mayhew	Principal Research Officer, Home Office Research & Planning Unit
James F. Orford	Senior Lecturer in Clinical Psychology, University of Exeter
Kenneth Pease	Head of School of Sociology & Social Policy, Ulster Polytechnic
Adrian R. Poole	Lecturer in Sociology, University of Exeter
Stanley Rachman	Professor of Abnormal Psychology, Institute of Psychiatry, London
Andrew Rutherford	Lecturer in Law, University of Southampton
Michael N. Smith	Director of Studies, Sociology, University of Bath
Keith Soothill	Senior Lecturer in Sociology, University of Lancaster
Nicholas Stern	Professor of Economics, University of Warwick
Nigel D. Walker	Wolfson Professor of Criminology, University of Cambridge
Gerald D.P. Wallen	Consultant Psychiatrist, Exe Vale Hospital
Dermot P. Walsh	Lecturer in Sociology, University of Exeter
Donald J. West	Professor of Clinical Criminology, Director of the Institute of Criminology, University of Cambridge

CONTRIBUTORS

Paul Wilkinson	Professor of Politics, University of Aberdeen
Karen Williams	Research Officer, Home Office Research & Planning Unit

A

Abduction Taking away: the law penalises those who would thus exploit women, intending marriage or unlawful sexual intercourse, where the taking is by force or for the sake of her property. The rights of parents are also protected over a girl under eighteen (or a mentally defective female of any age) who is taken away for unlawful sexual intercourse; if the girl is under sixteen it is an offence, whatever the motive, where there is no lawful authority or excuse.

See *Sexual Offences Act* (1956), ss. 17 and 19–21 (re-enacting earlier laws): a group of offences 'not suitable for a modern statute'. (Criminal Law Revision Committee, *Working Paper on Sexual Offences* (1980), p. 54. See also their 14th Report, *Offences Against the Person* (Cmnd 7844, 1980), p. 102.) Proposed revision of the law would penalise the abduction of a child under fourteen from lawful parental control; the *Working Paper* ponders the need for any more extensive regulation. (See also comments by Hogan (1980), *CLR*, 584.) Few cases of abduction appear in police statistics.

See also *Child stealing*; *Kidnapping*. ARP

Abortion Unlawfully taking or administering a poison or something noxious or using an instrument intending to procure a miscarriage is proscribed by the *Offences Against the Person Act* (1861), s. 58. The *Abortion Act* (1967) provides a defence where pregnancy is terminated by a registered medical practitioner, if two such doctors are of the opinion, formed in good faith,

(a) that the continuation of the pregnancy would put the woman's health or that of her existing children at risk, mentally or physically, *or*

(b) that the child, if born, would be substantially likely to be seriously handicapped, mentally or physically. Ancillary provi-

1

sions relate to emergencies, to the location of treatment and to certification of the relevant facts by the doctors to the DHSS.

The hundred years between these two enactments had seen much controversy, especially over situations where the health of the woman was at risk. The leading case of R *v*. Bourne (1939), IKB 687 established a defence on these lines but controversy continued – and still continues – between those who would allow women fuller rights and those who would restrict them.

Committee on the Working of the Abortion Act, *Report* (Cmnd 5579, 1974); G. Williams (1978), *Textbook of Criminal Law*, pp. 249 *et seq.*; illegal abortions currently appear in police statistics at less than twelve per annum.

See also *Child destruction*; *Concealment of birth*; *Infanticide*.

ARP

Absconding. See *Escapes*.

Addiction. See *Alcoholism*; *Drug abuse*.

Affectionless character, the. See *Deprivation*.

Affray (from Fr. 'effroi'). Unlawful fighting which would terrify a bystander of reasonably firm character. An ancient offence (the punishment being in the court's discretion) prosecuted not infrequently nowadays in the maintenance of public order. As it is an indictable offence, though, and taken to the Crown Court, prosecutors 'should think hard before charging affray, which should be reserved for serious cases which were not far short of riot' (R *v*. Crimlis (1976), *CLR*, 693: comment in the Court of Appeal). The Law Commission's Working Paper no. 82, *Offences against Public Order* (1982), suggests that there should be a new statutory definition of the offence.

See also *Public order*; *Riot*. ARP

After-care It is the responsibility of Social Services Depart-ments to provide after-care supervision on release for a *young person* (q.v.) released from custodial institutions (for twelve months) and for people released on *parole* (q.v.) (until the date on which they would normally have been released on remis-sion). For parolees given *life imprisonment* (q.v.), supervision can be for the rest of their natural lives. The provision of such support involves assistance in obtaining housing, training and employment as well as the management of relationships. In addition various religious and voluntary organisations informally provide means of assisting settlement.   DPW

Age of criminal responsibility. See *Child*.

Aggression   Injurious and destructive behaviour that is socially defined as aggressive on the basis of a variety of factors to do with both the performer and the person making the evaluation.

The social reaction to violent acts and the frequency of such acts both depend partly on cultural factors. Even today many crimes of violence are carried out not for gain or for any other criminal purpose but occur in social groups in which it is normal for a verbal quarrel to lead quickly to physical combat.

Aggressive behaviour is more likely to be learned in certain social settings than others, both by direct experience and by observing other people. Much work has been expended in testing the assertion that the television viewing of violence is related to real-life aggression. The evidence is still unclear and it is difficult to separate out televised violence as a specific influence from all others, such as copying real models in the school, the street, pub or workplace.

Once aggressive behaviours have been acquired by someone, whether or not they will be performed depends on: the presence of a model already behaving aggressively; a higher than usual level of emotional arousal; whether or not the person has just had an unpleasant experience, whether physical or verbal, has lost a valuable reinforcer (reward), has been frustrated in attaining an important goal, or has been ordered to aggress (the more removed is the victim the higher the probability of aggression).

It is often assumed that alcohol inevitably increases aggression; it does so if the person already knows how to behave aggressively and is in a setting in which alcohol gives one a licence to do so.

The nature of the opponent is important. Aggressive behaviours are less likely if the opponent not only has at least an equal capacity to retaliate but is known to be prepared to do so. Physical strength and skill also matter – many forms of combat require one or both. It is for these reasons that only a small minority of viewers at the most are likely to copy in real life the unarmed combat techniques so often shown on television.

3

ALCOHOL AND CRIME

Aggressive actions are often followed by outcomes satisfying to the aggressor. They may be material, or less tangible, such as social approval or enhanced status. Aggressors learn to deal with the distress of the victim by derogating his importance or social value, by denying the severity of his pain, or by displacing the responsibility for the aggressive actions on to superiors – 'I was only obeying orders' is a familiar excuse for atrocities in many parts of the world.   MPF

Alcohol and crime Alcohol is a depressant drug the abuse of which has for centuries had strong connections with crime (Glatt, 1977). Crime may be committed to obtain it, or by those addicted to it or by those under its influence whose inhibitions and self-control are temporarily lowered. Beyond the Licensing Laws, legislation to limit its use does not exist and much crime is committed by people who are drunk at the time, and by habitual drunkards (Washbrook, 1976). Just how much is impossible to say, given the prevalent tolerance of its use (with its concomitant reporting implications), since convictions for drunk and disorderly behaviour are only part of the problem (see Great Britain, Home Office, 1979).

Its involvement in serious crime, driving offences (Selzer, 1977) and trivial nuisance offences is likely to be high, and its heavy use by teenagers generates special difficulties (Heather, 1981).

M.M. Glatt (1977), 'The English drink problem through the ages', *Proc. Roy. Soc. Med.*, 70(3), 202; Home Office (1979), *Offences of Drunkenness*: *England & Wales, 1978*, Cmnd 7707; N. Heather (1981), 'Relationships between delinquency and drunkenness among Scottish young offenders', *Brit. J. Alcohol & Alcoholism*, 16(2), 50; M.L. Selzer *et al.* (1977), 'The drunken driver: a psychological study', *Drug and Alcohol Dependence*, 2(4), 239; R.A.H. Washbrook (1976), 'The criminology of the chronic alcoholic offender', *J. Alcoholism*, 11(I), 9.

See also *Alcoholism*; *Drug abuse*.   DPW

Alcoholism Although the potential of alcohol for doing harm has been recognised throughout history, the recognition that individuals may be personally addicted to alcohol has probably achieved widespread recognition only within the last hundred years. Significant landmarks were the publication, around 1885, of the American Dr Benjamin Rush's *An Enquiry into the* *effects of Spiritous Liquors upon the Human Body and their Influence upon the Happiness of Society*, the beginnings of the self-help organisation Alcoholics Anonymous in the USA in the 1930s and the publication in 1960 of E.M. Jellinek's *The Disease Concept of Alcoholism*.

The connection between alcoholism and crime is complex. A large proportion of offenders report drinking alcohol shortly before the commission of their crimes. Apart from drunken driving offences, which give particular cause for concern, the number of offences of drunkenness in England and Wales per 10,000 of the population aged fifteen years and over rose from 14.0 in 1950 to 28.1 in 1978. A survey of drunkenness offenders appearing in two London courts revealed that a high proportion had drinking problems (D. Gath, C. Hensman, A. Hawker, M. Kelly and G. Edwards (1968), 'The drunk in court: a survey of drunkenness offenders from two London courts', *Brit. Med. J.*, 4, 808). Surveys of prisoners such as those of C. Hensman (1969), 'Problems of drunkenness amongst male recidivists', in T. Cook, D. Gath and C. Hensman, eds, *The Drunkenness Offender*, and T. Gibbens and M. Silberman (1970), 'Alcoholism among prisoners', *Psychol. Med.*, I, 73, have found percentages with serious drinking problems varying between 10 and 65. In 1971 a Home Office Working Party recommended the provision of detoxification centres and rehabilitation hostels to serve the needs of chronic drunkenness offenders (*Habitual Drunken Offenders*). The latter now exist on a considerable scale in the UK, USA and Canada. Detoxification centres, although widespread in the USA and Canada, have been set up in Britain, only on an experimental basis, in Manchester and Leeds. Police are empowered to take people straight to a detoxification centre without charging them. The role of the alcohol detoxification centre illustrates how alcoholism lies at the interface of medical, social and legal domains.

The term alcoholism has come under increasing criticism recently, and has now disappeared from the International Classification of Diseases, and from the vocabulary of such bodies as the World Health Organization and the Department of Health in Britain. In its place has appeared the 'alcohol dependence syndrome', a concept which implies that the degree of an individual's dependence upon alcohol can vary independently along a number of dimensions – physiological, behavioural, subjective – and that the pattern of dependence is at least partly determined by social and cultural factors. Others

5

would go further and abandon any pretence that alcohol problems take the form of a syndrome, an -ism or, to use the language of the late nineteenth and early twentieth centuries, a 'mania'. Others have pointed to the similarities between different forms of excessive behaviour: alcoholism, drug addiction, compulsive gambling, compulsive eating, and even 'workaholism' and 'hypersexuality'.   JFO

Alienation   A vague (and much abused) term; originally used by Marx, it is clarified by M. Seeman (1959), in 'On the meaning of alienation', *ASR*, 24(6), 783, who lists its varieties as a sense of powerlessness, meaninglessness, normlessness, isolation and self-estrangement. It is in this latter sense that it has been most used, to describe the feelings of individuals estranged from social existence as a result of the division of labour in the economic system.   DPW

Amplification, deviancy   The term given to a process whereby social reaction against deviation functions to increase it. Originally coined by L.T. Wilkins in *Social Deviance* (1964, p. 85), 'deviation amplification', as he called it, was seen as affecting the population incarcerated and perhaps even crime rates.
   Amplification is a function of the degree of (in-)tolerance of non-conformity in the culture, in turn regulated by the information flow concerning the original deviance.   DPW

Anomie   A concept developed by E. Durkheim (1858–1917) in his *Suicide* (Paris, 1897) to refer to a situation where there are no social norms to ensure order, or where the norms conflict with each other. If and when social regulation breaks down (for example after a natural disaster, war or abrupt change in circumstances), individuals are left to their own devices and engage in unregulated behaviours. Anomie does not refer to a state of mind, but to a property of the social structure, and during an anomic period, when social norms no longer control men's actions, aspirations become unlimited. This concept has been extremely influential, e.g. M.B. Clinard, ed. (N.Y., 1964), *Anomie and Deviant Behaviour: a Discussion and Critique*; R. K. Merton (N.Y., 1968), *Social Theory and Social Structure*.   DPW

Anthropology, criminal.   See *Constitutional factors*.

Appeals procedure.   See *Criminal appeals*.

Approved schools.   See *Community homes*.

Area studies   This is a generic term for research studies of many different kinds which are united by a common concern with specific geographical areas and the criminal activities associated with them. Some area studies are purely *descriptive*: these may, for example, plot the statistical incidence of recorded crime in a given area or areas, or describe the life of a 'criminal area' through the eyes of its residents. Other studies are *policy-oriented*, aiming to discover ways of reducing the crime level in particular kinds of area. However, most areal research is explicitly or implicitly *explanatory*. Since the explanation of crime or offender levels in any one area necessarily involves some explicit or assumed comparison with other areas, it can be said that this kind of research is concerned *to explain the geographical distribution of crimes and/or offenders*. Ultimately, such research involves nothing less than the daunting task of understanding the way in which economic and social forces may create and/or interact with features of the physical environment (housing, land use variations; hill and valley patterns, etc.), and in turn with the perceptions of user populations, to shape the observed geographical distribution of crime.

In principle, area studies can be conducted at many different levels. For example, one might be concerned to explain differential crime patterns (i) in the different regions of a country; (ii) in different small areas within a city; (iii) in different streets on a given housing development; or (iv) in different houses or shops within a single street. In practice, most research has been conducted at the second of these levels, though there is a recent growth of interest in more micro-level studies. Worth-while results from the first type of study (regional comparisons) have been meagre.

Area studies are virtually as old as criminology itself. As soon as official criminal statistics were produced in the nineteenth century, scholars like A.M. Guerry (1802–66) began to plot the geographical incidence of recorded crime, showing substantial regional and local variation, but also persistence in high or low rates over time. A different tradition of area studies emerged a little later with the work of Henry Mayhew (1812–87) and his colleagues, who supplemented maps of recorded crime in the counties of England and Wales with first-hand observations, tramping the criminal areas of London on foot and sensitively recording details of prostitution, sneak-thieving, etc.

These promising nineteenth-century European developments were largely eclipsed by the advent of *positivism* (q.v.), with its individualistic and biological emphases. The second major phase of area studies did not begin until the 1920s: it came from America, from the sociologists of the *Chicago School* (q.v.), especially Clifford Shaw and Henry McKay. These men worked within the Chicago theoretical tradition of social ecology (though Shaw and McKay used this less than some of their urban sociology colleagues), and for this reason many modern area studies are still called 'ecological', although the term is not always strictly appropriate. Important findings from the massive Shaw/McKay research in Chicago and other US cities included (i) confirmation of the 'zonal hypothesis' that delinquency was highest in the inner city zone close to the central business district, then declined towards the periphery of the city; (ii) high rates of delinquency persisted in the inner zone despite successive waves of immigration and therefore of population turnover. These and other findings became standard background assumptions for most American criminologists, and formed part of the basis for theoretical developments like *culture conflict* (q.v.) and *differential association* (q.v.).

Shaw and McKay's work concentrated on delinquency areas, i.e. the areas where juvenile delinquents live; they paid no systematic attention to crime site location, i.e. the place where offences actually occur. Many have subsequently assumed the two to be identical or nearly so, but research has shown this to be sometimes false. (Offences are often committed close to home – especially by juveniles – but not necessarily so; in particular, 'crime-attracting' areas like city centres, industrial areas, suburban shopping complexes, etc., may have high crime rates but little or no offender residence.) Hence, modern area studies draw a sharp distinction in principle between *high offender rate areas* and *high offence rate areas*.

After the Second World War, many smaller empirical studies of census data and crime data, influenced by the Shaw/McKay tradition, were carried out in the USA. Some of these authors used more complex statistical techniques than their Chicago predecessors, especially factor analysis; others based their typology of census tracts upon the so-called *social area analysis* developed by Eshref Shevky and his colleagues. It is now

A

generally agreed that much of this work was methodologically or conceptually faulty, and area studies advanced little at this time.

Two issues of general concern were highlighted during this phase of work. First, some area studies were shown to contain examples of the so-called ecological fallacy. Because census data are available only on an areal basis, it is easy, but false, to assume that an areal correlation necessarily reflects individual behaviour. For example, in Britain one might find that high offender rate areas contain a disproportionately high number of Asian immigrant families; one might then conclude that Asian immigrants themselves have high offender rates – which is not, in fact, the case.

Second, many criminologists have strongly questioned the implicit reliance of most area studies upon recorded crime and offender rates, in view of the known severe limitations of official statistics (under-reporting, non-recording, etc.: see *crime rate*). Hence some recent area studies have sought to incorporate other measurements of crime, e.g. from *victim surveys* (q.v.). There is now a little evidence to suggest that, as between the different areas of a city, the comparative spatial distribution of 'street crimes' – theft, burglary, etc.; i.e. excluding *white-collar crime* (q.v.) – may be more valid in the official statistics than many have supposed. This clearly requires further testing.

By the late 1960s some criminologists were concluding that area studies had become repetitious and had little more to offer. Ironically, very soon afterwards, this kind of research was strongly revived, mainly as a result of the 'CPTED' approach.

'CPTED' (Crime Prevention through Environmental Design) is a generic term derived originally from the title of a book by C. Ray Jeffrey; a particular variant of CPTED is the *defensible space* (see *prevention*) movement associated with the architect Oscar Newman. Both these authors, writing independently in the early 1970s, argued that changes in urban form (design of cities, design of apartment buildings, etc.) could reduce crime levels. Whilst policy-oriented in their concern with crime *prevention* in specific areas, their work has led also to a renaissance of interest in the explanation of urban crime patterns.

A major difference in this phase of work, as against earlier area studies, has been the primary stress upon *offence* distributions rather than *offender* distributions (this reflects a shift in crime-prevention thinking from attempts to alter criminal motivation to attempts to reduce *opportunity* (q.v.) and to influence response to specific situations by environmental manipulation). This has raised a number of fresh problems of measurement, and has also led to the recent interest in micro-level analysis. A further important topic to emerge very strongly has been the spatial dimension of the offender/offence linkage – the so-called 'journey to crime' – which is being analysed in relation to perceptions of parts of the city by offenders, and their habitual patterns of movement within the city (journey to work, routes to usual leisure resorts, etc.).

A feature of this recent phase of area studies has been an entirely new interest in crime by many scholars (e.g. architects, urban planners) outside the established 'feeder' disciplines for criminology. In particular, there has been a great increase in the number and quality of contributions from the field of *human geography*. These and other innovations make the field of area studies one of considerable intellectual excitement at the time of writing, yet by the same token it is as yet difficult to make any clear judgment as to how much real progress in scholarship is being made.

Ever since Shaw and McKay, most of the intellectual impetus in area studies has come from the USA. However, there has also been a steady stream of (mostly small-scale) British studies, especially since 1950. A particularly distinctive feature of the British contribution has been the analysis of the *public housing sector*, which is much larger in Britain than in North America – a factor which, incidentally, has led to the modification of Shaw and McKay's zonal gradient when data for post-war British cities are examined. There have been a number of important British studies of the creation and maintenance of so-called 'problem council estates'. In particular, these studies have shown interest in (i) the direct and indirect effects of *local authority housing allocation systems* (and hence, more generally, in the housing market in cities as a key means of distributing populations spatially); and (ii) the *reputations of areas*, the ways in which these are constructed, and their social effects (including effects on the actions of police and other social controllers, and the consequent possibility of an areal *deviance amplification* (see *amplification*) effect). North American criminologists are now beginning to take an interest in similar issues.

See further J. Baldwin and A.E. Bottoms (1976), *The Urban Criminal*; P.J. and P.L. Brantingham, eds (Beverly Hills,

1981), *Environmental Criminology*; D.T. Herbert (1982), *The Geography of Urban Crime*; T. Morris (1957), *The Criminal Area*. AEB

Arrest To deprive a person of his liberty with the ultimate aim of bringing him to trial for a criminal offence. Common law and statute specify when an arrest may be made: most frequently the police use s. 2 of the *Criminal Law Act* (1967) when they must have at least reasonable cause for suspecting the person has committed, is committing or is about to commit an offence. Moreover, the offence must be sufficiently serious (an 'arrestable offence' being one carrying a sentence of five years' imprisonment or more). Reasonable force may be used.

There are various other powers of arrest (e.g. under warrant from a magistrate and numerous statutory provisions) and the law's uneven erosion of civil liberty is complicated, as it is also with reference to detention which may then ensue. Legal reform is urged. (See *Report of the Royal Commission on Criminal Procedure* (Cmnd 8092, 1981), pp. 40 *et seq.*)

In practice 40 per cent or so of alleged offenders (and nearly all motoring offenders) will be brought to trial by summons. Moreover, arrest will be half as frequent where the offence is petty ('summary') as when it is not. All told, 634,000 arrests were made in 1980; probably 10 to 20 per cent, though, would have been released without further proceedings being taken. The police have related powers of interrogation, search and seizure, but these are beyond our scope. (See the *Report of the Royal Commission*, above.) ARP

Arson Fire is a crucial element in our world. The abuse of fire creates a unique danger because of its propensity to spread uncontrollably and cause widespread destruction. The term arson has a long history, but in 1969 the Law Commission considered there was no need to retain the word 'arson' in their attempt to consolidate the law on criminal damage. Interestingly, the House of Commons took another view, feeling its retention in law preserved the overtones of horror in the public mind and so emphasising the seriousness of the offence. Hence, while the common law offence of arson has been abolished, the *Criminal Damage Act* (1971) still enables the offence of destroying or damaging property by *fire* to be charged as arson (s. 1(3)).

Pollock and Maitland (1911, p. 492) have observed that the

crime of arson 'is of some interest as being one of the first in which the psychical element, the intention, becomes prominent. At a very early time men must distinguish between fires that are and fires that are not intended'. Despite the range of possible damage and the degree of malicious intent, historically there was a general tendency not to allow the courts any discretionary power regarding the punishment of arson. By the eighteenth century all acts of arson – almost without exception – carried the penalty of death without benefit of clergy. (N.B. Until the 1971 Act it was still a *capital* offence to set on fire, burn or otherwise destroy Her Majesty's ships, dockyards and stores.) Nowadays the maximum penalty for arson is life imprisonment (s. 4(1)). Around half a dozen arsonists are so sentenced each year. Around 700 offenders appear each year in the Crown Courts charged with arson, of whom about two-thirds receive a custodial sentence.

The commission of arson is comparatively easy but the detection of the offender is often particularly difficult. Hence, arsonists who get caught may not be very representative of undetected arsonists. Offences of arson are frequently connected with mental disturbance on the part of the offender, but the motivational pattern prompting the act of arson is notoriously difficult to determine. While there is a small minority who commit further arson offences after being convicted, the behaviour is perhaps not so repetitive as some psychiatrists have in the past tended to believe.

F. Pollock and F.W. Maitland (2nd ed., 1911), *The History of English Law before the Time of Edward I*, vol. 2; L. Radzinowicz (1948), *A History of the English Criminal Law*, vol. 1; K.L. Soothill and P.J. Pope (1973), 'Arson: a twenty-year cohort study', *Med. Sci. Law*, 13(2), April.   KS

Assassination   The killing of individuals by treacherous means is as old as human history. The modern term 'assassination' derives from the *Assassins*, a fanatical Shiite Muslim sect active from the 11th to the 13th centuries, which dispatched chosen followers to murder leading members of the Sunni Muslim establishment and Christian princes as a sacramental duty. However, murder for motives of political ambition and rivalry was already well known to the ancients. The Greeks developed a doctrine of *tyrannicide* which claimed that the murder of a tyrant was not only justified, it was a heroic act deserving the people's gratitude.

The belief that the elimination of the oppressive ruler would bring down the edifice of autocracy and free the people was still a major driving force behind many of the nineteenth-century terrorist groups. When *Narodnaya Volya* (*People's Will*) succeeded in assassinating Tsar Alexander II in 1881, using a team of bomb-throwers, they declared that he had been killed because, among other crimes, he had hanged or exiled anyone who resisted on behalf of the people or in the cause of justice. Noble though these motives may have been, the assassination did not lead to liberty for the Russian people. It provoked a period of severe repression and retarded the prospects of gradual reform. Perhaps the most dramatic illustration of evil consequences flowing from an assassination was the murder of the Austrian Archduke Francis Ferdinand and his wife at Sarajevo, 28 June 1914, by Gavrilo Princip. The terrorist group involved can scarcely have imagined, let alone intended, the world war that they helped to ignite.

Monarchs and political leaders have always had to face the danger of assassination from two main directions: the lone killer motivated by jealousy, hatred or revenge or some private fantasy, and the political group using coup d'état, insurrection or terrorism to destroy the existing order and to seize political power. In a society such as the USA, where there is a tradition of maximum freedom of individuals, the laxest gun-laws in the world, and constant media and public contact with elected politicians, presidents and other major figures have been increasingly at risk from both kinds of killer. President John F. Kennedy, his brother Robert and Martin Luther King all died at the hands of assassins, and attempts were made on the lives of Presidents Truman, Ford and Reagan.

In almost every region of the world political assassination is one of the fastest-growing crimes. It has been assisted by the wider availability of more accurate and lethal man-portable weapons, and of bomb-making material and techniques, to an ever-increasing number of terrorist groups. Recent trends have been the targeting by certain groups (for example Red Brigades and the Provisional IRA) of middle-ranking and minor functionaries, for example in the police and prison services, members of the judiciary, businessmen and diplomats. Attacks on diplomats increased 400 per cent between 1976 and 1981. Assassination is an extremely difficult crime to combat, and for that reason is likely to remain popular with terrorist groups of all types as a low-cost, high-yield 'propaganda of the deed'.

PW

ASSAULT

Assault The law governing non-fatal violence to the person largely stems from this ancient crime and that of battery. In origin, and in theory still, an assault means an act causing someone to *apprehend* immediate and unlawful personal violence and battery means the actual infliction of such violence. The term 'common assault' in the *Offences against the Person Act* (1861), however, means assault and battery together. This Act provides that common assault may be penalised summarily or on indictment. Various rather higher penalties are provided where the victim's social position is material (e.g. police officers, clergymen, magistrates) or where the circumstances are special. The Act also provides substantial penalties for assaults occasioning actual bodily harm and for wounding and grievous bodily harm. The complicated law relating to these offences is currently being revised. (See Criminal Law Revision Committee, 14th Report, *Offences against the Person* (Cmnd 7844, 1980), pp. 68 *et seq.*)

In summary proceedings assaults on police officers feature most frequently; 14,000 or so, four times the number of common assaults. On indictment, 'wounding or other act endangering life' appears in police statistics at a current level of 4,000 per annum and 'other woundings' at a current level of 75,000 per annum.

In all, violence of the kind dealt with above accounts for about 4 per cent of crime in police statistics.

See also *Official statistics*.   ARP

Attempt A person who 'does an act which is more than merely preparatory' to the commission of an intended offence is guilty of an attempt. The law applies only when the intended offence is triable on indictment. (Sentence may be up to the maximum applicable to the intended offence.) (*Criminal Attempts Act* (1981), s. 1.) See I. Dennis (1982), 'The Criminal Attempts Act, 1981', *CLR*, 5.   ARP

Attendance centres Part-time (usually Saturday afternoon) attendance may be ordered for young offenders at places provided by the Home Secretary (as yet only in more populous areas). Junior centres are for boys under seventeen, senior centres for those between seventeen and twenty-one. The court will specify the total number of hours of attendance – maximum 24 for juniors, 36 for seniors (*Criminal Justice Acts* (1948) and (1982)). The centres are run by police officers in their free time and sometimes by prison officers. The hours are occupied with physical training, constructive work and useful talks, but there is room for initiative and individual assistance.

F. McClintock (1961), *Attendance Centres*; A. Dunlop (1980), *Junior Attendance Centres*, HORS no. 60.   ARP

Attitude change   This refers to a relatively permanent change in an individual's predisposition to evaluate a social object in a characteristic way. The phrase is commonly differentiated from other forms of social influence by its reference to non-transient changes in behaviour, and by its reference to evaluation.

The study of attitude change has been dominated by two major perspectives: that is those deriving from learning theory and cognitive consistency theories. Viewed from the learning theory perspective, attitude change is a change of internal implicit responses, as a result of external influences which are incongruent with the existing attitude. Research work in this tradition has thus concentrated upon external influences which can lead to attitude change, and these have often been grouped together into categories of the *communicator*, the *message*, the *channel* and the *audience*. Viewed from a cognitive consistency viewpoint, attitude change is seen as the consequence of changes in the internal relationships between attitudes and beliefs within the person rather than as the direct result of external influences. The basic assumption in this approach is that individuals seek to maintain consistency between their beliefs and evaluations, and that attitude change is a consequence of a person's need to maintain consistency between a set of existing cognitions and an attitude which is found to be incongruent with them. External influences lead to attitude change indirectly, according to this viewpoint, via their influence on the internal relationships between an individual's cognitions.

More recently attention has focused on the relationship between attitude change and behavioural change which have not always been found to be consistent with one another. Some theorists have suggested that attitude change is not a precursor for behavioural change, but is instead a change in personal attribution of attitude as a consequence of a directly instigated change in behaviour. Others have concentrated attention on defining other determinants of behaviour (e.g. normative influences arising in the behavioural setting) which operate together with attitude in the determination of behaviour.

NL

AVERSION THERAPY

Aversion therapy   One of the methods of behaviour therapy; a range of techniques developed mainly for the treatment of neurotic disorders (S. Rachman and T. Wilson (1980), *The Effects of Psychological Therapy*). It has a limited range of uses and its applications are governed by ethical guidelines because of the possibilities of misuse (British Psychological Society (1980), *Report on Behaviour Modification*). The purpose of aversion therapy is to produce an association between an undesirable behaviour pattern and unpleasant stimulation, or to make the unpleasant stimulation a consequence of the undesirable behaviour. In either case, it is hoped that an acquired connection between the behaviour and the unpleasantness will develop. There is a further hope that the development of such a connection will be followed by a reduction of the target behaviour. Ideally, the therapeutic programme includes attempts to foster alternative, acceptable behaviour. Aversion therapy is used predominantly for the treatment of those behaviour disorders (e.g. alcoholism and sexual deviations) in which the patient's conduct is undesirable but nevertheless self-reinforcing. In forensic work, aversion therapy has been used mainly to reduce, modify or eliminate sexual activities such as exhibitionism, transvestism or aggressive sexual acts. The appetitive characteristics of these disorders frequently require the introduction of other, suitable forms of satisfying behaviour. Sometimes it is not sufficient only to eliminate the unsuitable behaviour; the therapist attempts to foster alternate forms of behaviour that are incompatible with the unacceptable behaviour. In recent years, increasing attention has been given to helping sexual offenders improve their (often inappropriate/ inadequate) social skills, as part of the overall treatment plan. A variety of unpleasant (aversive) stimuli have been employed in aversion therapy but the most widely used are electrical or chemical forms of aversion.

In the electrical form of treatment, the therapist administers a mildly painful shock to the patient whenever the undesirable behaviour, or its imaginal equivalent, is elicited. In the chemical method, the patient is given a nausea-producing drug (emetine or apomorphine), and is then exposed to the deviant stimulus, or required to carry out the deviant act when the drug is having its maximal effect. The chemical method has found its widest application in the treatment of alcoholism, and the electrical method is used predominantly in the treatment of sexual disorders. The advantages and disadvantages of these two techniques are discussed by S. Rachman and J. Teasdale (1969), *Aversion Therapy and Behaviour Disorders*.

Aversion therapy is based on a conditioning paradigm, the basis of which is to be found in Pavlov's *Conditioned Reflexes* (1927). The earliest clinical application of aversion therapy appears to have taken place in Russia some fifty years ago. One of the earliest Western accounts of aversion therapy was provided in 1935 by Max, who described the treatment of a patient with a homosexual fixation by the administration of electrical shocks. During the late 1930s and 1940s, however, chemical aversion therapy was widely employed – predominantly in treating alcoholics. The resurgence of interest in this form of therapy occurred as a result of the development of behaviour therapy from 1950 onwards.

There is sufficient evidence to conclude that the treatment is an effective procedure but it is widely recognised that the technique requires refinement, and the underlying theory is only partially satisfactory. It has become increasingly clear that the classical conditioning theory is limited, and that greater importance must be attached to the cognitive factors which are part of this or any other form of treatment. This theoretical development is paralleled by the exploration of a new form of aversion therapy based largely on cognitive manipulations. Covert sensitisation, like aversion therapy proper, attempts to build up an association between an undesirable activity and an unpleasant effect (Cautela (1967), 'Covert sensitization', *Psychological Reports*, 20, 459). However, this treatment is carried out entirely at the imaginal level – the patient is required to imagine some extremely undesirable consequence, such as nausea, shame, pain and so forth. The refinement of this form of cognitive treatment coincided with, and indeed was part of, the shifting emphasis from a purely conditioning approach to a more cognitive view of aversion therapy.

Currently, the forensic use of aversion therapy is confined mainly to the treatment of sexual offenders, and generally forms only one part of a wider treatment programme designed to promote more satisfactory alternative means of sexual satisfaction.   SR

B

Bail Release on bail is a procedure dating back to Anglo-Saxon times (Holdsworth, 1956; Stephen, 1883). The first legislation dealing with the subject was the Statute of Westminster, 1275. Today, the general principles are to be found in the *Bail Act* (1976). When granted bail a person charged with an offence and held in custody may be released while awaiting or during committal proceedings or trial; or, after conviction, before being sentenced or while appealing. He is under a duty to surrender to the custody of the court or police, as the case may be. In order to enforce this duty a person granted bail by a court (but not the police) may be required to provide one or more sureties and to comply with such other conditions as appear to be necessary to ensure that he surrenders to custody, commits no offence while on bail, does not interfere with witnesses or otherwise obstruct the course of justice and is available for the purpose of enabling enquiries or a report to be made to assist the court (*Bail Act* (1976), s. 3). Failure without reasonable cause to surrender to custody at the time appointed is an offence. Arrest without warrant is possible if there are reasonable grounds for believing that this is likely to happen, or that the conditions on which bail has been granted have been or are likely to be broken, or if a surety gives written notice to the effect that the person bailed is unlikely to surrender to custody and that he wishes therefore to be released from his obligations as a surety (s. 7). It is also an offence to agree to indemnify another against liabilities the latter may incur as a surety (s. 9). The conditions on which bail may be granted may be varied on application (s. 3).

Except in the case of bail granted by the police (White, 1977), the general principle is that, subject to certain exceptions, bail is to be granted in all cases; it is for the prosecution or police opposing bail to satisfy the court that the defendant is within the

B

exceptions and therefore should not be granted bail (s. 4 and Schedule 1; but see Hayes, 1961). An appeal lies to the High Court against a decision by a Magistrates' Court to withhold bail (*Criminal Justice Act* (1967), s. 22). Depending on the circumstances, bail may be granted by the police, a Magistrates' Court, the Crown Court, the High Court, or the Court of Appeal (*inter alia, Magistrates' Courts Act* (1952), ss. 7, 29, 38, 89, 93; *Criminal Justice Act* (1967), s. 22; *Administration of Justice Act* (1960), s. 4).

In 1980, out of a total of 288,300 persons remanded by Magistrates' Courts, 42,300 (15 per cent) were held in custody. In the same year, 74,100 were committed to the Crown Court for trial, 14,000 (19 per cent) in custody. At some stage of the Crown Court proceedings 39 per cent of those being tried were remanded, 6,300 (22 per cent) in custody. In all cases, those not held in custody were released on bail. The police granted bail to 544,300 persons, of whom 4 per cent failed to appear – i.e. absconded. The Magistrates' Courts bailed 258,100, and the number who absconded was again 4 per cent of that figure. Roughly the same percentage of those granted bail to appear in the Crown Court failed to appear (Home Office, 1981).

M. Hayes (1981), 'Where now the right to bail?', *CLR*, 20; W.S. Holdsworth (1956), *A History of English Law*, 7th ed. by A.L. Goodhart and H.W. Hanbury; Home Office (1981), *Criminal Statistics, England & Wales, 1980*, Cmnd 8376; J.F. Stephen (1883), *A History of the Criminal Law of England* (3 vols); R.C.A. White (1977), 'The Bail Act: will it make any difference?', *CLR*, 338.   MB

Bankruptcy. See *Compensation*.

Baroning The term 'baron' is the slang for a prison inmate who obtains wealth and power through selling tobacco. A baron with a surplus of tobacco gives it to other prisoners and later demands its return with interest accruing. Those who cannot pay are then physically assaulted. It is for this reason that the amount of tobacco a man may hold at any one time while in prison is restricted.   DPW

Behaviour modification Behaviour modification techniques are based on the assumption that the likelihood of occurrence of a behaviour depends on its consequences. If a behaviour is followed by a reward, it becomes more likely to occur in future, while if it is followed by a punishment, it becomes less likely. This assumption has a long history. It has formed the basis, implicitly or explicitly, of many training methods used in the past by parents, teachers, institutional staff and others with the power to shape people's behaviour. What is new in behaviour modification research is the systematic and explicit use of rewards and/or punishments to modify behaviour, and the emphasis on a research design which will permit an evaluation of the effectiveness of any treatment.

Many behaviour modification techniques are said to be derived from the operant conditioning ideas of B.F. Skinner. The techniques have been used much more in the USA than in England, in institutions, in semi-custodial 'community-based' settings, in families, schools and even in the community. (For a review see G.B. Trasler and D.P. Farrington, eds (1979), *Behaviour Modification with Offenders*.)

Most institutional and community-based programmes have used a 'token economy' in which offenders received tokens for approved behaviour (e.g. cleaning rooms or doing chores) which could then be exchanged for tangible rewards (e.g. money, time spent watching television). Often, token economies were combined with a system in which offenders were required to progress through a series of levels, each succeeding one providing more opportunity for rewards but requiring more desirable behaviour. Sometimes, release was conditional on a successful progression through the levels. Two of the most famous of these kinds of American programmes were 'START' and 'Achievement Place' (see V.S. Johnson (1977), *Criminal Justice and Behaviour*, 4, 397). Token economy programmes have also been used in English institutions (see M.S. Hoghughi (1979), *BJC*, 19, 384). In the USA, some of these programmes have been closed down by lawsuits alleging that it is unconstitutional to make privileges (which had previously been enjoyed unconditionally) conditional on specified behaviour.

The major problem with behaviour modification is that, while non-delinquent behaviour within institutions can be modified, it is much harder to modify delinquent behaviour in the community. (For a review of delinquent behaviour modification in the community, see D.P. Farrington (1979), *BJC*, 19, 353.) The most hopeful techniques seem to involve contingency contracting within families of delinquents, as used for example by G.R. Patterson and his collaborators. However, at the present time the effectiveness of behaviour modification in changing delinquent behaviour has not been conclusively demonstrated in well-designed research. DPF

Bestiality. See *Buggery*.

Betting and gaming. See *Gambling*.

B

Bifurcation A.E. Bottoms (1977), 'Reflections on the renaissance of dangerousness', *HJ*, 16 88, introduced this term to refer to the difference in treatment envisaged for the 'really serious offender' (for whom severe treatment is usually recommended unquestioningly) as opposed to the 'ordinary' offender, who is treated more tolerantly. DPW

Bigamy This offence will be committed by one who 'being married, shall marry any other person during the life of the former husband or wife, whether the second marriage shall have taken place in England or Ireland or elsewhere' (*Offences against the Person Act* (1861), s. 57).

The Act creates exceptions to cover: 1. Second marriages contracted elsewhere by any other than a subject of Her Majesty. 2. The first spouse being absent for at least seven years and not known to be living. 3. Divorce. 4. Decree of nullity. It is also likely to be no offence if the person accused reasonably believed that his former marriage was at an end through death, divorce or decree of nullity (Smith and Hogan (1978)).

Bigamy is inappropriately included under the heading 'Sexual Offences' (as in the Home Office *Criminal Statistics*), for although the bigamous ceremony does not create a marriage, there is nothing criminal in extra-marital sexual intercourse should it thereafter take place. It is better thought of as offensive to the institution of monogamous marriage and a desecration of its solemnisation, whether in Church or Register Office. J. Smith and B. Hogan (1978), *Criminal Law*, pp. 676 *et seq.*, suggest that a severe punishment is likely today only 'when the other party is innocent and is deceived into taking a highly detrimental course of action'. ARP

Binding over One is bound over when one undertakes to the court (technically enters into a recognisance) 'to keep the peace' or 'to be of good behaviour' or 'to come up for judgment'. What is recognised is that a sum of money specified by the court will become payable to it on failure to abide by the undertaking; sureties may also be required and, in default of payment, will have to pay. All courts may bind over to keep the peace or to be of good behaviour, even without convicting; even against witnesses; thus it may be used as a preventive measure, e.g. 'to restrain political agitators from repeating or encouraging violence or from inciting other persons to break the law . . . to prevent persons from behaving in a way likely (though not intended) to provoke others to commit breaches of the peace, and to inhibit the activities of transvestites, prostitutes, protestors against nuclear weapons and increased car-parking charges, and gentlemen who peep into ladies' lavatories and bedrooms' (de Smith (1975), *Constitutional and Administrative Law*, p. 461). In exercising this power, as distinct from the following, nothing more than keeping the peace or being of good behaviour may be required. On failure to comply, payment must be made under the recognisance but no further penalty may be imposed. Only the Crown Court may take a recognisance to come up for judgment (which is then respited), and this only on conviction and when the punishment is not fixed by law (as it is in murder). Keeping the peace and being of good behaviour will be conditions of the recognisance, but further conditions may be inserted: e.g. leaving the country and not returning for five years (see R *v*. Williams, *The Times*, 12 March 1982). On failure to comply, payment must be made under the recognisance and judgment may be passed for the original offence. See D. Thomas (2nd ed., 1979), *Principles of Sentencing*, p. 228.　　　　ARP

Biological factors.　See *Constitutional factors*.

Birth cohort　A group born in the same year, selected for study as they march through time to assess the nature and influence of factors affecting their behaviour.
　　See also *Longitudinal research*.　　　　ARP

Blackmail　In Western societies the criminal law punishes three kinds of blackmail: by physical intimidation, threats to accuse the victim of a criminal offence and threats to reveal discreditable information about the victim. In all cases the central illegality is theft through terror, the victim being forced to part with goods or services.
　　Of the three kinds of blackmail, the use of physical intimidation has the longest history. Until the nineteenth

century the word 'black mail' was generally only used to describe the payment of 'black money' enforced by threats against life, limb or property. During the early decades of the last century the courts gradually recognised that individuals could be equally vulnerable in their reputations or 'good names' and an increasing number of successful prosecutions for threats to destroy an individual's public reputation added the extra strand to the modern law of blackmail.

B

The concern in contemporary society over reputational blackmail has not resulted in a great deal of systematic research. One reason, of course, is the difficulty of obtaining 'hard' data and reliable information. While it is not difficult to find analyses of extortion by physical threats in the literature on organised and 'business' crime, especially in the USA, there is only one sociological study of reputational blackmail, M. Hepworth (1975), *Blackmail: Publicity and Secrecy in Everyday Life*. This book reviews the history of all three kinds of blackmail in Britain and assesses the social factors that have contributed to the rise of reputational blackmail, which is divided into four types. First, entrepreneurial blackmail where a victim is deliberately lured into a compromising situation (often sexual); second, opportunistic blackmail resulting from the accidental discovery by the blackmailer of damaging information about the victim; third, commercial research or the deliberate pursuit of discreditable information which may be used, for example, against a political or business rival; and fourth, participant blackmail arising from a pre-existing relationship between blackmailer and victim where both share what might become a damaging secret.   MH

Blasphemy   It is an offence at common law to publish, orally or in writing, blasphemous matter, i.e. reviling or scurrilous attacks on Christianity; and providing the matter was intended to be published it is no defence that its author did not intend it to be taken that way. It may or may not be necessary to show that the matter had a tendency to lead to a breach of the peace.

Law Commission (1981), *Offences against Religion and Public Worship*, Working Paper no. 79; J. Spencer (1981), 'Blasphemy: the Law Commission's Working Paper', *CLR*, 810.   ARP

Board of Visitors   A body of independent, impartial, men and women appointed by the Home Secretary to monitor conditions

23

in each approved place of detention (borstal, prison, detention centre, etc.). Boards were first formed alongside Visiting Committees (used in county jails only) by the *Prison Act* (1877), where they were used only in prisons which did not receive prisoners direct from the courts. This distinction continued until they completely replaced Visiting Committees in 1971 (*Courts Act*, s. 53(3)). Their activities are detailed in the *Prison Rules* (1964) ss. 88, 92–7. Broadly they have a two-fold function. (1) An inspectorial role, to examine periodically standards of care and custody in their institution, involving receiving from prisoners and staff formal complaints, applications, requests and grievances and processing these. Also to bring to the institution's attention any observed weaknesses or stress-points and to supply advice and guidance to prisoners where requested. Visits are undertaken by single Board members; in addition prisoners may apply to see the full Board at its monthly meeting. Prisoners have a *right* to see Board members, and the Board members' aim on every visit is to make themselves available to see as many prisoners as is feasible. (2) To deal with serious offences against prison discipline (which a Governor cannot deal with, and where the police will not be involved) in the form of an adjudication. Board activities and composition have recently been subject to closer scrutiny; cf. Home Office (1975), *Report of the Working Party on Adjudication Procedures in Prisons*; Jellicoe (1975), *Boards of Visitors of Penal Institutions*; Report of a Committee set up by Justice, the Howard League for Penal Reform and NACRO; G. Borrie (1976), 'The membership of Boards of Visitors of penal establishments', *CLR*, 281; J.P. Martin (1975), *Boards of Visitors of Penal Institutions*; D. Smith, C. Austin and J. Ditchfield (1981), *Board of Visitor Adjudications*, Home Office Research Unit Paper no. 3. DPW

Body build. See *Constitutional factors*.

Born criminal, the. See *Constitutional factors*; *Criminal type*.

Borstal As an alternative to imprisonment, the *Prevention of Crime Act* (1908) enabled courts to pass a sentence of 'detention under penal discipline in a Borstal Institution' on offenders over sixteen (reduced to fifteen in 1961) and under twenty-one, the term being not less than one year and not more than three (from 1961, two years). The provision was the brainchild of E. Ruggles-Brise (see *prison*), who experimented with special adolescent training institutions based on Elmira Reformatory (New York State). The first, which gave the system its name, was set up in 1902 at the village of Borstal, Kent.

Within the period of the sentence, an offender who had served six months could be released on licence, remaining under supervision until six months after the sentence had expired.

The official aim of borstal has always been to provide such training as would be conducive to reformation, and in the years before the Second World War the system was thought to be having some success. In the post-war years it gradually became clear that the situation had changed for the worse and the Advisory Council on the Penal System report, *Young Adult Offenders* (1974), saw no point in retaining it as a separate system. The outcome of the long debate that followed may be found in the provisions of the *Criminal Justice Act* (1982) relating to the new sentence of *youth custody* (q.v.).

R. Hood (1965), *Borstal Re-assessed*; Home Office (1978), *The Sentence of the Court*.

See also *Young adult offender*.   ARP

Brainwashing.   See *Attitude change*.

Bribery   The offer or acceptance of bribes is penalised in various contexts: judges and other judicial and public officers, at common law; members and officers of public bodies, under the *Public Bodies Corrupt Practices Act* (1889) and other statutes; in transactions where an agent so acts to the disadvantage of his principal, under the *Prevention of Corruption Act* (1906) and other statutes; in connection with the grant of honours, under the *Honours (Prevention of Abuses) Act* (1925); at elections, at common law and under the *Representation of the People Act* (1949); and in obtaining information about 'spent convictions' under the *Rehabilitation of Offenders Act* (1974) (see *Halsbury's Laws of England* (4th ed., 1976), vol. 2, paras 921–7 and 1285). The small number of cases that come to public attention are highly unlikely to be typical of all, since successful cases are unlikely to be reported. Bribery remains a buried figure.   ARP

Bridewell.   See *House of Correction*.

Buggery Anciently joined with heresy and apostasy as a form of treason against God, buggery involves sexual penetration *per anum* by a man with a man or a woman; or *per vaginam* as well, with an animal; or between a woman and an animal. (Buggery between humans is also known as 'sodomy', between humans and animals as 'bestiality'. In law these terms are no longer in use, though the Criminal Law Revision Committee would create a distinct and lesser offence of bestiality.)

No offence is committed if the act involves two men (and two men only) over twenty-one, in private and mutually consenting (*Sexual Offences Act* (1967), s. 1). Otherwise buggery remains proscribed by the *Sexual Offences Act* (1956).

The Criminal Law Revision Committee would lower to eighteen the minimum age of all consensual male homosexual acts, including buggery, and would treat consensual heterosexual buggery similarly. In their view, consensual adult sexual intimacy admits to a wide variety of conduct which is no concern of the law.

Convictions for buggery or attempted buggery are most likely when a boy under fourteen has been involved.

Criminal Law Revision Committee (1980), *Working Paper on Sexual Offences*, pp. 20 *et seq.*; T. Honoré (1978), *Sex Law*; R. Walmsley and K. White (1979), *Sexual Offences, Consent and Sentencing*, HORS no. 54.   ARP

Burglary As defined by the *Theft Act* (1968), a person is guilty of burglary if he enters any building as a trespasser and with intent to commit an offence, or having entered the building he steals anything, harms anyone inside or attempts to do so. Aggravated burglary is where the burglar has with him a weapon of any kind. The maximum sentence for aggravated burglary is life imprisonment, and for ordinary burglary, fourteen years imprisonment.

E.M.W. Maguire (1982), *Burglary in a Dwelling: the Offence, the Offender and the Victim*; I. Waller and N. Okihiro (Toronto, 1978), *Burglary: the Victim and the Public*; D.P. Walsh (1980), *Break-ins: Burglary from Private Houses*.
                                                        DPW

C

Capital punishment With gaps of some years capital punishment by hanging was used from before 1016 to 1964 for a wide variety of offences. The number of those executed is not known but at Tyburn tree (Marble Arch), one place of execution in use from 1177 to 1783, the minimum number executed is estimated to be 50,000 and from 1900 to 1949 in England and Wales only, 751 people were executed, of whom 87 were women.

Early hanging was by strangulation which prolonged death. The patent drop (designed to instantly break the neck) was introduced in 1760, but not generally adopted until 1783. Since the object of capital punishment was to combine both retribution and deterrence, originally public hanging was felt to be necessary (abolished in 1868).

Capital punishment became an increasingly popular sentence with the judiciary throughout the eighteenth century, so that by 1819 there were over 220 capital offences. Due largely to the work of Romilly (1757–1818) and Peel (1788–1850) this list was whittled down until by 1861 the only offences subject to it were murder, treason, piracy and arson in HM dockyards. As late as 1908 children could technically be subject to capital punishment. In 1949 Ernest Gowers chaired a Royal Commission on it, reporting as the *Royal Commission on Capital Punishment 1949–53* (Cmnd 8932, 1953). Sidney Silverman MP began campaigning for the abolition of it and in 1955 formed the National Campaign for the Abolition of Capital Punishment. Partly as a result of this in 1957 the *Homicide Act* was passed which had a new defence for murderers of *diminished responsibility* (q.v.) and also a distinction between capital murder (subject to the death penalty) and non-capital murder (subject to *life imprisonment* (q.v.)). By the early 1960s there was a strong abolitionist lobby and in 1965 the *Murder (Abolition of Death Penalty) Act* was passed. This provided for a trial period (without the use of capital punishment) of five years, actual abolition occurring in December 1969. (The last men to be hanged were executed in 1964.) The Act provided for three exceptions: *arson* (q.v.) in HM dockyards, piracy and *treason* (q.v.), where capital punishment could still be used. The latter only now remains as an exception. Henceforth the punishment for murder is life imprisonment. DPW

Care Order *Juveniles* (q.v.) may be 'ordered into care' when guilty of an offence punishable in the case of an adult with imprisonment. This gives the local authority the powers and duties of a parent and the power to restrict liberty. The Order, unless discharged or extended by the Court, ceases to have effect at age eighteen or, if the Order was made after sixteen, at age nineteen. The local authority has a duty to review all cases in care at least every six months, to consider discharge.

The local authority, that is, its Social Services Department, usually arranges for an assessment of the juvenile to be made in a residential centre and then he may be sent to a *community home* (q.v.), though there are other possibilities, e.g. boarding with foster parents or even returning to his own, the local authority retaining control. There are community homes with secure accommodation for those thought to need it.

The Care Order, introduced by the *Children and Young Persons Act* (1969), has met with strong criticism from magistrates and police; its welfare orientation derogates from the more punitive (supposedly deterrent) stance that they would prefer, at any rate with the more troublesome in this age range. Before the Act, the courts had direct power to commit a juvenile to an approved school (now a community home) and this is what they miss. The *Criminal Justice Act* (1982) returns it to them to some extent to enable them so to deal with those who offend again while already in care.

H. Giller and A. Morris (1976), 'Children who offend: care, control or confusion?', *CLR*, 656; A. Morris (1978), 'Juvenile justice: where next?', in A.K. Bottomley, ed., *Criminal Justice*, p. 252. ARP

Care proceedings These replaced the 'care, protection and control' proceedings of previous legislation and, like them, are civil proceedings before a juvenile court. The *Children and Young Persons Act* (1969), (ss. 1–3) thereby re-emphasised the need for a procedure without the stigmatising effect of prosecution, but went further in that: (1) the situations which the court could deal with in this way included that of a juvenile who had committed an offence (except homicide). Requirements of justice insist though that this ('the offence condition') has to be established in the same way as in criminal proceedings (ibid., s. 3(3)). (2) Provision was made for care proceedings to replace the prosecution (except for homicide) of all children, and for them to be the preferred method for dealing with young persons. In this the 'welfare orientation' of the 1969 Act was at its most pervasive; but criticism mounted against it and it has not been brought into force.

Care proceedings under (1) operate over a wide area of social problems and the outcome for a juvenile may well be a *Supervision Order* (q.v.) or a *Care Order* (q.v.), though there are certain differences compared with the outcome on prosecution. Where an offence is involved it is still much more frequent to proceed by way of prosecution. See Home Office (1978), *The Sentence of the Court*, pp. 55, 61–6.   ARP

Career, criminal role   The notion of a criminal 'role-career' emerged in the USA partly out of dissatisfaction among sociologically-oriented criminologists with earlier attempts (e.g. Glueck and Glueck, 1950) to describe and explain criminality in terms of individual psychological characteristics. Gibbons (1965) argued that criminal behaviour could be seen as socially-determined 'role-playing' which often produced a clear career pattern. He put forward a complex typology of role descriptions. These included the 'professional thief', 'professional heavy criminal', 'one-time loser',. 'naïve cheque-forger' and 'white-collar criminal'. He produced a profile of each type under five major headings: offence-behaviour, interactional setting, self-image, attitudes and role-career. For example, the typical 'professional heavy criminal' engages in armed robbery, operates with a team or 'mob', defines himself as criminal, displays negative attitudes to work and continues in crime until early middle age. Gibbons correlated each type with 'background dimensions' such as social class, upbringing and peer-group associations. Alternative typologies were provided by Roebuck (1965), based upon the proportion of offences of a similar kind found in criminal records, and Clinard and Quinney (1967), whose 'criminal behaviour systems' were defined by the variables of previous career, group support, societal reaction and correspondence with legitimate behaviour patterns. Wolfgang *et al.* (1972) contributed a longitudinal study following the careers of a 'birth cohort', and considered the phenomenon of 'crime-switching' and other changes over time.

Critics of such typologies have claimed that they use arbitrary 'common-sense' categories which frequently overlap and that they are neither theoretically rigorous nor based upon sufficient empirical evidence. Homogeneous criminal careers have since been shown to be relatively unusual and many offenders cannot be fitted into the schema. Moreover, the notion of 'career' is dubious when applied to occasional or 'one-off' offenders.

Nevertheless, there has been a recent revival of interest in 'role-careers' in the USA. Petersilia *et al.* (1977) analysed self-report data about the 'careers' of 49 felons, concluding that they could be classified as either 'intensive' or 'intermittant' criminals, but that accurate categorisation was impossible from ordinary records of convictions. They suggest that if those likely to fall into 'intensive' career patterns could be identified in other ways (e.g. using more detailed information held in police files), special measures could be taken to 'incapacitate' them at an early age. Such conclusions are resisted by many criminologists on moral grounds as well as through doubts about the existence of clear patterns.

M.B. Clinard and R. Quinney (N.Y., 1967), *Criminal Behaviour Systems*; D.C. Gibbons (Englewood Cliffs, N.J., 1965), *Changing the Law-breaker*; S. Glueck and E.G. Glueck (Cambridge, Mass., 1950), *Unraveling Juvenile Delinquency*; J. Petersilia, P.W. Greenwood and M. Lavin (Santa Monica, 1977), *Criminal Careers of Habitual Felons*; J.B. Roebuck (Springfield, Ill., 1965), *Criminal Typology*; M. Wolfgang, R. Figlio and T. Sellin (Chicago, 1972), *Delinquency in a Birth Cohort*.   MM

Causes, Causation Proof of causality takes two forms, evidence that A did not occur *before* B or evidence ruling out all other causes of C apart from D. In human behaviour such clear causal evidence is rarely available simply and even more is this the case with criminal behaviour due to the secretiveness of the act (and of the actor), the lack of clarity about the circumstances that permitted it, and subsequent pressure for the actor to represent his motivation in a personally favourable light, and as being simple rather than complex (see also *motive*) and due to inevitable suggestibility at the time of apprehension. (Causality amongst undetected criminals is even more problematic and various.)

The search for the causes of crime was the starting point in criminology arising from pressure to know and then check. When it began to be clear that for any given crime, let alone all crime, there may be thousands of 'causes' (rather than a few) and a complex degree of interaction, the search for causes was abandoned and attention turned to the *process* of crime commission which led in two directions: (a) *prediction* studies (q.v.), ignoring cause and focusing on the isolation of concomitant factors and triggers, and (b) phenomenological studies aiming to describe a crime as a separate phenomenon, again ignoring cause. Interest in causes re-emerged in different guise with *labelling theory* (q.v.) and its offspring *radical criminology* (q.v.)

DPW

Cautioning   The word has two distinct meanings, each relating to a separate area of the legal process.

1 *Cautioning under the Judges' Rules*. This occurs in the course of police investigation, when they have a suspect before them. The suspect has a 'right of silence' all the way through English criminal procedure (there are limited exceptions), implying, *inter alia*, that he may not be forced, pressured or induced into making statements: they must be voluntary. From this has devolved the rule that once the police have sufficient admissible evidence for reasonable suspicion, they must caution their suspect in this manner:

> You are not obliged to say anything unless you wish to do so but what you say may be put into writing and given in evidence.

Prior to this point what the suspect has said may form part of the police case, and frequently does, without any such warning: at this point a change is perceived in the legal view of the relation between police and suspect: the police are seen as dominant. The suspect may yet make (further) utterances and, again, frequently does. The police, however, should not in general press further questions. What justice requires, it seems, is that the ordinary suspect be fully aware of the pressure (the imminence of formal charge and prosecution) now upon him and that juveniles and the mentally handicapped get independent advice. Furthermore it is regarded as wrong to draw any inference as to guilt from his silence at any stage. The main sanction – it is not very powerful – against the police for failing to caution at the relevant point is that anything said thereafter *may* be inadmissible as part of their evidence.

On being charged, the accused must be cautioned again, in similar manner, and yet again, should he be asked further questions.

The continuance of the 'right to silence' in present times and the advantage allegedly conferred on the guilty, especially among persistent offenders who 'know the ropes', has been widely criticised. None the less, the 'golden thread' that runs through English criminal procedure, that the prosecution must prove guilt, appealed more to the Royal Commission on Criminal Procedure reporting in 1981 and it is likely that the 'right to silence' will be maintained. The Royal Commission made further proposals as to the clarity, publicisation and enforcement of the Judges' Rules.

D. Barnard (1979), *The Criminal Court in Action*, pp. 61 *et seq.*; *Report of the Royal Commission on Criminal Procedure* (Cmnd 8092, 1981), pp. 80 *et seq.* Note particularly the empirical findings cited; D. McBarnet (1981), 'The Royal Commission and the Judges' Rules', *Brit. J. Law & Society*. 8(1), 109.

2 *Cautioning: 'Don't do it again!'* If cautioning as just discussed reveals a vital aspect of the judicial control of police procedure, this second usage relates to its very opposite: the well-nigh complete discretion vested in the police to decide whether or not to take a case to court. If they decide not to prosecute, one thing they can do instead is to 'let the offender off' with a caution. This may happen with complete informality on the beat or on the highway where the incident is of minimal significance.Cases like this do not get into official statistics. The published *Criminal Statistics*, however, have sets of tables indicating that many quite serious offences are disposed of by caution as well: but there is more formality to these decisions, made in the presence of the offender by a senior police officer, and the offender must admit his guilt. Over the last thirty years, these statistics show that an increasingly greater use has been made of cautioning, though it has now levelled out. The reason lies in the tendency to caution juvenile offenders, especially the ten-to-fourteen age group, at any rate for non-violent crimes. The practice was linked originally with the development of Juvenile Liaison Schemes, now operating as Juvenile Bureaux. The Juvenile Liaison Scheme of the Liverpool police force was

one of the first examples of *diversion* (q.v.) from the prosecution process known to the English system.

D. Steer (1970), *Police Cautions: a Study in the Exercise of Police Discretion*; J. Ditchfield (1976), *Police Cautioning in England and Wales*, HORS no. 37. ARP

Chicago School, The   The name given to a group of sociologists based at Chicago University and operating from the 1920s onwards, whose focus of interest was predominantly urban growth and urban problems, which they investigated in a number of empirical surveys, chief among which are: N. Anderson (1923), *The Hobo: the Sociology of the Homeless Man*; E.W. Burgess, ed. (1926), *The Urban Community*; R.S. Cavan (1928), *Suicide*; R.E. Faris and H.W. Dunham (1939), *Mental Disorders in Urban Areas*; R.E. Park and E.W. Burgess (1925), *The City*; C.R. Shaw (1929), *Delinquency Areas*, (1930), *The Jack-Roller: a Delinquent Boy's Own Story*, (1931), *Natural History of a Delinquent Career*, (1938), *Brothers in Crime*; C.R. Shaw and H.D. Mackay (1942), *Juvenile Delinquency and Urban Areas*; F.M. Thrasher (1927), *The Gang*; W.F. Whyte (1943), *Street Corner Society*; L. Wirth (1928), *The Ghetto*; H.W. Zorbaugh (1929), *The Gold Coast and the Slum*. Their work has been extremely influential as a result of the fruitfulness of the concepts generated and because it embraced both intensive ethnographic studies and highly theoretical (cartographic-based) ones, and shed much light on the criminal area (see also *area studies*), but its principal importance arose because of the way members recorded the world of reality as seen by the criminal actor, rather than distorting it or denying its significance. DPW

Child, The   One who is under the age of fourteen years. In law it is conclusively presumed that no child under the age of ten can be guilty of an offence (*Children and Young Persons Act* (1969), s. 16). Ten is therefore the so-called 'age of criminal responsibility', though from ten to fourteen it is still necessary to satisfy the court that the child knew that what he was doing was wrong: the 'rebuttable presumption' of the common law is that up to fourteen he lacks such understanding.

Confusingly, in the legislation and arrangements relating to child care (e.g. Pt II of the *Children and Young Persons Act* (1969)), 'child' means a person under the age of eighteen.

See also *Juvenile*; *Young person*. ARP

CHILD BATTERING

Child battering. See *Child neglect*.

Child destruction The law governing *abortion* (q.v.) does not apply if a child is born alive and its life then terminated, even though it may not yet have an existence independent of its mother. When it does, the law of homicide applies: in the meantime the offence of child destruction will be committed under the *Infant Life Preservation Act* (1920), s. 1. In fact, the offence will be committed as soon as the child is 'capable of being born alive' (*prima facie* presumed after twenty-eight weeks of pregnancy), so there is an overlap with the law on abortion. The Act provides a defence which has been interpreted to cover acts done in good faith for preserving the life or health of the woman. See J. Smith and B. Hogan (1978), *Criminal Law*, p. 341.   ARP

Child molestation A majority of the victims of sex offenders prosecuted in the English courts are juveniles, but as recent Home Office research reveals (Walmsley and White, 1979), many of them, especially the boys, are consenting victims. Sexual contacts between adults and children are surprisingly common. An American survey (Finkelhor, 1979) found that 19.2 per cent of women students and 8.6 per cent of males reported having had such an experience. The great majority of the incidents were never mentioned to anyone by the children at the time. Their first experience most commonly took place when they were aged eight to twelve.

The boys' experiences are usually, but by no means exclusively, with older males, who are often encountered outside the home, whereas the girls' contacts generally take place with persons in their own household or immediate family circle. Although some children co-operate, appear to enjoy or may actually seek out contacts with adults for purposes of petting or masturbation, a frequent reaction to an adult approach is one of unresponsiveness, withdrawal or terrified fright.

The term molestation, although commonly used for all kinds of sex incidents involving children, seems to imply an act of unwanted intrusion, if not of actual aggression. Many so-called molesters are child-lovers or paedophiles who have a real attachment to their victims and wish them no harm. The act of sexual exhibitionism or indecent fondling, which is usually all that occurs, is probably not in itself damaging, although the child may subsequently feel anxious or guilty. More traumatic are the rarer incidents in which the child is intimidated by threats, physically overpowered or subjected to painful penetration. Where the aggressor is a parent, or a girl is coerced reluctantly into actual incest, the trauma can be considerable, because the victim is in a position of dependency upon the offender and can see no way of escaping from an intolerable situation. Sometimes the questioning by shocked parents, interrogations by police and lawyers, and ultimately appearance in a court room are more damaging to the victim than the sexual misbehaviour itself.

C

Many child molesters are lonely social inadequates who seek solace with children for lack of access to more mature partners; others are sexually fixated upon children and turned off by signs of physical maturity. Detected paedophiles are virtually always male. A minority of them are attracted exclusively to boys, but it is doubtful whether paedophilia is any commoner among homosexuals in general than it is among heterosexuals.

D. Finkelhor (N.Y., 1979), *Sexually Victimized Children*; R. Walmsley and K. White (1979), *Sexual Offences, Consent and Sentencing*, HORS no. 54.   DJW

Child neglect   The *Children and Young Persons Acts* (1933 to 1969) provide for the care of children and, in particular, the 1933 Act, s. 1, penalises those who have the custody of a *child* (q.v.) if their conduct is wilful and 'likely to cause him unnecessary suffering or injury to health'. Other provisions of the criminal law relating to violence apply in appropriate circumstances, and when a child dies the person responsible may be guilty of manslaughter or murder. See P. Bromley (1981), *Family Law*.

See also *Homicide*.   ARP

Child stealing   Taking away a child under fourteen, by force or fraud and with intent to deprive the parent or guardian of possession. *Offences against the Person Act* (1861) s. 56; J. Smith and B. Hogan (1978), *Criminal Law*, p. 386.   ARP

Chromosome abnormality.   See *XYY chromosomes*.

Civil disorder.   See *Public order*.

Civil rights   Since there is no written Constitution, 'rights in the UK are based on the negative concept that anything is

35

lawful unless it is expressly forbidden by Act of Parliament or common law' (*Civil Liberty: the National Council for Civil Liberties Guide to Your Rights* (1979)). The concept may be negative but it is none the less jealously safeguarded, as by the NCCL itself and in general by the legal system. In the context of criminology it enters into all discussions of penal laws, public order, police powers, judicial and penal administration, mental health, public safety, racial equality, censorship and personal privacy. The latest NCCL report, P. Hewitt, *The Abuse of Power* (1982), is useful.   ARP

Class, social.   See *Social class*.

Classification.   See *Typology*.

Coining.   See *Counterfeiting*.

Community homes   This is a general term covering residential accommodation available to local authorities in exercising discretion as to the placement of children in care. There are three main categories: (a) community homes with education on the premises (CH(E)s). These to a large extent replaced approved schools in 1973 under the *Children and Young Persons Act* (1969); (b) community homes where children attend local schools; and (c) Observation and Assessment centres (O and A centres). In 1980 there were about 34,000 places in local authority provided and controlled community homes. Of these about 5,000 places each were in CH(E)s and O and A centres. There were a further 5,000 places in assisted community homes provided by voluntary organisations.

There were 31,000 children in community homes in 1979, of whom 20 per cent were in care as a result of an offence. Forty per cent of children in care for offences were in community homes, compared with 31 per cent of non-offenders in care. Sixty per cent of children in CH(E)s were in care as the result of an offence.

There was an increase in secure places during the 1970s, especially as a result of central government capital finance provided through the *Children Act* (1975). By 1981 there were 400 secure places in community homes; children in care can also be placed in Youth Treatment Centres which are run by the Department of Health and Social Security.

Since the *Children and Young Persons Act* (1969) the proportion of juvenile offenders placed in care has declined while the proportion receiving custody has increased. Magistrates and other groups complained throughout the 1970s that the discretion as to placement under the Care Order resided solely with the local authority and that the courts' dissatisfaction with the manner in which this discretion was exercised had resulted in a greatly increased use of penal custody. These concerns culminated in the provision of the Residential Care Order in the *Criminal Justice Act* (1982), which enables courts to impose a determinate period of removal from home of up to and including six months.

C

The *Criminal Justice Act* (1982) left intact most of the discretionary powers of the local authority with reference to care placements and community homes. Care Orders are for periods of up to the child's eighteenth birthday. Research has shown that children coming in care as the result of an offence change placements frequently (P. Carson, *Young Offenders in Care*, DHSS, 1981), and that the typical pattern of placement of offenders in CH(E)s is a child coming into care at fourteen, spending two or three months in an O and A centre and then rather over a year in a CH(E) before leaving at sixteen (DHSS, *Offending By Young People*, 1981).

The declining use of community homes for juvenile offenders may in part be due to high operating costs borne by local authorities. A number of facilities have been closed and there has been a decline in purchased places from other local authorities. By contrast, custodial provision is provided by central government at no cost to local government. See generally, *Children in Care*, annual statistical report by DHSS; Department of Education and Science, *Community Homes with Education* (1980).   AR

Community policing   The concept of communal responsibility for maintaining social order is probably as old as that of society itself. Most cultures have manifested some variant of the form at one time or another. The term 'community policing' in the English language appears to have come to the fore in Anglo-American usage during the 1970s. It is primarily concerned with the concept of prevention of crime and disorder through co-operative effort. It is still in the process of development as a modern concept and lacks adequate theoretical bases as well as organisational form.

COMMUNITY POLICING

Community policing might be held to describe at least four distinct styles of social control involving community effort.

Primitive community policing   It is first seen in its ancient form in tribal or undeveloped societies. In civilisations where only small and vulnerable settlements existed, social control through the immediate family, or group of families in combination, provided early examples of community policing.

The concept is also found under ancient Anglo-Saxon law where the groups of families owe duties for the keeping of the peace to the tythingman or headman of the tens and hundreds who in turn owes allegiance to the king. 'From very early times, certainly from the reign of King Alfred, the primary responsibility for maintaining the King's peace fell upon each locality under a well-understood principle of social obligation, or collective security' (Critchley, 1978).

Totalitarian community policing   Totalitarian community policing is the arm of the ruling party and is associated with the political left (e.g. USSR) and the right (e.g. Nazi Germany). The latest example of this kind of social/political control has been seen in the People's Republic of China. T. Bowden (1978) records the growth of the Red Sentinels in the factories as guards and as controllers of discipline and ideology on the factory floor in 1969.

Unofficial community policing   Unofficial community policing is to be found in areas where official policing is weak, allowing various power groups to arise in neighbourhoods and localities to exert an unofficial control. This can be a benign or malign control.

Kibbutzim in the Israeli culture, where the residents subscribe to the rules, offer one example of benign unofficial community policing. Malign unofficial community police systems can be seen where power groups get their ascendency through violence or intimidation. This can happen within a democratic state where a criminal sub-culture pervades a neighbourhood. Local social control of this kind sometimes flourishes in spite of the existence of official police.

Modern community policing   Community policing is difficult to find in a modern developed country, since there are many forces working against it. It would exist where all the elements in a community, both official and unofficial, would conceive of the common good and combine to produce a social climate and an environment conducive to good order and the happiness of all those living within it. It leaves legal policing to the police and concentrates on social measures for its success. In the first place it has to define the term 'community' and seek to strengthen or create such a phenomenon through fraternity. Community should be seen as a group of people who live in sympathetic proximity with, to a greater or lesser degree, some significant factor in common. Residential commonality is one thing but it may contain animosity, even hatred. Thus where a community exists it should be strengthened; where it does not exist it should be created.

C

The aim of modern community policing should be based on a concept and understanding of the common good. The creation of a neighbourhood or community climate free from fear and uncontrolled delinquency and crime would be its primary aim. In respecting the dignity of the individual nobody should be regarded as unworthy of its concern. On the other hand it should have due regard for the privacy, individuality and freedoms of all, including the freedom to be left alone. Community based, it should be motivated only for the community as a whole and not for narrow political or sectarian causes or concerns.

In setting out to achieve its aims it should involve all the statutory bodies and agencies whose work in any way affects the quality of community life so far as control of crime and delinquency is concerned. The common interest lies in the creation of lower social tensions through a more wholesome environment. The statutory agencies should then come together with the voluntary bodies whose social aims bear relevance, and with individuals whose concern is to represent the residents of the community.

J. Alderson (1979), *Policing Freedom*; T. Bowden (1978), *Beyond the Limits of the Law*; T.A. Critchley (1978), *A History of Police in England and Wales*; C. Moore and J. Brown (1981), *Community versus Crime*. JCA

Community Service Orders 'The most ambitious proposal' of the Report of the Advisory Council on the Penal System (1970), *Non-custodial and Semi-custodial Penalties*, was that 'in appropriate cases, offenders should be required to engage in some form of part-time service to the community' (Wootton

Report, para. 31). Translated into the statutory provisions of the *Criminal Justice Act* (1972) and then the *Powers of the Criminal Courts Act* (1973), courts were thereby enabled so to sentence an offender over seventeen convicted of an offence punishable with imprisonment. The work required of him (and the order may be made only if he agrees to it) will be of not less than 40 hours and not more than 240 hours and will be unpaid. The *Criminal Justice Act* (1982) brought in sixteen-year-old offenders too, but the maximum for them is 120 hours. An offender who fails to do what is required may be brought before the court and fined (leaving the Order in force) or the court may revoke the Order and deal with him in any way appropriate to the original offence. Community service is organised by the Probation Service and now operates in all parts of England and Wales. It appears to be used mostly for the seventeen-to-twenty-one age group for those who might otherwise have received a short custodial sentence. There is little indication from research as yet as to its effectiveness.

Home Office (1978), *The Sentence of the Court*; R. Cross and A. Ashworth (3rd ed., 1981), *The English Sentencing System*; W. Young (1979), *Community Service Orders*; B. Wootton (2nd ed., 1981), *Crime and the Criminal Law*. ARP

Compensation The separation of criminal jurisdiction, where the outcome is traditionally 'punishment', from the civil makes for difficulties in compensating victims; compensation often requires the more appropriate procedures of the civil courts. What is more, criminals may remain undetected or unconvicted or be without the means to pay, especially if subject to a custodial sentence. To assist victims, though, the following arrangements have been made. (a) The Criminal Injuries Compensation Board, set up in 1964, makes *ex gratia* payments to victims of violent crime. See Samuel's full account (1973), *CLR*, 418, and the annual reports of the Board itself. (b) The Criminal Courts may, in addition to sentence, make Compensation Orders against the offender for personal injury, loss or damage. (Magistrates' Courts may not award more than £1,000). Criminal Bankruptcy Orders may be made by the Crown Court in addition to sentence (but not for personal injury) where loss or damage exceeds £15,000; these are far less frequent – about thirty per annum (*Powers of the Criminal Courts Act* (1973), ss. 35–41).

R. Cross and A. Ashworth (3rd ed., 1981), *The English*

Sentencing System, p. 64; P. Softley (1978), *Compensation Orders in Magistrates' Courts*, HORS no. 43; Advisory Council on the Penal System (1978), *Sentences of Imprisonment: a Review of Maximum Penalties*, Ch. 15 on Criminal Bankruptcy.

See also *Restitution*.   ARP

Computer crime Types include: theft and receiving of parts or peripheral devices; given that systems are valuable and vulnerable, damaging or destroying them (out of spite, revenge, etc); producing false printout to facilitate *fraud* (q.v.) through alterations or additions to programme or data, and extracting information for criminal purposes (e.g. theft or blackmail). All of this is serious in direct proportion to what is stored in the system. High potential gains, low victim awareness and widespread computer education make this a flourishing crime.

DPW

Concealment of birth The difficulty of proving how an infant life might have been terminated led to the creation of this offence by the *Offences Against the Person Act* (1861), s. 60. It covers the 'secret disposition' of the dead body, whether the death took place before, at or after birth.   ARP

Conditionability Individual variations in response to 'conditioning' (by which is meant a highly specific learning process involving the manipulation of rewards and punishments to produce desired behaviour). H.J. Eysenck (3rd ed., 1977), *Crime and Personality* has argued that differences in conditionability in childhood (leading to differential absorption of pro-social values) directly relate to adult criminality.

See also *Behaviour modification*; *Extraversion*.   DPW

Conditioning. See *Behaviour modification*; *Conditionability*.

Confidence tricks There are numerous forms (Jackson, 1962, pp. 383–7), many of great antiquity (e.g. the *hokano-baro* described by Vesey-FitzGerald (1973), and all based on the greed and gullibility of the victim, who is often also out to break the law. In essence, a confidence trick is either a promising-looking gamble which the victim cannot win (e.g. the three-card trick or the three-pea trick), or involves the criminal developing a trusting relationship – lending and borrowing money – with the victim, the trust being abruptly terminated when enough

41

money is in the hands of the criminal. Maurer (1940) divided such tricks into the 'short con', usually one operator involving a fast take from an individual, and the 'big con', usually worked by a group which takes a much longer time to set up, with correspondingly higher gains. A higher level of education and increased awareness of duplicity due to the media have probably slightly reduced incidence, although estimates of current numbers are impossible to make since victims will only rarely report such actions.

R.L. Jackson (1962), *Criminal Investigation*; D.M. Maurer (N.Y., 1940), *The Big Con*; J.B. Roebuck and R.C. Johnson (1964), 'The "short con" man', *Crime and Delinquency*, 10, 235; E.M. Schur (1957), 'Sociological analysis of confidence swindling', *JCLCPS*, 48, 296; B. Vesey-FitzGerald (1973), *Gypsies of Britain*.   DPW

Consensual crime.   See *Victimless crimes*.

Conspiracy With the enactment of the *Criminal Law Act* (1977), the offence of conspiracy, developed hitherto by the courts, has taken on a statutory definition. (But see below for certain cases where the old law has been temporarily retained.) S. 1 of that Act (as amended by the *Criminal Attempts Act* (1981), s. 5) provides:

> if a person agrees with any other person or persons that a course of conduct shall be pursued which, if the agreement is carried out in accordance with their intentions, either –
>
> (a) will necessarily amount to or involve the commission of an offence or offences by one or more of the parties to the agreement, or
>
> (b) would do so but for the existence of facts which render the commission of the offence or any of the offences impossible, he is guilty of conspiracy to commit the offence or offences in question.

Conspiracy is sometimes referred to as an inchoate offence, along with attempt and incitement, in that it is the activity in contemplation of a substantive offence which is itself criminal; the prevention or inhibition of a substantive offence is its rationale. In conspiracy, group activity in particular is what may make the matter one of some gravity. The penalties are set out in s. 3 of the Act and, roughly, the maximum corresponds with what is permissible for the substantive offence.

The incidence of conspiracy is impossible to estimate from the published statistics, which collate most inchoate offences along with the substantive offence.

Two forms of conspiracy remain actionable under the old law: (a) Conspiracy to defraud, even when the fraud does not amount to a crime; and (b) conspiracy to do an act which tends to corrupt public morals or outrage public decency, again even if such acts are not themselves criminal. Were these forms of conspiracy not retained there would be gaps at the moment in the criminal law. It is intended that changes in the law relating to fraud and to obscenity and indecency will be made, so that the conspiracy definition of s. 1 may then prevail.

Law Commission (1976), *Conspiracy and Criminal Law Reform*, Report no. 76; I. Dennis (1982), 'The Criminal Attempts Act (1981)', *CLR*, 5; J. Smith and B. Hogan (1978), *Criminal Law*, pp. 216 *et seq*. ARP

Constitutional factors/theory Constitutional theories attempted to prove that the origin of crime could be found in a person's genetic make-up or physique (and see *heredity*; *XYY chromosomes*). Now discredited, they have been extremely influential and represent the earliest attempts to examine crime scientifically and to isolate causes. Theorists argued that ownership of certain inherited physical conditions directly caused crime, hence allegedly simplifying the identification of criminals as those who possessed these conditions. The results of early 'tests' of these theories were uncritically accepted since they justified the *status quo* of penal treatment. Optimum treatment then merely consisted of containment only, without hope of improvement, and society was absolved of any responsibility for its criminals, if they were produced by biology rather than by social conditions. (This view, which logically presumes that no treatment can conceivably have any effect, curiously co-existed with deterrent beliefs.) Stages in the generation of such theories (which usually involved a failure sufficiently to accept the influence of environmental factors) are: (a) identification of a prevalent characteristic in a captive population of prisoners (ignoring, for example, conditions of custody and characteristics of the catchment area), (b) correlating crime with the characteristic, (c) arguing that the characteristic was inherited, (d) uncritical ideological acceptance of its

43

causal role in creating crime. Given, however, that crime is socially defined and alterable, there is no likely connection at all between it and biology (but see *physical abnormality*).

See also *Criminal type*; *Intelligence*; *Somatotype*.   DPW

Contagion   A concept first considered by Howard to refer to a situation in which prison inmates, kept together without any attempt to divide them by extent of involvement with crime, would transmit to each other the means to commit further crime once outside prison, prison in fact becoming a school for crime.

See also *Prison classification*.   DPW

Contra-culture   A term used by J.M. Yinger (1960) in 'Contra-culture and sub-culture', *ASR*, 25, 625, to delineate a sub-culture in direct opposition to the values held by society.

See also *Sub-culture*.   DPW

Control theory   According to Hirschi (1969), who is credited with first formulating a coherent statement of 'control theory', criminology should pay more attention to answering the question 'Why *do* men *obey* the rules of society?' As a starting point this has been neglected, as for example in *strain theory* (q.v.) and theories of cultural deviance like *differential association* (q.v.) in favour of the more obvious question 'Why do men *not* obey?'

Hirschi takes his lead from Hobbes (*Leviathan*): 'Of all passions, that which inclineth men least to break the laws, is fear. Nay, excepting some generous natures, it is the only thing, when there is appearance of profit or pleasure by breaking the laws, that makes men keep them.' Control theory does not, however, assume that man is basically amoral; but it does assume variations in the strength of the moral bond. Criminal behaviour occurs when societal controls have weakened; when the individual's 'bond to society is weak or broken' (Hirschi, p. 16). With this, his respect decreases; he has less to fear from society's reproof and he acts increasingly in self-interest.

In Hirschi's analysis the bond involves 'attachment', 'commitment', 'involvement' and a belief in conventional morals. Conforming behaviour is thereby 'explained' and with it its counterpart in deviance. His research, and much since, was designed to test the empirical basis for this and the link with deviance. What is valuable in this approach is the assertion of man's freedom and rationality as opposed to the social determinism which has characterised much else. 'Control theory's major claim to novelty is that it reconceptualises the starting point of something which might turn into a deviant career. By stressing the boundlessness of human nature and the necessity for the powerful in an established institutional order to *caress*, *coax* and *convert* newcomers into conformity, control theory reveals that when this object is not achieved individuals remain at liberty to explore, and that exploration may lead to behaviour labelled as deviant by the powerful' (Box, 1981).

C

S. Box (1981), *Deviance, Reality and Society*; T. Hirschi (Berkeley, 1969), *Causes of Delinquency*. ARP

Control units After the prison riots of 1972 (see *prison security*), control units were introduced, over and above the extant *segregation units* (q.v.) for persistent troublemakers who could be confined for long terms under an austere regime until they showed willingness to behave. Control units were abandoned in 1975 as a result of a public outcry.

P. Birkinshaw (1981), 'The Control Unit régime: law and order in prison', *HJ*, 20(2), 69; J.E. Thomas (1975), 'Special units in prisons', in K. Jones, ed., *The Year Book of Social Policy 1974*. DPW

Convict, the. See *Convict prison*.

Convict prison The idea of the convict prison has a number of origins. First, the notion of a prison as an architectural structure within which might occur rational, measured, reclamatory, deterrent and retributory training of convicted offenders received great impetus in the late eighteenth and early nineteenth centuries, mainly through the remarkable growth of evangelicalism and utilitarianism. Second, the belief that certain prisons ought to be administered by the central authority rather than by local dignitaries flowed from the fact that the government had responsibility for the administration of transportation, the decline of which was intimately bound up with the growth of the convict prison. Third, the state determined to introduce long prison sentences as an alternative during the decline of transportation. Fourth, it was believed that local magistrates lacked the financial, organisational and theoretical basis for the construction and maintenance for such prisons. Fifth, well before the decline of transportation, philanthropic reformers and prison discipline theorists had

45

conducted a campaign of vilification against the prison hulks which held transportees until the convict ships could take them to their destination.

As early as the 1770s, John Howard and others, aware that the American revolution had temporarily ended transportation, had been closely involved in an unsuccessul project to establish a long sentence prison for transportees, but in the early nineteenth century the first government-constructed long-sentence prison was opened at Millbank in London. Two more followed it: Parkhurst in 1838 (for juveniles) and Pentonville in 1842 (as a model prison for the imposition of the *separate system* (q.v.)), and by 1877 there were thirteen of them, other examples of which were Dartmoor (1850) and Portland (1853).

These prisons were initially aimed at two groups of offenders. In part they were intended to hold transportees until such time as the voyage was undertaken but, particularly after *penal servitude* (q.v.) replaced *transportation* (q.v.), they were intended as prisons of long sentence.

Initially these new prisons were each administered by state-appointed committees (e.g. Millbank and Pentonville) but after 1850 their administration was collectively assigned to state–appointed Directors of Convict Prisons and this directorate retained a separate identity until 1898, when its functions were absorbed by the Prison Commission. The prisons themselves were especially suitable for the separation, classification and labour systems required in penal servitude. Typically, their long cell-lined corridors, radiating from massive administrative centres, offered maximum opportunities for constant surveillance and control of prisoners; while their sombre menacing exteriors shrouded from public view the process of punishment of convicted prisoners at the long-term disposal of these most notable additions to the carceral power of the Victorian state:

WJF

Conviction The formal judicial determination of a case on a finding of guilt or the acceptance of a plea of guilty, though the word is sometimes used simply to refer to a finding of guilt.

ARP

Coroner, the An officer of the Crown appointed, in medieval times, to attend to the king's interests in local areas, the coroner has now specific functions under the *Coroners' Acts* (1887 to 1954) as amended by the *Criminal Law Act* (1977). The principal function is to enquire into deaths in his area where there is reasonable cause for suspecting that death was violent or unnatural, or sudden and of unknown cause, or where it had occurred in prison. (A subsidiary function relates to 'treasure trove'.) He may summon a jury to enquire into the facts (only in limited circumstances is he required to do so), and their findings are recorded in their written 'inquisition'.

Until the 1977 Act (above) discontinued it, a coroner's inquest could find a person guilty of murder, manslaughter or infanticide and the case could go straight to the Crown Court for trial. What now remains of his former function consists in the safeguard of a public enquiry into a death which may cause concern. This may, of course, be dissipated should there be a trial, and the law now provides that the coroner must adjourn the inquest to await the outcome; it also provides that any finding of his inquest should not be inconsistent with the outcome of the trial.

The coroner must be a solicitor, barrister or registered medical practitioner of at least five years' standing.   ARP

Corporal punishment Used to be available in prisons for mutiny or incitement to mutiny or gross personal violence against a prison officer, under s. 18 of the *Prison Act* (1952), which allowed a maximum of eighteen strokes of the birch rod for those twenty-one and over, and twelve for those younger, until it was abolished by s. 65 of the *Criminal Justice Act* (1967). Prior to this, whipping with the cat-o'-nine-tails was available (1743–1948) for offences against prison discipline and as a separate punishment awarded by the courts for crimes of violence (as was birching). The 'cat' consisted of nine leather whips each tipped with a knot, attached to one handle, which inflicted severe lacerating injuries. There is no evidence that either form of corporal punishment had any deterrent effect; rather the opposite.   DPW

Corrective training Introduced by the *Criminal Justice Act* (1948), s. 21 and repealed by the *Criminal Justice Act* (1967), s. 37, this was intended for offenders who while apparently committed to a criminal career were not so far advanced in criminal sophistication that a period of intensive and constructive training might succeed in rescuing them.

The youngest age at which a person could be sentenced was twenty-one; there was no statutory maximum, but the Court of

CORRUPTION

Criminal Appeal (R *v*. Boucher (36 Cr. App. R. 152)) advised that the sentence should not unless in exceptional circumstances be used on men over thirty-five and generally should be used only on an offender whose age did not exceed thirty. The offender had to be convicted on indictment of an offence punishable with imprisonment of two years or more. He further had to have been convicted on at least two previous occasions since reaching the age of seventeen of similar offences. The court, if these criteria were met, also had to satisfy itself 'that it is expedient with a view to his reformation and the prevention of crime that he should receive training of a corrective character for a substantial time followed by a period of supervision if released before the expiration of his sentence.' The sentence was between two and four years and the offender received one-third remission. Treatment in prison was the same as for a person sentenced to imprisonment and then transferred to a regional training prison. A prisoner was released on licence to the supervision of a probation officer, the licence being for the period of the sentence which remained unexpired at the time of the prisoner's release. Any breach of imposed conditions led to recall to prison.

The White Paper, *The Adult Offender* (Cmnd 2852, 1965), which proposed abolition of the sentence, gives the number of sentences per year of CT as about 200 and says that in 1965 there were 260 men and women serving them.   DPW

Corruption As 'the perversion of integrity by bribery or favour' (*Oxford English Dictionary*), see *bribery*. As the corruption of morals, see *conspiracy* and *obscenity*.   ARP

Counterfeiting A popular craft-crime throughout the nineteenth century which is still occasionally engaged in. Coins might be manufactured from worthless metal in plaster of paris moulds and then 'coloured' (i.e. silvered by electroplating) and milled. (Milling itself was originally introduced to prevent the 'clipping' of pieces off gold coin, an alternative to 'sweating', i.e. shaking them in a bag and collecting their dust.) Alternatively, low-denomination coins were coloured to make them resemble coins of higher denomination. Treasury notes were faked by engraving a plate and using a printing press (more recently by photocopying) or by prising a note apart edgeways-on with a needle and then backing each of the two constituent pieces with stiffening paper and passing them off as separate notes. Increasingly detailed genuine coins and notes made to fine tolerances (which are difficult to copy realistically) and forensic aids have caused a fall-off in counterfeiting. Counterfeiting currency notes and coins used as money is penalised by the *Forgery and Counterfeit Currency Act* (1981), Pt II.

See also *Forgery*.   DPW

Crank. See *Prison*.

Crime There is no word in the whole lexicon of legal and criminological terms which is so elusive of definition as the word 'crime'. Yet an understanding of the meaning of the word is of central importance to the study of the making and breaking of law and to the justification and measurement of punishment.

Crime in the law One way of exploring the resonances of the word is to consider the different contexts in which it has been used. In law and jurisprudence, for example, crime is defined as those acts or omissions which are specifically proscribed by law. This proscription, however, always involves sanctions or punishments and it is this connection between crime and its punishment that has remained the key element in the lawyers' concept of crime.[1]

For Sir James Stephen (1829–1894), whose *History of Criminal Law* (1883) gave the standard legal view of the time, crime was 'some act or omission in respect of which legal punishment may be inflicted'. From this definition we must infer that the criminality of an act is defined in an important way by the punishment which follows it. It is for this reason that the age and state of mind of the offender must be taken into consideration. If, for example, a person is killed or injured by another, the killing or injury would not be criminal if the aggressor were too young, too deranged or too weak-minded to form the kind of evil intention that would render him liable to punishment. For lawyers, then, crime is a concept whose necessary elements are proscribed action, evil intention and prescribed punishment. This is the stuff of legal argument and decision-making in the courts. It also fixes the definition of crime firmly in the person and the intention of the criminal. There is no crime without a willing criminal.

Crime and sin Among moralists there has been some attempt to construct a relationship between acts or omissions which are contrary to accepted religious or moral teaching and acts or omissions which are proscribed by secular law. From this attempt there has grown up a huge and confusing literature on 'crime and sin'. This is an important aspect of any study of the meaning of crime but its interest is historical rather than epistemological. The evolution of moral feeling and moral systems is on a different historical time-scale from that of any system of secular legislation. It is easy to chart the passage from crime to non-crime of attempted suicide, homosexual acts or adultery; it is also possible to give some social explanation for the change. We cannot synchronise with these short-term movements the long sweeps of continuity and evolution in whole systems of religion or morality. For some time now the arguments on this matter have been regarded as of interest only to philosophers and therefore largely academic.

Crime as disease The late nineteenth and early twentieth century saw the development of a new theory of criminal behaviour and thus a new definition of crime. It was thought of as a disease, not in the body politic, but in those who committed criminal acts as they were legally defined. Murders, thefts and robberies were committed by men and women who were abnormal in body and in mind. Crime was a function of their 'diseased or defective' condition (Lombroso, 1836–1909). This theory, although it began as an explanation of criminal behaviour, provided an analogy that was comforting and easy to assimilate. Crime was like a disease. It appeared non-randomly among the weaker, more defective of the human race, but its threat could be contained because disease was curable or at least treatable. Such a definition need not incorporate the legal niceties of intention and malice. It could accommodate the notion that the very commission of a wrongful act itself justified intervention – a notion that lawyers call 'strict liability' and apply to a few, very special offences. Therefore the connection between crime and punishment, so vital to legal rationalisations, need not be made.

Crime as a social organisation The consideration of crime as a function – or a malfunction – of social organisation itself allows for many different kinds of definitions which can be tailored to suit the needs of Marxists, Durkheimians, the Chicago School, followers of Edwin Sutherland and many others. These definitions, however, are vague about the phenomenon of criminal behaviour itself. Is it any breach of the law which attracts punishment? Is it an attempt, deliberate or unintentional, to frustrate the social and political rules that others accept? Is it any kind of behaviour that can be used as an excuse for excluding certain classes and kinds of people from participation in the social activity of the community? Whatever the content of these definitions, the notions that they describe do not separate the ideas of crime and punishment. If anything, they emphasise the importance of punishment in the same way that lawyers do. It is the sanction which lays bare and defines the crime.

Crime as a social process   One of the many other attempts to unravel the strands that are woven into the notion of crime begins with a consideration of the whole process of definition. Here it may be helpful to return to the analogy of crime as disease, if only to see how the process of crime-making begins. Disease has no existence until it is complained about or discovered. Many people may be suffering from kidney disease, bilharzia or fibrositis, but until they complain about their symptoms or are recognised to be exhibiting symptoms, their disease does not exist.

So it is with crime. Victims of offences which have the characteristics of robbery, rape or burglary may not wish to make any complaint of what they have suffered. If these incidents do not come to light in any other way, by police activity, for example, or by the reports of witnesses, they remain without formal definition as crime. In effect, crime does not exist.[2] Calculations of the extent of this non-existent crime can be made where there are studies of victim response to what might be called criminal behaviour.[3] A further stage in the process of crime creation is the acceptance or rejection by law-enforcement agencies (mostly the police) of reports of crime. There is extensive evidence in the USA and some evidence in this country that a sizeable proportion of reported offences never reach the official statistics.

This last notion of crime, therefore, has to do with a series of interactions – the reaction of the victim to the assault upon him or upon his property and the reaction of the police both to reports of what may be criminal acts and to offences they may discover for themselves. There is a final stage in this process which may be of less importance – it is the decision of magistrates, judges or juries that there are not the ingredients of crime in the offence that is described to them.

CRIME RATE

All these definitions of crime are part of the texture of the complex social and political organisations within which such human activity is devised, organised, controlled and defined. Legal definitions are neither so restrictive nor so inapposite as they seem, for they find a place for sanctions and limit their use. Moral definitions point to deep and long-held beliefs that may colour some of our perspectives on crime and punishment. Medical and social explanations and analogies contribute to the definition of crime. They also point forward to the consideration of criminal activity as a social process by which its existence and recognition depend upon the reactions of victims and law-enforcement agencies almost as much as upon the perpetrator of the act which comes to be labelled a crime.

NOTES

1 The first analysis of such a connection was, however, made by an economist rather than a lawyer. Cesare Beccaria (1738–1794) pointed to the necessity of some kind of economic relationship between crime and its punishment, which should be reasonable, just and effective.

2 Earlier theorists, who did not take the view that crime was a social process, included in the universe of crime both that which came to light and that which was never seen. The latter they called the 'dark figure' (see *hidden crime*) of crime.

3 The extent of under-reporting by the victim is thought to be around 50 per cent on average in this country, the USA and the Netherlands. US studies of victim reporting have been going on since 1967. A Dutch report, *Criminal Victimisation in the Netherlands 1974–1977*, was published by the Ministry of Justice in 1978. A general survey in this country by M. Durant, M. Thomas and H.D. Willcock was published in 1972, OPCS, *Crime, Criminals and the Law*.   SM

Crime rate The rate at which crime occurs in reference to population, measured either by *offender* rates or more usually by number of *offences* in a time period. The interest lies in attempting to make comparisons (over time for a particular offence or group of them, between different offences at a particular time, or between regions comparing similar offences), and then in drawing inferences which would account for variation. Difficulties arise in that statistics may be unreliable and hence conclusions may be invalid. With increased awareness of these problems, authoritative discussions of rates so popular in the past have tended to diminish in number.

K. Bottomley and C. Coleman (1981), *Understanding Crime Rates*; R.A. Carr-Hill and N.H. Stern (1979), *Crime, the Police and Criminal Statistics*, ch. 3.

See also *Hidden crime*.   DPW

Crime wave A sudden increase, out of all proportion to expectations, either in all crime or in particular offences. This is very difficult to distinguish from a *moral panic* (q.v.), when it is alleged that a 'wave' is occurring, or from an increase in *reporting*, which gives the impression that more is occurring. Increases in reporting are of course more likely after moral panics. They may also occur because certain behaviours have suddenly become more visible or where tolerance of the behaviour has diminished as a result of changed social or technical circumstances. Changed circumstances may lead to *displacement* (q.v.) to sections of society more prepared to report acts as crimes, and as with anything else there are fashions in criminal behaviours. Emulative carbon-copies of certain (usually bizarre) offence forms undoubtedly do occur, but are usually so limited as not to justify being classed as a 'wave'.

Genuine crime waves are probably associated with affluence and with the aftermath of major social crises but it is really only feasible to identify them retrospectively. R.A. Carr-Hill and N.H. Stern (1979), *Crime, the Police and Criminal Statistics*, argue that 'the process generating criminal statistics differs substantially from year to year' (p. 271) and on this basis do not accept that it is possible to say whether actual offences have increased or decreased over a long term, far less to identify a 'wave'.

See also *Anomie*; *Criminalisation*; *Differential association*.

DPW

Criminal, the To say that a criminal is simply a person who has committed a crime is inadequate; the word suggests a continuing state, though expressions like habitual or persistent offender, or recidivist, are used for the more chronic. The difference between *primary* (q.v.) and secondary deviance makes a similar point. Its usage also reflects some of the variations to be observed in the use of the word *crime* (q.v.) in its different contexts.   ARP

CRIMINAL APPEALS

Criminal appeals   Persons convicted have the following rights of appeal against conviction and/or sentence: note that the prosecution may not appeal against an acquittal or sentence, though, exceptionally they may raise points of law in this way.

1   *Against conviction*
   A From Magistrates' Courts   (a) A person convicted may appeal to the *Crown Court* (q.v.), consisting for this purpose of a circuit judge or recorder plus at least two and not more than four magistrates. There will be a complete rehearing of the case.
   (b) Where the person convicted asserts that an error of law was made, the matter is referred to the Divisional Court of the Queen's Bench Division of the High Court, consisting of at least two judges. This proceeding may also be instigated by the prosecution.
   B From the Crown Court   A person convicted may appeal to the Court of Appeal, Criminal Division – consisting of at least three judges – on matters of fact or of law; if factual errors are asserted, though, the appeal lies only with permission from the trial judge or the Court of Appeal. On legal matters the appeal lies 'as of right' and the Attorney General may also refer a point of law to the Court of Appeal (the outcome not affecting an acquittal).
   C The House of Lords   hears appeals from the Divisional Court of the Queen's Bench Division (A(b) above) and from the Crown Court, but in either case only if the lower court certifies that a point of law of general public importance is involved, and then only if the lower court or the House of Lords gives leave to appeal. In its judicial capacity the House of Lords normally consists only of the 'Law Lords' and at least three will hear an appeal.
   In dealing with points of law, the Court of Appeal has no small say in the development of the criminal law, and similarly the House of Lords. However, it has been suggested that the English system inhibits this development in any 'consistent, coherent or principled way'. (See J. Spencer (1982), 'Criminal law and criminal appeals: the tail that wags the dog', *CLR*, 260.)
   The annual *Criminal Statistics* contain tables of appeals against conviction (in 1980 they totalled 7,800) and around 80 per cent come from Magistrates' Courts, 20 per cent from the Crown Court. Only a handful of cases go to the House of Lords.

2 *Against sentence*

A From Magistrates' Courts Appeal lies to the Crown Court, composed as above, against any sentence or order made by a Magistrates' Court, except orders for probation or conditional discharge or costs. The Crown Court may also review a sentence on an appeal only against conviction. If an error of law in the sentencing process is alleged, the Divisional Court may review the matter as above.

B From the Crown Court Appeal lies to the Court of Appeal except where the sentence is fixed by law (as in murder). Permission to appeal must be obtained from the Court of Appeal – meaning, though, just one of the judges; if he refuses, the full Court may be asked. The appeal itself will be heard by at least three judges.

The Court's work in the promotion of uniformity in the sentencing process and in the production of principles of *sentencing* (q.v.) is of great importance (see D. Thomas (2nd ed., 1979), *Principles of Sentencing*).

The *Criminal Statistics* show 16,000 appeals against sentence for 1980. 69 per cent were from Magistrates', 31 per cent from the Crown Court. But *proportionately* fewer appealed from Magistrates', the estimate being 0.5 per cent as against 7 per cent from the Crown Court. ARP

Criminal damage The *Criminal Damage Act* (1971) penalises conduct ranging from minor damage and 'vandalism' to serious damage and *arson* (q.v.) with intent to endanger life. It all amounts to about 13 per cent of serious crime recorded by the police, but most of it is such as to be dealt with by Magistrates' Courts. Of those found guilty or cautioned, juveniles tend to form a fairly high proportion (38 per cent of all ages in 1980). See R. Clarke, ed. (1978), *Tackling Vandalism*, HORS no. 47.

ARP

Criminal Injuries Compensation Board. See *Compensation.*

Criminal responsibility. See *Responsibility.*

Criminal type, the The founder of scientific positivist criminology, C. Lombroso (1836–1909), in his (1876) *L'Uomo Delinquente*, who based his work on meticulous anthropometric measurement, argued that a distinct criminal type existed, both atavistic and degenerate – the born criminal. This type was recognisable by stigmata (physical peculiarities and malformations). From the 3rd edition of *L'Uomo* he began to modify this view, stating that perhaps only 35 per cent of criminals were of this type, the rest being either insane or occasional criminals. In his (1893) *La Donna Delinquente* (Eng. trans., 1895) with G. Ferrero, he noted the rarity of the criminal type among females, arguing that prostitution was the female substitute for crime.

See also *Constitutional factors*.   DPW

Criminalisation, Over-criminalisation   The process whereby more and more behaviour becomes subject to regulation by the criminal law as this expands under public pressure, 'creating' as a result more criminals. De-criminalisation is the opposite, whereby acts that previously were criminal have ceased to be. As applied to an individual, criminalisation and decriminalisation respectively refer to the processes of becoming criminal, and of re-entering law-abiding society.

See also *Diversion*.   DPW

Criminology   The study of crime, of attempts to control it, and of attitudes to it. Crime is interpreted in its widest sense, so as to include minor as well as major law-breaking, and also conduct which, but for the special status or role of those involved, would be regarded as law-breaking; e.g. excessive punishment of children by parents, anti-social practices of commercial undertakings.

Description   Much of the modern research literature is descriptive, due to recognition of the fact that official statistics deal only with *reported* offences, and that most law-breaking is unreported, whether because unobserved (e.g. traffic offences), unresented (e.g. consensual sexual offences), too trivial (e.g. pilfering by employees), unlikely to be cleared up (e.g. pocket-picking) or for other reasons. This can to some extent be remedied by *victim surveys* and *self-report studies* (qq.v.): and these have demonstrated that – with exceptions such as homicide – reported offences are the atypical tip of a very large iceberg. Another reason for their atypicality is that even offences reported by the public are not always recorded by police or other recording agencies (e.g. minor domestic violence, because police experience is that complainants often change their minds about giving evidence).

Explanation Advances in descriptive research have affected explanations of law-breaking, especially by demonstrating that in industrialised societies many kinds of violence, dishonesty, sexual misbehaviour and vandalism are endemic, and not, as was thought, confined to unusual individuals or sub-groups. (This can be exaggerated: even self-report surveys of adolescents, the age-group most prone to law-breaking, reveal a substantial minority whose infringements are trivial and infrequent.) Explanations can be divided into those which seek to account for differences between the *incidence* of this or that type of crime in *groups* (whether distinguished by age, ethnically, occupationally or otherwise) and those seeking to account for the *frequency* of some sort of law-breaking by *identified individuals*. Explanations of the former type use concepts such as conflicts of interest, availability of opportunities for legitimate and illegitimate gain, or sub-cultural values. The latter type feature family differences in child-training methods, the influence of siblings, friends or leaders, defects of intelligence or education, and – in special cases – congenital defects such as brain damage. *XYY chromosomes* and poor *conditionability* (qq.v.).

Prevention A large part of criminological literature is concerned with this, and is sometimes called 'penology'. The most traditional technique is deterrence, that is, the prospect of penalties which will discourage both those who have experienced them ('individual deterrence') or those who have not ('general deterrence'). Research suggests that differences in severity of penalty, though not unimportant, matter less than the probability of incurring it. Since this is low in the case of traffic or acquisitive offenders, they are not easily deterred. Sexual or violent offences, on the other hand, though more often leading to detection if reported, are frequently committed in states of mind which do not consider the consequences. Another traditional approach was to eliminate serious offenders ('felons') by hanging, transportation or very long sentences. This survives in the *life sentence* and in *Restriction Orders* (qq.v.) which commit offenders indefinitely to mental hospitals. Increasing doubts, however, about both the ethics of indefinite precautionary sentences and the ability of courts and experts to identify those who are future dangers to life or limb have made such disposals unpopular, except with the man-in-the-street. The emphasis therefore shifted in the course of this century to techniques for 'reforming' offenders: i.e. altering their dispositions by enlightened custodial régimes or supervision. Follow-up studies, however, have shown that the offenders (if any) who will benefit are in the minority and that it is very hard to identify them at the sentencing stage.

'*Just deserts*'   Recognition that none of these approaches can contribute much to crime-reduction has led to a revival of the classical principle that penalties should be 'just deserts'; that is, should be what are deserved by offenders, whatever future benefits may or may not result. The consequence has been to dilute penology with jurisprudence, although sometimes of a superficial sort. In the USA, for example, reaction against the flexibility of treatment-oriented sentencing has taken the form of rigid scales of penalties ('tariffs'). This has traditionally been the approach of countries whose penal codes are modelled on the Code Napoléon; but they have developed sophisticated rules for mitigating or aggravating standard penalties so as to discriminate between degrees of culpability in individual cases, whereas the American 'just deserts' approach is designed to limit discrimination of this kind.

Denunciation   This retributive approach, however, is distrusted by those who see it as sterile and moralistic. An alternative is the 'expressive' or 'denunciatory' justification for penalties which – at least in the usual form – claims that the penalty expresses society's disapproval of the offence, and thus maintains public standards of behaviour. Such evidence as there is does not suggest that this effect is any stronger than that of deterrence; and, since it depends on the extent to which individual sentences (not sentencing statistics) are made known to the public, this is not surprising.

Technology   A comparatively recent development has been a marked advance in the technology of crime prevention. Architects and city planners have seen the advantages of 'defensible space', and have designed flats, office buildings, shopping precincts, car parks and other public places so as to maximise the possibilities of surveillance by residents, neighbours and security staff. Burglar alarms have become more sophisticated, and – together with other devices for preventing thefts – are now the basis of a profitable industry. An increasing percentage of wage-earners are paid by cheque instead of ready cash (trade unions are less cautious about this than they used to be). Private posses of security staff can be hired for special or routine protection of people or property. Advances in *police science* (q.v.) have not only made fingerprint searches much faster but have enabled convincing evidence to be based on other physical traces such as hairs, blood-stains, semen.

These developments have their dangers. The transition from a cash society to a credit-card society means that for offenders who are skilled enough to abuse the system the gains are bigger. The criminal manipulation of computers can yield spectacular hauls for expert employees, who are sometimes not prosecuted even when detected, in case the bank or firm in question suffers from loss of customers' confidence. Security firms are sometimes unwary enough to employ men with criminal records, to their regret. The computerisation of personal records – whether for security or other reasons – may make them vulnerable to misuse. Forensic scientists sometimes present evidence to juries with more confidence than it merits. Nevertheless, technology seems to offer better prospects than some traditional ways of waging war on crime.   NDW

Critical criminology.   See *Radical criminology*.

Crown Court The Crown Court, set up by the *Courts Act* (1971), is the higher court for trying criminal cases; it also has functions on *appeal* (q.v. at *criminal appeals*) or referral for sentence from the lower courts, i.e. *Magistrates'* (q.v.). It replaced the old Assizes and Quarter Sessions.

The Court, although properly referred to in the singular, sits in various towns throughout England and Wales. In the 'circuits' (i.e. administrative regions) into which England and Wales is divided, circuit judges (appointed from recorders of three years' standing or barristers of ten years' standing) and recorders (appointed from barristers or solicitors of ten years' standing) function at all locations. The most serious cases, though, are dealt with by High Court judges visiting only certain towns. The Crown Court in London is known as the Central Criminal Court – the 'Old Bailey'. The Crown Court provides trial 'on indictment' (the document specifying the offences alleged) and before a *jury* (q.v.). The vast majority of cases (96–98 per cent) heard by all courts are, however, heard 'summarily' by magistrates. See D. Robinson (1972), 'The Crown Court', *CLR*, 14.   ARP

CULTURE CONFLICT

Culture conflict   The expression dates back to the work of T. Sellin (N.Y. 1938), *Culture Conflict and Crime*, and refers to his analysis of the ways in which conflicts between the norms of divergent cultural codes may arise: '(1) when these codes clash on the border of contiguous culture areas; (2) when, as the case may be with legal norms, the law of one cultural group is extended to cover the territory of another; or (3) when members of one cultural group migrate to another.'

The focus within this framework on the effects of immigration in the USA was of great importance, though it was for later writers to give it a fuller theoretical form.

See also *Anomie*; *Area studies*; *Contra-culture*; *Opportunity*; *Sub-culture*.   ARP

Cultural deviance theory   What characterises this type of theory is the supposed conformity of the deviant to a set of norms and values not accepted by more general society or by its power elite.

See also *Culture conflict*.   ARP

Dangerous class(es) An expression widely and uncritically used by the elite (from at least the eighteenth century onwards well into this century) to refer in general to the poor, criminals and vagrants and their particular propensity to riot or engage in other 'dangerous' activities. The expression is important since its existence more readily permitted the use of repressive legislation and penal measures. L. Chevalier (1973), *Labouring Classes and Dangerous Classes: in Paris during the first half of the Nineteenth Century*.

See also *Dangerousness*.   DPW

Dangerousness While classical theorists such as Beccaria advocated fixed penalties for given offences, this view was opposed by nineteenth-century adherents of *positivism* (q.v.), for whom punishment should ideally be individualised, forward-looking and corrective. A problem then posed for positivists was what to do with 'incorrigible' offenders unaffected by ordinary penalties. A typical answer was that they should be subjected to special preventive measures 'according to the degree of their degeneration, *or of the danger which they threaten*' (International Union of Penal Law, 1890).

Garofalo (1852–1934) is generally accredited as the first positivist criminologist to develop clearly this notion of 'dangerousness' (*pericolosità*). Commonly suggested target groups for special preventive confinement were *habitual offenders* (q.v.) and those with some *mental abnormality* (q.v.). The discredited measure of *preventive detention* (q.v.) in England was a kind of 'dangerousness sentence' for habitual criminals.

From these beginnings, the term 'dangerousness' in criminology has been used especially in connection with (i) the identification of individual offenders said to pose a special threat to society, and (ii) the provision of special protective measures against such offenders. Whilst associated historically with *positivism* and *social defence* (qq.v.), this is not a necessary connection; some recent advocates of 'dangerousness sentences' have held other theoretical perspectives.

Since about 1974, a particularly lively debate on 'dangerousness' has developed in several countries, focusing especially upon those offenders believed to threaten serious violence. In Britain this debate has been given special impetus by proposals from three official committees to create new preventive sentences for the 'dangerous', or to incorporate 'dangerousness' as a key concept in a revised general sentencing structure.

The recent controversies have centred upon three main issues. First, there is an *empirical debate* about how successful criminologists are, or in principle could become, in predicting future serious violence among specified groups of offenders. The limited number of relevant research studies has been given widely different interpretations; nevertheless, most scholars agree that *on present evidence* predictions of *serious* violence are likely to be wrong at least as often as they are right. This leads, second, to an *ethical debate*: given such figures, is the state morally justified in locking up (say) three offenders for extended terms in order to prevent one serious assault? This debate raises intricate questions in ethical theory; e.g. as regards the scope of utilitarianism, the meaning and content of 'rights', etc. Third, a *socio-political critique* challenges the whole framework of the above debates, arguing that concentration upon 'traditional' violent offenders (assaultists, etc.) as potential candidates for 'dangerousness sentences' fails completely to recognise that more 'modern' crimes (like keeping unsafe factories, or persistently drunken driving) are much more 'dangerous' because they cause more deaths and injuries. Typical replies to this are that 'traditional' and 'modern' crimes are usually different; e.g. in intentionality, potentiality for control by measures short of protective custody, etc. The debates continue.

M. Ancel (1965), *Social Defence*; J. Monahan (Beverly Hills, 1981), *Predicting Violent Behaviour*; J. Floud and W. Young (1981), *Dangerousness and Criminal Justice*; *BJC* Special Issue on Dangerousness, July 1982, 22.

See also *Incapacitation*; *Indeterminate sentence*.   AEB

Dark figure number.   See *Hidden crime*.

Decarceration A term first made prominent by Rothman, and defined by Scull in his book of the same name as 'shorthand for a state-sponsored policy of closing down asylums, prisons and reformatories. Mad people, criminals and delinquents are being discharged or refused admission to the dumps in which they have traditionally been housed. Instead, they are to be left at large, to be coped with "in the community".' Such a definition is both broad and value-laden. Decarceration appears to refer not merely to the discharge of long-term inmates but also to the exclusion of those who would have been admitted for relatively long periods of time under the *status quo ante*, and even to the development of short-stay 'revolving-door' policies with regard to those who are admitted under community-oriented programmes of control.

D

Most of Scull's evidence for the development of such policies comes from US and British adoptions of 'community care' and the running down of long-stay beds in mental hospitals. The evidence for the decarceration of adult and juvenile criminal offenders is not as firm as that of the mentally ill. Few post-war examples of a major decline in the size of prison and reformatory populations can be found in either country. Those that are known involve the closing down of juvenile rather than adult institutions. Although the experience of other nations, such as the Netherlands, might be relevant, Scull does not refer to it. He thus has to rely largely on imprisonment rates which, indeed, have fallen in recent decades, but this is to incorporate a policy of diversion into his definition of decarceration.

Thus Scull extends the concept of decarceration well beyond his original definition to encompass a critique of diversionary and community treatment policies in general. These he regards as methods of social control which are a 'response to the changing exigencies of domestic pacification and control under welfare capitalism'. Whatever the liberal rhetoric of community treatment, he contends that its latent function is to reduce the cost of managing deviants through 'non-segregative' methods of control that, in practice, pauperise and ghettoise them.

In sum, the concept of decarceration is an imprecise but powerful antidote to excessive enthusiasm for community care and de-institutionalisation.

Y. Bakal, ed. (Lexington, Mass., 1973), *Closing Correctional Institutions: New Strategies for Youth Services*; D. Rothman (1973), 'Decarcerating prisoners and patients', *Civil Liberties Review*, 1, 8; A.T. Scull (Englewood Cliffs, N.J., 1977),

DECRIMINALISATION

Decarceration, Community Treatment and the Deviant: a Radical view.
    See also *Diversion*.   MNS

Decriminalisation.   See *Criminalisation*.

Defensible space.   See *Prevention environmental*.

Deferment of sentence   A court may defer its *sentence* (q.v.) for up to six months in order to have regard to the offender's subsequent conduct, including his making reparation (where appropriate) for his offence, or any change in his circumstances as might occur, for example in his employment, accommodation or marital status. It is a somewhat veiled inducement to him to change his ways – though what is expected of him should be made clear even if the final outcome is not. The power to defer sentence can be exercised only when the offender consents and the court is satisfied that it would be just. If he is convicted of any offence during the period of deferment he may thereupon be sentenced for both offences. At the end of the period the court, preferably constituted as before, will enquire into his conduct and if satisfied may impose a non-custodial sentence or discharge him.

Corden and Nott (1980) report a growing use of deferment since its introduction, though even so it does not come the way of more than 2 per cent of all persons sentenced by the courts. The procedure has some affinity to *diversion* (q.v.) and should be carefully distinguished from *binding over* and *remand* (qq.v.).

The Criminal Justice Act (1972) gave the courts this power, now contained in the *Powers of the Criminal Courts Act* (1973).

J. Corden and D. Nott (1980), 'The power to defer sentence', *BJC*, 20(4), 358; D. Thomas (2nd ed., 1979), *Principles of Sentencing*, p. 380.   ARP

Defilement   The word has come to refer to a group of offences involving a person who permits premises to be used for sexual intercourse with a girl under sixteen or who causes or encourages prostitution of or intercourse with or indecent assault on a girl under sixteen for whom he is responsible. The word itself does not feature in modern statutes; indeed it simply means 'unlawful sexual intercourse'; but it has lived on, as described, in legal usage. The offences in point are to be found in ss. 25, 26 and 28 of the *Sexual Offences Act* (1956). See Archbold's *Pleading; Evidence and Practice in Criminal Cases* (1979), paras 2948–9.   ARP

Delinquency areas.   See *Area studies*.

Delinquent/Delinquency   In its literal meaning delinquency is the omission of a duty or the commission of a fault, not necessarily a crime. Frequently, however, it is used almost synonymously with crime, particularly with reference to crimes that are not thought to be very grave or to offences committed by young persons. Juvenile delinquency is commonly used to include behaviour, such as truancy or being 'beyond' parental control, which would not be considered criminal in an adult. American writers call these status offences.

The term 'delinquent' is sometimes applied to an individual who has not merely committed some offence, but who is generally unruly or antisocial. There is some empirical justification for this usage in connection with young offenders who make repeated appearances before the juvenile courts. They are often found to be troublesome in a variety of ways, resistant to parental discipline, liable to aggressive outbursts, unpopular and difficult in the eyes of their teachers, irregular attenders and backward scholastically, apt to mix with companions of a similar character and to participate in group offences of vandalism or illicit drug use and prone to carry offensive weapons and to become involved in fights. They adopt aggressively macho attitudes, are intolerant of ethnic minorities and hostile and suspicious towards all authority figures, especially the police. As they grow up, their life-styles become noticeably hedonistic, characterised by heavy drinking, sexual promiscuity, choice of short-term jobs that require no training, frequent unemployment and no organised or constructive use of leisure time.

This generalised antisociality of the young recidivist is frequently associated with poor upbringing, deprived home circumstances and parental deviance or criminality. Fortunately, most young delinquents cease to acquire further convictions when they reach their twenties and settle down to a more conformist existence. Those who come from the worst backgrounds and who are the most recidivistic as juveniles are the ones most likely to have criminal careers persisting into adult life, usually in the form of small-scale, disorganised crimes leading to repeated imprisonments.   DJW

Deprivation (parental)   Ever since Bowlby's (1946) seminal work on broken homes and maternal deprivation as a possible generator of psychopathy, controversy has blazed over the impact of parental (especially maternal) deprivation and its role in the creation of criminals. Bowlby found that 40 per cent of his sample of delinquents had been maternally deprived in the first five years of life and he related this to the development of affectionless, antisocial characters. It is now generally recognised (Rutter, 1981) that it is the *quality* of bonding experiences (coming not only through contact with the biological mother) the child has in the early years which is critical in determining whether it learns to relate to people sociably or not. The absence of the biological mother need not produce behaviour problems (including crime), providing there are surrogates available who teach bonding, offer sensitive responsiveness to the child's needs and provide a background of low stress, consistent behaviour and discipline (West and Farrington, 1977). Multiple separation experiences, the absence of substitute mothers or similar figures, high stress, the experience of inconsistency and bonding deficiencies may create conditions favourable to the development of *psychopathy* (q.v.). Yet it is possible that the effects of these may be *reversed* by subsequent social experiences; infantile experiences do *not* 'fix' the personality (Rutter, 1981, ch. 9). Rutter makes it clear that the experiences included under the term 'maternal deprivation' are too diverse and the effects too varied for it to continue as a useful term.

   J. Bowlby (1946), *Forty-four Juvenile Thieves: their Characters and Home-Life*; M. Rutter (1981), *Maternal Deprivation Reassessed*; D.J. West and D.P. Farrington (1977), *The Delinquent Way of Life*.

   See also *Conditionability*.   DPW

Detection   By detection may be meant either discovering the occurrence of a crime in the first place (see *reporting, self-report studies, victim surveys*) or, more usually, discovering the offender or resolving or clearing up the crime in a satisfactory fashion. This latter is partly a matter of level of public concern, partly of police manpower and partly of *police science* (q.v.). Different offences have different clear-up rates (see annual

Criminal Statistics). For a discussion of the detection rate see R.A. Carr-Hill and N.H. Stern (1979) *Crime, the Police and Criminal Statistics*, ch. 3(I).   DPW

Detention centres   These were set up by the *Criminal Justice Act* (1948) following discussions, going back to the 1920s, to the effect that what was needed for some young offenders was a 'short and sharp punishment'. The Act, as amended by the *Criminal Justice Act* (1961) enabled the courts so to sentence offenders between fourteen and twenty-one who had committed offences, punishable in the case of adults with imprisonment, for a period of three months (nine months maximum as cumulative sentences). On release, after-care supervision took over for one year. *The Criminal Justice Act* (1982), re-emphasising the short and sharp punishment approach, now enables the courts to pass a sentence from three weeks to four months; normal remission of one-third the period is allowable and after-care supervision provided. Even before the 1982 Act, the Home Office were experimenting with a new and more rigorous régime for detention centres, appropriate also to the shorter periods and the results are still awaited. There are some nineteen detention centres in the system; no provision has ever been made for females and the 1982 Act applies only to males.

Advisory Council on the Penal System (1970), *Detention Centres*; Home Office *et al.* (1980), *Young Offenders*, Cmnd 8045.   ARP

Determinism   In contrast with the doctrine of free will, determinism suggests that human actions (like physical events) are not chosen but caused. Determinists argue that the only reason why human beings speak of decisions, choices, moral dilemmas, etc., is that we have not hitherto been able to discover and specify all the causes of our actions. Even when we consider we have chosen a course of action (for instance, when we claim to have been persuaded by rational argument), determinists suggest that we are only describing a certain response to a set of stimuli, and that this outcome could have been predicted by scientific study of these influences on us, and the patterns of our previous behaviour.

At various times in the history of criminological thought, sociologists and psychologists have advanced deterministic accounts of criminal behaviour (either of specific crimes, or of crime in general). Resistance to such claims has been strong, both by philosophers and by lawyers. This has mainly centred on the ability that people have to specify their motives for action. Although we are not always truthful about the factors which influence our behaviour, we can usually give some account of them, and specify the reasons why we did one thing rather than another. In particular, we can distinguish between, for instance, actions performed mainly for rewards, and actions undertaken from convictions, and according to principles. Both philosophers and lawyers would tend to claim that all actions follow rules, rather than simply patterns, of conduct, and that people are generally aware both of their own rules and of society's laws, and are conscious of the ways in which their behaviour either conforms to these, or deviates from them. Some recent criminological writing has adopted a position of compromise in the causation of criminal acts called 'soft determinism'. This includes elements of choice and constraint and recognises the need to distinguish between different kinds of causes of action, and the circumstances in which choices are made.

See also *Drift*. WJOJ

Deterrence Criminal deterrence is an important aim of a criminal justice system; it is also presented as a justification for punishment, especially by utilitarians. Broadly, criminal deterrence refers to crime prevention *per se*: any measure which acts to prevent crime is a deterrent. Strictly, criminal deterrence refers to crime prevention only when this is achieved by threatening consequences (arrest, trial, conviction, penalties) which the prospective law-breaker is unwilling to risk. Imprisonment, if it prevents crime only by keeping an offender 'out of circulation', is a deterrent in the broad sense. If it prevents crime by being a consequence which potential offenders are unwilling to risk, then it is a deterrent in the strict sense. In the strict sense, in particular, general deterrence must be distinguished from individual (or special, or specific) deterrence. Imprisonment of one offender has a general deterrent effect if it makes other potential offenders refrain from crime. It has an individual deterrent effect if it makes the imprisoned offender refrain from crime after his release.

There is a considerable research literature on the general deterrent effectiveness of various penalties (see D. Beyleveld (1980), *A Bibliography on General Deterrence Research*). This research tends to show an inverse relationship between various crimes and the probabilities of arrest and conviction, but no relationship between crime and the severity of penalties. The demonstrated inverse relationship cannot, however, be conclusively interpreted as deterrence evidence as negative correlations between crime and arrest probabilities are compatible with other hypotheses which cannot be discounted. Econometricians have recently brought their statistical techniques to bear on this problem, most notably in relation to the deterrent effect of capital punishment. Their results, contrary to earlier evidence, indicate that capital punishment may exert a deterrent effect on murder in excess of that hypothetically exerted by terms of imprisonment, but the assumptions upon which they are based are too controversial to sustain any definite conclusions.   DB

Deviance   The 1960s saw an explosion of interest in deviance, deviancy and deviancy studies which initially aimed to put criminology into perspective through supplying information on issues that often correlated with crime or were possible alternatives to it, such as alcoholism, drug abuse, suicide, mental abnormality and homosexuality. There followed a succession of studies on scarce or rare behaviours which although they are very frequently not proscribed by the law are regarded with disapproval by the community.

A shift in emphasis then occurred whereby it was argued by some that the term 'deviance' should subsume 'crime' rather than being a separate list of 'topics'. The rationale for this was in part that common pressures might generate either deviance or crime, depending upon individual and local factors. The pressures, identified as largely economic, were alienation, frustration, blocked opportunities, unemployment, and so on (see *strain theory*), all of which could give rise to deviance. The central point was that the economically disadvantaged, unlike the economically advantaged, derive no rewards from conformity, and so engage in a range of behaviours (including crime) in an attempt to obtain rewards. These are likely to be disapproved of or forbidden by society, and, given their common origin, they should be studied without discrimination. A necessary corollary to this approach is the rejection of *positivism* (q.v.).

See also *Deviant, the*; *Radical criminology*.   DPW

Deviancy amplification.   See *Amplification, deviancy*.

Deviant, the A person whose behaviour *at a point in time* is abnormal. Such people may be eccentric, foreign, mad, bad, normal people who engage in episodic abnormality to enable them to continue to behave normally, or the assessment may be mistaken. S.L. Halleck, *Psychiatry and the Dilemmas of Crime* (1971), has pointed out that the 'eye' of society demands only a one-dimensional picture (of a multi-dimensional personality). Hence it is possible for a person to be judged deviant on one day and normal the next. Without clear definitions of normality only prejudice and ignorance can isolate deviants from normals, depending upon whose standards are being invoked, 'society's' or those of the group. Theoretically, deviants could be assessed statistically as those who for a given behaviour are outside the 95 per cent confidence interval (mean $\pm$ 1.96 sd) for the behaviour. In practice there is insufficient information on what normality is (the mean actual, as opposed to ideal) to use a statistical definition. As a result many studies of deviants are merely demonstrating the breadth of normality as defined by the group, the only unit which has immediate meaning for the individual. Critical issues are the degree of tolerance for the behaviour in question in the community and its *visibility* (q.v.). Society requires some deviants to provide vigour, to act as moral catalysts and to prepare for social change. The usual grounds for the suppression of deviance are contagion-potential, violation of another's rights and (circularly) the amount of money previously spent on suppressing the behaviour.

See also *Amplification, deviancy*; *Crime*; *Criminalisation*; *Deviance*; *Media*; *Moral panic*.   DPW

Differential association This extremely influential theory of criminal behaviour was first developed by E.H. Sutherland, in *Principles of Criminology* (1927), although an earlier somewhat similar theory had been used by Tarde (1843–1904). Sutherland's aim was an attempt to generate a theory of all criminal behaviour in cultural transmission terms. The theory denies that criminal behaviour is invented, inherited or explicable in terms of general needs and values; instead crime is seen as being learned by individuals in small groups in a process of communication. The learning includes techniques and 'the specific direction of motives, drives, rationalisations and attitudes'. The key principle is that a person becomes criminal because of an excess of *definitions* favourable to violation of the law over definitions unfavourable to violation of the law. The emphasis is on definitions rather than associations and although everybody has contact with both kinds of definition, what is critical is the ratio of one to another for the individual. The occurring differential associations are of unequal weight which varies with frequency, duration, priority and intensity. Glaser (1956), 'Criminality theory and behavioural images', *AJS*, 61, 434, summarises the theory thus: 'a person pursues criminal behaviour to the extent that he identifies himself with real or imaginary persons from whose perspective his criminal behaviour seems acceptable.' The theory was developed and refined by Sutherland's colleague Cressey and has since been widely criticised, discussed and tested.

D

See D.R. Cressey (The Hague, 1964), *Delinquency, Crime and Differential Association*; A.J. Reiss and A.L. Rhodes (1964), 'An empirical test of differential association theory', *Journal of Research in Crime and Delinquency*, 1, 5; C.R. Jeffery (1965), 'Criminal behaviour and learning theory', *JCLCPS*, 56, 294.   DPW

Diminished responsibility   The term used in s. 2 of the *Homicide Act* (1957) for 'such abnormality of mind (whether arising from a condition of arrested or retarded development of mind or any inherent causes or induced by disease or injury) as substantially impaired (a defendant's) mental responsibility for his acts and omissions in doing or being a party to the killing (of another)'. On a charge of murder it is for the defence to prove that the charge should be reduced to manslaughter for this reason; but the jury need be satisfied of this only on a balance of probabilities, and not beyond reasonable doubt. The plea can be offered only to a charge of murder, not of any other crime, even attempted murder. This anomaly is traceable to the origin of the plea in Scots law, from which it was borrowed only in order to resolve disagreements over the widening of the insanity defence in cases of murder. Successful pleas of diminished responsibility have all been based on psychiatric diagnoses (of various kinds of mental illness, psychopathic disorder or mental impairment). The effect is to enable the sentencing judge to choose any disposal, ranging from absolute discharge to life imprisonment or (if the necessary conditions are fulfilled) a Hospital Order. The drafting of the section has been much criticised, notably the phrase 'mental responsibility', which envisages responsibility as a faculty or ability. Criticism has also been directed at the notion that responsibility can be anything but complete or totally absent. The Butler Committee, in *Mentally Abnormal Offenders* (Cmnd 6244, 1975), recommended that it be abolished when their wider definition of the insanity defence was adopted; but the Criminal Law Revision Committee disagreed in their 14th Report, *Offences against the Person* (Cmnd 7844, 1980).

See also *Infanticide*; *Responsibility*.   NDW

Discharge (absolute and conditional)   On convicting an offender, the court may none the less discharge him either absolutely or conditionally (except when the sentence for the offence, e.g. murder, is fixed by law). It may do so when it thinks it inexpedient to inflict punishment (which includes fining) or inappropriate to make a Probation Order. A conviction followed by discharge does not count as a conviction except for the purpose of those proceedings (subject to what is said about conditional discharge below).

An offender *absolutely* discharged is thereupon free from all further liability; however, it happens relatively rarely. Much more frequently an offender is discharged *conditionally* on his committing no offence during such period not exceeding three years as the court specifies. If he does, he may be sentenced for the original offence as well as the subsequent one and the original conviction revives. See *Powers of the Criminal Courts Act*, (1973), ss. 7–9, 12, 13.   ARP

Discretion   Defined as 'the liberty of deciding as one thinks fit absolutely or within certain limits' (*Concise Oxford Dictionary*), discretion operates at many points in the criminal process, some of them, e.g. the discretion to initiate a *prosecution* (q.v.), of great significance.   ARP

Displacement   Displacement of crime can be defined as the reappearance of criminal activity following preventive measures which increase the difficulty of committing a particular offence (see, for example, *target hardening*) or which increase the risks of being caught. Various types of displacement are possible; offenders can choose a different *time* to offend; they can shift their attention to other *places* where there are unprotected targets; they can employ a different *method* of committing crime; or they can turn to different *forms* of illegal activity. Displacement effects are crucial in assessing the value of opportunity-reducing crime-prevention measures, since any gains made may be ruled out by displacement. It is, however, difficult to measure in all its various forms, and to date geographic displacement has received most attention. What evidence there is suggests that some displacement often follows restrictive practices, but this is often less than the amount of crime prevented. Intuitively, one would expect differences in motivation underlying different sorts of crime to be important. Displacement among 'professional' criminals is relatively likely, as evidenced, for example, by the switch to over-the-counter armed bank robbery when safe security was improved. Conversely, 'opportunist' offenders who commit crimes which are easy and unrisky may be unlikely to persist in offending when crime is made harder. For what may be the bulk of offenders in the middle, displacement effects are more at issue; the balance between deliberate intent and opportunities for offending is less easy to judge, as is the degree to which different crimes can be functionally equivalent. However, for many offences, displacement may be likely to the extent that there are other targets for the offender to switch to – or other methods to apply – which do not present greater risks or costs for the same reward.   PM

Diversion   This mainly involves the use by prosecuting authorities of alternatives to traditional criminal justice measures in dealing with breaches of the criminal law. The effect is to remove a suspected offender from the criminal process. This may occur at any stage. It is achieved informally through the exercise of official discretion in proceeding with a case, and through the implementation of formal schemes. Use of police discretion is well documented in the literature (see e.g. Fisk, 1974; Goldstein, 1960; Pasnas, 1971).

The decision by the prosecuting authority (whether police or other, such as the Procurator-Fiscal in Scotland) not to initiate or proceed with a prosecution may be taken at any time before the trial. Charges may be withdrawn, or no evidence offered.

Formal diversion projects tend to be directed at specific groups. During the 1960s, the idea developed and was later embodied in the *Children and Young Persons Act* (1969), that juveniles should, where possible, be diverted from court proceedings. One popular means of doing so is the practice of cautioning. Section 34 of the *Criminal Justice Act* (1972) empowered the police to take a drunken offender to an approved medical treatment centre for alcoholics, thereby avoiding bringing a charge. Section 72 of the *Mental Health Act* (1959) enables transfer of prisoners diagnosed as mentally disordered to mental hospitals. *Mediation* (q.v.) provides one means of settling disputes without resorting to criminal proceedings.

Decriminalisation of offences, which excludes potential offenders from the criminal justice system, is another form of diversion.

Often offences are not referred to the police by a complainant or investigator, so that disputes are settled without reference to a specialised legal apparatus. Examples of this are disciplinary tribunals within professional bodies; employees dealt with by dismissal or warnings, breaches of the pollution laws, tax and social security frauds dealt with by the relevant government departments.

When referring to the sentencing stage, the term 'diversion' is used to designate dispositions which avoid the immediate incarceration of the offender. Bail and deferment of sentence offer the court two means of diverting the offender from custody prior to sentence. When sentencing, a range of non-custodial dispositions is available.

Early release from custodial sentences can be effected by offering remission and/or parole.

In 1974 a NACRO Working Party was set up to consider what, if any, applicability the diversion concept had to this country. They concluded that the American emphasis was on alternatives to criminal justice, whereas English diversionary measures had so far concentrated on short-term early intervention and thus had an impact on lessening rather than avoiding criminal penalties.

J. Fisk (Los Angeles, 1974), *The Police Officer's Exercise of Discretion in the Decision to Arrest: Relationship and Organisational Goals and Societal Values*; J. Goldstein (1960), 'Police discretion not to invoke the criminal process; low-visibility decisions in the administration of justice', *Yale Law Journal*, 69(4), March; R.I. Pasnas (1971), 'Police discretion and the diversion of incidents of intra-family violence', *Law and Contemporary Problems*, 36, 539.   RG & KW

Drift   With the aid of this concept D. Matza (*Delinquency and Drift*, N.Y., 1964) combines a 'free will' approach to *crime* (q.v.) with '*determinism*' (q.v.) – an epistemological compromise called 'soft determinism'. On the one hand 'drift' means that the delinquent has *chosen* to break the law, while on the other it indicates the social processes affecting him (see especially *neutralisation*). 'The delinquent *transiently* exists in a limbo between convention and crime, responding in turn to the demands of each, flirting now with one, now the other, but postponing commitment, evading decision. Thus he drifts between criminal and conventional action.' ARP

Driving offences   The very nature of motor vehicles results in a variety of offences being created specifically to secure their safe use. Other offences do not relate directly to operating a motor vehicle but to the circumstances in which it is operated; they may also be designed to promote safety or simply to enforce legislation intended to raise revenue from the ownership of a motor vehicle. Driving offences constitute overwhelmingly the largest number of cases heard by the Magistrates' Courts. Offences in the first class cover the manner in which the vehicle is used – the most important being causing death by reckless driving, reckless driving and careless driving (*Road Traffic Act* (1972), ss. 1, 2, 3). In addition, the criminal law is used to enforce compliance with mandatory road signs and markings, and the safe design and condition of vehicles. In principle there is no reason why a person whose driving may be described as reckless should not be convicted of manslaughter if he causes death (Smith and Hogan, 1978; Williams, 1978). A separate offence was developed owing to the reluctance of juries to convict motorists of manslaughter (Elliott and Street, 1968). The meaning of 'reckless' is somewhat unclear. In R v. Lawrence (1981), *CLR*, 409, it was said that it was necessary to show that the driver failed to give any thought of there being obvious and serious risk of causing serious physical injury to another road-user or of doing substantial damage to property; or, having recognised that there was some risk involved, went on to take it. The less serious offence of careless driving requires it to be shown that the defendant did not exercise the degree of care and attention of a reasonable and prudent driver in the circumstances (Simpson v. Peat (1951), 1 *All E.R.*, 447). Examples of offences of the second type are driving with a blood-alcohol concentration above the prescribed limit and driving while unfit through drink and drugs (*Road Traffic Act* (1972), ss. 5, 6), driving while uninsured for third-party risks (*Road Traffic Act* (1972), s. 143), and driving without holding a valid licence (*Road Traffic Act* (1972), s. 84). Unlicensed drivers are *ipso facto* generally also uninsured. Willett has argued that his research shows that more serious motoring offenders are more likely to have records for non-motoring offences than a random sample of the population, but his conclusions have been challenged by Steer and Carr-Hill (Willett, 1964; Steer and Carr-Hill, 1967). Conversely, there is evidence that a record of non-motoring offences may be a more powerful predictor of motoring offenders than exposure to risk, i.e. years driven multiplied by annual mileage (MacMillan, 1975).

D.W. Elliott and H. Street (Baltimore, 1968), *Road Accidents*; J. MacMillan (1975), *Deviant Drivers*; J.C. Smith and B. Hogan (4th ed., 1980), *Criminal Law*; D.J. Steer and R.A. Carr-Hill (1967), 'The motoring offender – who is he?', *CLR*, 214; T.C. Willett (1964), *Criminal on the Road*; G. Williams (1978), *Textbook of Criminal Law*.   MB

Drug abuse/addiction   Source books on abuse in general are A. Schecter *et al.* (1978) and National Drug Abuse Conference Inc. (1978). The sheer range of substances and their varying effects complicates generalisation, and in recent years the expanding list of both *materia medica* and abusable chemicals (e.g. the problem of solvent inhalation; J.M. Watson (1976)) has created new opportunities for drug dependence which may bear on crime. Addicts have little involvement with crime (being preoccupied with their addiction), except possibly through prostitution or theft to support their addiction, whereas experimenters and other users *may* show more involvement either because of uncontrolled behaviour facilitated by consumption of the drug in question, or as part of the general life-style of such groups. Young's (1971) description of this form of abuse remains unequalled.

National Drug Abuse Conference Inc. (Basle, 1978) *Critical Concerns in the Field of Drug Abuse*; A. Schecter, H. Alksne and E. Kaufman, eds (Basle, 1978), *Drug Abuse: Modern Trends, Issues and Perspectives*; J.M. Watson (1976), 'The growing problem of glue-sniffing', *Social Work Today*, 8(3), 10; J. Young (1971), *The Drugtakers: the Social Meaning of Drug Use*.

See also *Alcoholism*; *Drug trafficking*.   DPW

Drug trafficking   The illegal supply of drugs can take place at several levels: at the level of the 'capitalist' who organises and controls the availability and distribution of the drug in question, or at the level of the street pedlar who sells small amounts to addicts, passing the gains back up the 'system' via middlemen to the capitalist. Trafficking is punished under *The Misuse of Drugs Act* (1971).

See also *Smuggling*. DPW

E

Ecology. See *Area studies*.

Economic theory There are broadly speaking two ways in which economic theory has been introduced into the analysis of crime and punishment; the first concerns the individual decision to commit an offence and the second the design of policy towards crime; i.e. the specification of punishment levels and allocation of resources to the police and the judicial system. Theories which deal with the design of policy generally have, as an integral part, a theory of the individual decision to offend.

The standard approach in economics to the modelling of behaviour is to portray the individual as making choices how to act which depend on the likely consequences of his acts and on the alternative opportunities that are available. This was also the approach of some of the earliest theorists of criminal behaviour, for example Beccaria (1764, Eng. trans., 1768) and Bentham (1789). However, the first expression of this type of theory as a formal mathematical model of criminal behaviour did not occur, it seems, until Becker's article of 1968. In Becker's model the individual perceives a probability of apprehension, p, if he commits an offence, the level of punishment, f, if caught, and the gains if he is not caught. He offends if the expected utility from committing the offence exceeds the utility from not offending. The expected utility is calculated by forming the weighted sum of utilities for the events that he is caught or not caught, where the weights are the probabilities of the two events. Thus for the individual, and, if we aggregate across the individuals, society as a whole, the level of offending is a function of p and f. The approach may be extended (see Ehrlich, 1973) to take account of the allocation of time between legal and illegal activities.

In these models one can examine the likely effects on crime of poverty, unemployment and so on. The models have been subject to extensive empirical estimation: for a survey of the theory see Heineke (1978a) and of the attempts at estimation – mostly for the USA – Taylor (1978), for a development of the theory; its relation with criminological theories, and estimation on UK data for England and Wales see Carr-Hill and Stern (1979). The study of the use of statistical data to estimate economic models constitutes the subject of econometrics. The econometric estimation of models of criminal behaviour has led to considerable controversy (e.g. surrounding Ehrlich's work (1975) on capital punishment) and has too often ignored the fact that criminal statistics are numbers recorded by the police and not the total number of actual incidents. Thus, for example, an observed relation between unemployment and crime might possibly be explained by more unemployment leading to more policemen being recruited, who then record more incidents as crime.

Following the spirit of Beccaria and Bentham, Becker (1968) embodied the economic view of criminal behaviour just described in a model of policy. In the model the government chooses penalties and resources allocated to the police and judicial system to minimise some 'social loss function' which is made up from the damage done by offences and costs of apprehension and punishment. An attempt is made to show, for example, that this economic approach can lead to the conclusion that the punishment for an offence should be closely related to the damage caused; but there are serious logical objections (see Stern, 1978) to this approach to policy.

C. Beccaria (1768), *On Crimes and Punishments* (trans. from the Italian with a commentary attributed to M. de Voltaire); G. Becker (1968), 'Crime and punishment; an economic approach', *J. Political Economy*, 76, 169; J. Bentham (1789), *An Introduction to the Principles of Morals and Legislation*, (first published in 1789, but see 1948 ed. by W. Harrison); R.A. Carr-Hill and N.H. Stern (1979), *Crime, the Police and Criminal Statistics*; I. Ehrlich (1973), 'Participation in illegitimate activities; a theoretical and empirical investigation', *J. Political Economy*, 81, 521; I. Ehrlich (1975), 'The Deterrent Effect of Capital Punishment: A Question of Life and Death', *Amer. Econ. Review*, 65, 397; J.M. Heineke, ed. (Amsterdam, 1978), *Economic Models of Criminal Behaviour*; J.M. Heineke (1978a), 'Economic models of criminal behaviour: an overview', in Heineke (1978), p. 1; N. Stern (1978), 'On the economic theory of policy towards crime', in Heineke (1978), p.123; Taylor (1978), 'Econometric models of criminal behaviour: a review', in Heineke (1978), p. 35.   NS

Education   The generalised assumptions about education – that it is a beneficial prophylactic against crime, but that working-class children suffer both from reduced pre-school preparation for deriving benefit from it and from differential access to it by comparison with the middle class – have become increasingly displaced as areas of interest by the problems ethnic minorities experience in acquiring education and by a growing concern with problem behaviour occurring in schools, such as violence and vandalism.

M.D. Casserly, S.A. Bass and J.R. Garrett (Lexington, Mass., 1981), *School Vandalism*; B. Gillham, ed. (1981), *Problem Behaviour in the Secondary School*; D.H. Hargreaves, S.K. Hester and F.J. Mellor (1975), *Deviance in Classrooms*; J.M. McPartland and E.L. McDill, eds (Lexington, Mass., 1977), *Violence in Schools*.   DPW

Embezzlement.   See *Theft*.

Emergency laws   The rationale generally invoked to justify the introduction of *emergency laws* in a liberal democratic state is that at moments of grave national crisis the normal system of democratic decision-making and checks and balances is inadequate to deal with the emergency. The circumstances in which *states of emergency* and *emergency powers* may be used range from natural disasters, epidemics and famines (which may be restricted to specific areas of the country) to major strikes and disruptive industrial action, riot, terrorism, rebellion, revolution and war. According to liberal constitutional theory the extent of emergency laws should be commensurate with the severity of the emergency. A basic distinction is between a *local emergency* and a *national emergency*. The latter inevitably involves the demand for more extensive powers and resources to be placed at the disposal of central government and carries far greater risk of a mutation from constitutional democracy to dictatorship or semi-permanent *government by decree*.

An example of a local emergency is the decision of a US State governor to declare a part of his State an emergency area in the wake of severe flooding or tornado damage.

EMERGENCY LAWS

A dramatic case of a national emergency occurred in France in April 1961 when President de Gaulle assumed full powers under Article 16 of the Constitution to deal with the crisis of the generals' putsch in Algiers. Under the French Fifth Republic Constitution the President is permitted to invoke Article 16 only in exceptional circumstances, such as when the Republic is under 'grave and immediate' threat and when there has been an interruption of the regular functioning of the constitutional public authorities. The French Constitutional Court judged that President de Gaulle's use of this power in 1961 was legitimate on the grounds that the clearly stated ultimate aim of the putschists was to seize power in France. Nor was Article 16 the sole weapon available: the government had already declared a state of emergency and they could have declared a state of siege and requested powers from Parliament under Article 38, to rule by ordinance.

The revolt which led to de Gaulle assuming full powers in fact collapsed after several days. Yet the President of the Republic was left holding vast and ill-defined personal powers for five months. During this period special military courts were established, the maximum period for the holding of suspects by the police was extended to two weeks, and certain publications were suppressed. It is quite clear that a ruthless politician with dictatorial ambitions could have used the vast potential emergency powers to destroy democracy. Fortunately for France de Gaulle did not wish to become a Caesar and he returned the country to normal constitutional government.

The most dramatic illustration of emergency powers designed to preserve constitutional government being used to destroy it is Germany between the World Wars. Article 48 of the Weimar Republic Constitution gave sweeping powers to the President to circumvent parliamentary legislation by crisis decrees and to enforce these federal emergency laws in the German States by military force. These very powers which were used as a temporary measure by the socialist President Ebert to save the Republic from insurrection in 1923 became the device used by Hitler to achieve absolute power over Germany in 1933. Sweeping emergency powers have also been used as the stepping-stone to dictatorship at various times in this century in Turkey, Portugal, Spain, Austria, and many other states.

Citizens of democracies which have no explicit provisions for general emergency government (for example Great Britain, Switzerland and the USA) should therefore be able to sleep more easily in their beds. However no western democracy is without some contingency legislation for emergency powers, for example to deal with major industrial strikes, severe disturbances or terrorist campaigns. For instance, in the USA presidents have been able to use their implied and inherent powers to deal with severe urban riots. And the British government has felt the need to introduce the Emergency Provisions (Northern Ireland) legislation to deal with prolonged and severe terrorist violence. It should be remembered that these limited emergency measures are firmly subject to parliamentary agreement, accountability and review. Nevertheless, the powers given to the police to strengthen their hand in dealing with terrorism (such as the power under the British *Prevention of Terrorism (Temporary Provisions) Act* (1974) to detain for questioning for up to seven days, subject to the authorisation of the Secretary of State) do to some extent impinge upon civil liberties, and on this ground some jurists are totally opposed to them. Others argue that they may be a distasteful necessity if it can be shown that they substantially reduce the terrorist threat to the innocent. There is, of course, always a danger that emergency measures intended to be temporary will become accepted as part of the permanent legal machinery, long after they have outlived their original purpose.

PW

Emulative crime. See *Crime wave*; *Modelling*.

Epilepsy. See *Physical abnormality*.

Equity theory A theory which discusses the relationship between the damage incurred and the reparation paid as compensation for harm done to a victim. Codified by E. Walster, E. Berscheid and G.W. Walster (1973), 'New directions in equity research', *J. Personality & Social Psychology*, 25, 151, the main propositions are: individuals try to maximise their outcomes, and as long as they feel they can achieve this by behaving equitably they will do so, but if they feel they can better do so by behaving inequitably they will; systems equitably distribute rewards and costs; groups reward members who treat others equitably and punish inequitable treatment; given an inequitable relationship individuals react with distress in direct proportion to the degree of inequity, and attempt to eliminate it by restoring equity (means of doing so are discussed).

DPW

Escapes from custodial establishments The largest group of escapes do not occur from the premises of custodial establishments but are abscondings, i.e. escapes from a court to which a man has been taken, escapes while being escorted to or from a court, failures to return from short paroles or escapes from working parties. Those that do take place from the premises usually consist of concealment or climbing perimeter fences or walls. In the mid-1960s there was a spate of escapes made possible by low security. From this there arose the Mountbatten Report (see *prison security*), and since 1966 perimeter security has been improved. Forms of escape using mechanical apparatus brought to the prison from outside have occasionally been employed where wealthy prisoners have been able to obtain outside assistance. Men who show by the frequency of their escape attempts that they will stop at nothing to do so are placed on the 'E' list, wear patches (see *prison uniform*) and are subject to increased observation.

R.V.G. Clarke and D.N. Martin (1971), *Absconding from Approved Schools*, HORS no. 12; C. Banks, P. Mayhew and R.J. Sapsford (1975), *Absconding from Open Prisons*, HORS no. 26; G. Laycock (1977), *Absconding from Borstals*, HORS no. 41. For information on number per year see the current edition of the annual *Report of the Work of the Prison Department*. DPW

Ethnicity There is no intrinsic reason why ethnic status should be closely related to crime at all. However, membership of an ethnic minority may increase the risk of involvement in three main ways:

1 Where different standards of normality and acceptable conduct (originating from a different culture) are held in the teeth of those of the host culture.

2 Where the minority is located in an adverse socio-economic position in society and hence particularly subject to low educational attainment, poverty and unemployment (Home Affairs Committee (1981); Scarman (1981)).

3 Where the minority is stigmatised through ignorance and prejudice and its members frequently selected as a scapegoat. The associative goading and taunting inevitably leads to retaliation which is seen as justification for the prejudice. Ethnic groups with high visibility (different language, skin colour) suffer more in this respect than do those more closely resembling host culture members (Pryce, 1979). If for any of

these reasons ethnic groups *do* commit much crime then ideology and politics step in to complicate understanding.

S. Field *et al.* (1981), *Ethnic Minorities in Britain: a Study of Trends in their Position since 1961*, HORS no. 68; House of Commons, Home Affairs Committee: Sub-Committee on Race Relations (1981), *Racial Disadvantage*; R.E. Kapsis (1976), 'Continuities in delinquency and riot patterns in black residential areas', *Social Problems*, 23 (5), 567; K. Pryce (1979), *Endless Pressure*; Scarman (1981), *The Brixton Disorders 10–12 April 1981*, Cmnd 8427; P. Stevens and C.F. Willis (1979), *Race, Crime and Arrests*, HORS no. 58.   DPW

Exemplary sentence   A sentence of greater severity than it might otherwise have been, passed with the aim of deterring potential offenders from crime of a like nature. The Court of Appeal Criminal Division has said that judges should still not exceed the *tariff* (q.v.) for the offence in question. None the less, there are regular instances of their doing so when dealing with an alleged spate of crime, though how effective it is remains doubtful. See D. Thomas (2nd ed., 1979), *Principles of Sentencing*.

See also *Deterrence*.   ARP

Experiments   The word 'experiment' is often used loosely to refer to any social action (especially if innovative) whose ultimate effects are uncertain. Following this definition, most methods of dealing with crime are experimental in nature. The technical meaning of an experiment, on the other hand, is a systematic attempt to investigate the effect of variations in one factor (the independent variable) on another (the dependent variable). In an experiment, the researcher has control over the independent variable. In a randomised experiment, the researcher also controls extraneous variables by random assignment.

It is easiest to explain the nature of experimentation by discussing a specific example. I. Berg, R. Hullin and R. McGuire (1979) (in D.P. Farrington, K. Hawkins and S.M. Lloyd-Bostock, eds, *Psychology, Law and Legal Processes*) wanted to investigate the relative effectiveness of two court dispositions, adjournment and social work supervision, in the treatment of truancy. They carried out an experiment in which truants were assigned by magistrates to adjournment or supervision according to a table of random numbers. During a six-month follow-up period, the supervised group truanted more and committed more offences, suggesting that adjournment was the more effective disposition in preventing truancy and delinquency.

In this example, the independent variable was the form of the disposition. The major dependent variable was truancy, and there was also a second dependent variable, delinquency. The random assignment meant that the adjourned and supervised groups were equivalent (within the limits of statistical fluctuation) in extraneous factors which might have been related to truancy and delinquency (e.g. age, sex, social class and school performance) and which might have been used as a basis for the dispositions in the usual uncontrolled situation. Therefore, in some way, the subsequent differences in truancy and delinquency must have been produced by the different dispositions.

E

Randomised experimentation is the best method of investigating the effect of one factor on another. One of the earliest and most famous American experiments was the Cambridge–Somerville study (see J. McCord (1978), *American Psychologist*, 33, 284) on delinquency prevention. In this, 325 pairs of boys were matched on rated delinquency potential, and one member of each pair was chosen at random to receive special help from counsellors. This special help lasted on average five years. However, thirty years after the end of the programme, the treated and control boys were not significantly different in recorded offending.

Apart from the Berg *et al.* study mentioned above, the most famous English criminological experiments are: (a) the IMPACT study of intensive probation, directed by M.S. Folkard; (b) the study of police juvenile liaison directed by G. Rose; (c) the evaluation of a 'therapeutic community' treatment of delinquents by D.B. Cornish and R.V.G. Clarke; (d) the studies of social work in prison by M. Shaw and A.J. Fowles; and (e) the evaluation of different borstal régimes by M. Williams. These and other criminological experiments have been reviewed by D.P. Farrington (1982) (in N. Morris and M. Tonry, eds, *Crime and Justice*, vol. 4).   DPF

Extended sentence The extended sentence of imprisonment (replacing *preventive detention* (q.v.)) was introduced by s. 37 of the *Criminal Justice Act* (1967) and re-enacted by s. 28 of the *Powers of Criminal Courts Act* (1973). Its use is for persistent adult criminals from whom it is judged expedient to protect the public for some considerable time. Its object is *incapacitation* (q.v.).   DPW

Extraversion/Introversion   One of the major dimensions in H.J. Eysenck's comprehensive theory of personality, the others being *neuroticism* and *psychoticism* (qq.v.). All three dimensions are measured by a self-administered personality questionnaire which yields quantitative scores. The extremes of the dimension are termed extraversion and introversion. The person scoring high in extraversion, E, displays sociability, activity, optimism and outgoing and impulsive behaviours, the low E scorer being the opposite of these.

Extraversion is considered to be related to the general level of cortical arousal, with extraverts having a higher level than introverts. The theory asserts that extraverts should learn less rapidly and less strongly than introverts. This applies to all types of learning including social rule learning, hence there is a possible connection between E and crime. According to Eysenck, social rules are learned through the punishment of forbidden behaviours, a process termed 'avoidance conditioning'. With equal opportunity the more extraverted the person the less well will he, and she, learn to keep the rules. Hence they will carry out more illegal acts, both as children and as adults.

The prediction that prisoners would be more extraverted than comparable groups outside prison has not been supported. It has been argued that prison samples are unsuitable for testing the theory: impulsiveness is a large contributor both to extraversion and to getting caught; prison does not allow much social mixing, thus having an introverting effect and reducing any initial differences between prisoners and those outside prison. Several studies have reported significant positive correlation between E and self-reported offending (the more extraverted, the more offending). However, it is still possible that extraverts are more likely to admit crimes than are introverts, so that a considerable degree of doubt remains.

On balance, it is likely that the Eysenckian personality variables, such as E, contribute a minor but useful part to a comprehensive theory of crime.   MPF

F

Female crime Relative to male crime, female crime has two distinct characteristics, a low *number* of offences and a narrow *range* of them. Pollak (1950) pointed out that females have males to commit crime for them which would reduce rates. He also argued that there is considerable under-reporting due to cultural definitions of femininity which means that males are reluctant to report females as criminals, but Mawby (1980) found this was not the case, concluding that girls do in fact commit fewer offences than boys. Explanations of the low female rate usually emphasise that the rate is higher for males because of their greater responsibilities as breadwinners *and* that there is greater socialisation for males into the acceptance of violence. (Female emancipation and the growth in single-parent families should therefore have produced higher rates of crime and changes in reporting.) Further, that socialisation and general supervision for girls and young women is anyway more intense than for males, so a lower crime rate should follow from this, and conceivably more psychiatric disturbance among those who *do* commit crime. The extant narrow range of offences has often been related to physiological crises and sexual factors (pre-menstrual tension, parturition and the menopause), where, of course, there is a danger of over-sexualising female crime, an issue much commented upon by feminists writing on the subject.

N. Goodman *et al.* (1976), *Further Studies of Female Offenders*, HORS no. 33; Institute of Criminology (1980), *Women and Crime*, Cambridge University Cropwood Series no. 13; R. Mawby (1980), 'Sex and crime: the results of a self-report study', *BJS*, 31 (4), 525; O. Pollak (Philadelphia, 1950), *The Criminality of Women*.

See also *Abortion*; *Infanticide*; *Prison*; *Prostitution*; *Shoplifting*. DPW

Fencing This is the activity of trading in stolen goods. There are three views of its nature. The traditional legal view focuses on the purchase or 'receiving' of stolen goods, and sees it as a passive, supportive and protective activity through which the 'fence' harbours the 'thief' and provides him with a means of converting stolen property into cash or kind; typically prostitutes, inn-keepers or second-hand dealers. Until 1602 it was not illegal to receive stolen goods, but an offence to receive a felon; thereafter receiving was made a misdemeanour, but in 1691 the receiver was made an accessory after the fact, liable to branding, whipping and/or seven years transportation. The offence was not made a substantive felony until 1827 (J. Hall (Indianapolis, 1952), *Theft, Law and Society*).

Under the 1968 *Theft Act* the offence was redefined as 'handling' stolen goods, 'knowing or believing them to be stolen'. The significance of this Act was to acknowledge that fencing was more than buying, as Hall and other social commentators had long recognised, and reflected a second view of fencing as 'dealing'. The 'master' fences, Jonathan Wild, Ikey Solomons and, more recently, 'Vincent Swaggi', were classic examples of such wheeler-dealer businessmen and criminal brokers, illustrating how the active view of fencing also involves organising thieves and placating police and politicians with gifts ranging from free goods to guilty men (G. Howson (1970), *Thief-Taker General*; J. Tobias (1974), *Prince of Fences*; C. Klockars (1974), *The Professional Fence*). In its most extreme form this view locates the fence at the centre of a 'stolen property system', a gigantic distribution circuit which locates, plans, facilitates and executes the acquisition, conversion and redistribution of stolen property and reintegrates it into the legitimate property stream (M. Walsh (Connecticut, 1977), *The Fence*).

A third view sees fencing not as the product of a 'Mr Big' but as the by-product of professionalised policing and legitimate business in a capitalist society. Fences are 'licensed' as informers and 'thief-takers' by police under pressure to convict thieves, and 'It is not that one species of actor, "the fence", buys stolen goods, whereas another, "the businessman", buys legitimate ones. Rather businessmen buy *cheap* goods to sell at a profit; a greater or lesser proportion of their purchases may be illicit' (S. Henry (1977), 'On the fence', *Brit. J. Law & Society*, 4, 133). Such duality and ambiguity render fencing indistinguishable from normal business and thereby legitimates it.

The third view also recognises amateur fencing whereby ordinary people in legitimate jobs buy and sell 'cheap' goods, pilfered, fiddled or legitimately acquired from workplaces and traded on-the-side as 'bargains' to friends, relatives and neighbours at cost price in return for status, prestige and reciprocal social favours.

S. Henry (1978), *The Hidden Economy*, (1981), *Can I Have it in Cash?*   SH

Fiddling   An English lay colloquialism. Even thus restricted, it may legitimately be used to describe, albeit contemptuously, the actions of violinists, ditherers (after Nero), idlers, etc. When further restricted to illicit activity, although the word has no legal coinage and appears in no law, it is used to describe surreptitious and illicit manipulation of accounts or procedures to facilitate and simultaneously conceal small thefts. It is frequently, but neither exclusively nor always, used to describe thefts by employees, particularly of small sums of money or materials of insignificant value.

Fiddling is rarely used of thefts of any size or type by persons who are not related to the victim in some appropriate material or fiscal (rather than consanguinial or affinal) way. Thus, those who over-claim social security benefits, or fraudulently pay insufficient taxation, or who pay inadequate or no fares on public transport, or who tinker with electricity or other meters to reduce their liability for payment, etc., may all sensibly be described as indulging in fiddling.

The first recorded and unequivocal use of fiddling to refer to theft is contained in a bitter tract written by Daniel Defoe in 1703, wherein he criticises the actions of 'stock-jobbers' on the London Stock Exchange who made a living by speculatively buying shares cheaply and speedily selling them dear. This semantically specialised and culturally particularised use became culturally universalised by 1850, when such existence by that form of sharp exchange had become commonplace on the streets of London (Farmer, *Lloyd's Weekly London Newspaper*, 3 February). Semantic generalisation of fiddling to a variety of other small deceitful practices among those appropriately related occurred over a similar period, as attested, *inter alia*, by Mayhew (*London Labour and the London Poor* (1862), vol. 1, p. 199). The word has gained currency, but the illegal activities to which it sometimes refers have attracted little serious, sustained or general study by criminologists. Available litera-

FINE

ture is chiefly ethnographic or anecdotal, and includes: G. Mars (1973), 'Chance, punters and the fiddle', in Malcolm Warner, ed., *The Sociology of the Workplace*, p. 200; J. Ditton (1977), *Part-Time Crime*; S. Henry (1978), *The Hidden Economy*.

JD

Fine The Crown Court may fine an offender by way of punishment and no maximum limit is set. Magistrates' Courts are limited by statute, now principally the *Criminal Justice Act* (1982), which provides a standard scale and enables the Home Secretary by Order to revise the levels in accordance with changes in the value of money. The Court has regard to an offender's ability to pay in fixing the amount. Collection and enforcement is dealt with by Magistrates' Courts.

Fines are imposed more frequently than any other form of sentence or order, and it has been suggested from Home Office research that they are also the most effective way of dealing with all types of offender (but see A. Bottoms (1973), 'The efficacy of the fine: a case for scepticism', *CLR*, 534).

Home Office (1978), *The Sentence of the Court*; P. Softley (1978), *Fines in Magistrates' Courts*, HORS no. 46.　　ARP

Firearms Ownership of firearms is drastically restricted by the *Firearms Act* (1968). Certain classes may not be owned at all (e.g. machine pistols, machine guns) and others (rifles, pistols, shotguns) may be bought or sold only after a licence has been obtained from the police. Unquestionably this policy of restriction has reduced offences involving firearms.

R. Carr and G. Campbell (1973), *The Control of Firearms in Great Britain*, Cmnd 5297; A.D. Weatherhead and B.M. Robinson (1970), *Firearms in Crime*, HORS no. 4.　　DPW

Follow-up studies These examine what happens to groups of offenders over a time period. They have their origin in a desire both to assess the effects of institutional treatment and to predict subsequent criminality. They were pioneered by S. and E. Glueck.

See also *Longitudinal research*; *Prediction*.　　DPW

Forensic medicine The application of medical practice as it relates to crime, including mental disorder, medical evidence and ethics, autopsies, causes of sudden death and changes after death, blood stains and groups, wounds, effects of injury, identification by bones, teeth, stains, hairs and fibres, sex offences, abortion, alcoholic intoxication, drug dependence, poisoning, occupational hazards and accidents. There are numerous textbooks, two excellent ones being F.E. Camps and J.M. Cameron (1971), *Practical Forensic Medicine*, and K. Simpson (1972), *Forensic Medicine*. DPW

Forensic psychiatry The mental state of an individual can have an important bearing in criminal and civil cases and this is the substance of forensic psychiatry. Reports to court are produced mainly by general psychiatrists and prison medical officers, but there are a number of forensic psychiatrists throughout the country who provide a specialised service to courts, prisons and remand centres.

In criminal cases, psychiatric opinion may be sought at a number of stages. Prior to trial, prisoners can be transferred to hospital under s. 73 of the *Mental Health Act* (1959) if they suffer from mental illness or severe mental impairment. At trial, the question of fitness to plead can be raised, for which a specially empanelled jury sits to hear medical evidence. Various medical defences can be raised during the trial, including the 'insanity' defence, diminished responsibility and automatism. The majority of psychiatric reports are requested after the defendant has been found guilty as an aid to sentencing. Under Pt V of the *Mental Health Act* (1959), mentally disordered individuals can be sent to hospitals on a s. 60 treatment order. A judge, in certain circumstances, can make a s. 65 restriction order which prohibits medical discharge by the Responsible Medical Officer. A Probation Order with a condition of psychiatric treatment (*Powers of the Criminal Courts Act* (1973), s. 3) can be made for a period of up to three years for patients who cannot be dealt with under the *Mental Health Act* (1959). Finally, if a sentenced prisoner's mental state deteriorates, there is provision under the *Mental Health Act* (1959), s. 72, for a transfer to a psychiatric hospital for treatment.

In civil cases, psychiatric opinion is sought as to testamentary capacity, ability to contract marriage, and for the evidence needed to place a patient's affairs under the jurisdiction of the Court of Protection.

An important recommendation of the Butler Committee *Report on Mentally Abnormal Offenders* (Cmnd. 6244, 1975) was the setting up of Regional Secure Units (run by the DHSS).

91

These units for mentally disturbed offenders will provide a focus for forensic psychiatric services throughout the country.

See also *Hospital Order*; *Mental abnormality*.   WMD

Forgery   It is the offence of forgery to make a false instrument intending it to be accepted as genuine, to someone's prejudice. This summarises the leading provision of s. 1 of the *Forgery and Counterfeit Currency Act* (1981), which, as the Law Commission put it, 'does away with the old law and the multiplicity of forgery offences . . . differentiated by the nature of the document forged.' An 'instrument' is defined in s. 8 so as to include documents, formal and informal; postage or inland revenue stamps; and any disc, tape, sound track or other device on which information is recorded or stored by mechanical or electronic or other means. See Law Commission (1973) *Forgery and Counterfeit Currency*, Report no. 55.

See also *Counterfeiting*.   ARP

Fraud   The essence of fraud is the use of false representations to obtain an unjust advantage or to injure the rights or interests of another individual or organisation. Statutes governing offences with elements of fraud are fairly numerous, ranging from the *Servants' Characters Act* (1792), whereby pretending to be a servant's master in order to give a reference for him was punishable by a fine of £20, to the *Prevention of Fraud (Investments) Act* (1958), whereby potential investors came to be protected from the consequences of false statements made to induce them to invest.

The aspect of fraud which most invites analysis by the social scientist is differential enforcement by social class. The argument that there is such a bias is powerfully made in an analysis of prosecutions by non-police agencies in England and Wales (Lidstone *et al.*, 1980). It was found that agencies such as the Inland Revenue (dealing with the taxpayer) and the Health and Safety Executive (dealing with businesses) typically dealt with infractions by means short of prosecution, preferring persuasion, education and negotiated settlements. In contrast, the Department of Health and Social Security (dealing with those in receipt of welfare benefits) saw infractions as unambiguously criminal, to be pursued through the deterrent and retributive mechanisms of the criminal law.

The relationship between political power, on the one hand, and the law and its enforcement on the other, is a leitmotif of radical sociology. The enforcement of fraud offences is a particularly fruitful area for the demonstration of this relationship, and one whose possibilities are far from exhausted. For example, the insurance industry uses the concept of 'moral hazard', whereby individuals are identified as bad risks, and once insured are regarded as more likely to make fraudulent claims of their insurers. The concept of moral hazard in the prosecution of fraud cries out for empirical analysis. A neat example of class-based double standards is provided by Box (see Henry, 1978), who describes jurors, immediately after convicting an offender of a minor property crime, discussing how much they could make on their expenses.

Computer fraud deserves special mention as a type of crime whose frequency and importance is likely to increase. We seem to be in a period in which innovation outstrips the investigatory process (see McKnight, 1973; Bequai, 1979). Bequai writes: 'the problem of computer crime is, in great part, the failure of our laws, jurists, lawyers and law schools to adapt to the needs of a changing environment . . . Our law schools prepare students for an era that has long since passed' (p. 197).

A. Bequai (Lexington, 1978), *Computer Crime*; S. Henry (1978) *The Hidden Economy*; K.W. Lidstone, R. Hogg and F. Sutcliffe (1980), *Prosecutions by Private Individuals and Non-police Agencies*, Royal Commission on Criminal Procedure, 1978–81, Research Study no. 10; G. McKnight (N.Y., 1973), *Computer Crime*.   KP

Free will   In philosophical terms, the notion of free will entails the choice of actions, and is contrasted with situations in which people act under compulsion. This does not imply that all actions stem from rational decisions, or that people are (or can be) free from powerful external influences on their behaviour. What it does imply is that human beings follow certain rules of conduct, are capable of recognising situations to which those rules apply, and of deciding which of them to observe. In ordinary life, many actions spring from motives which are undesired (for instance, 'a choice of evils'), but this form of compulsion is distinguishable from actions taken under physical force or physical necessity. The major problem (philosophically and criminologically) of the doctrine of free will occurs in cases where the actor claims that he was compelled to act as he did because of the intense demands, either of his external situation or of his inner psychological drives. Because obedience to the law is seen as an important aspect of conduct, citizens are expected to avoid illegal acts except in extreme situations. While the rules governing pleas of insanity have remained relatively constant since the first half of the nineteenth century, and mainly concern the ability to recognise the application of laws to particular circumstances, various forms of mitigation of the seriousness of offences have gradually eroded the notion that offenders always freely choose criminal acts. For instance, in 1981 the decision not to impose a custodial sentence on a woman who killed her fiancé by crushing him with a car because she was suffering from pre-menstrual tension was widely recognised as establishing a new kind of mitigating stress factor. One paradoxical consequence of the proliferation of these factors in serious cases, in conjunction with the strict interpretation of *mens rea* in less serious ones, is that penalties for certain examples of murder and rape are sometimes little higher than those for trivial property offences. Of the latter, shoplifting is a contentious example, since a constant proportion of these offences are committed by middle-aged people (usually women) of previous good character. The case of Lady Barnett in 1980 drew attention to the notion of a psychological compulsion to steal from shops, which might be compared with the addiction to alcohol or drugs but which, like these, is unlikely to be recognised in law as grounds for an acquittal.

WJOJ

Frustration When a person's attempt to reach a particular target is blocked for whatever reason, the result is a state of subjective discomfort, termed 'frustration'. Earlier theorists (e.g. J. Dollard *et al.* (1939)) asserted that frustration leads inevitably to aggression (and conversely that aggression follows frustration). Recent findings (e.g. A. Bandura (1973)) indicate that the situation is much more complicated. An aggressive act aimed at achieving the original target is only one possible consequence. Others include an increase in activities of all types, as well as a sense of helplessness associated with making no response of any kind. The latter is of great current relevance. Life in the inner areas of large cities may so reduce the expectation of rewarding outcomes for 'trying harder' that their inhabitants may fall into a state of apathy (in behavioural language, non-responding).

The determining factors for a reduction, or an increase, of activity include the success or failure of past attempts – either by oneself or by other people well known to one – to overcome obstacles, and the relative deprivation suffered from the frustrating experience. If matters have been going well, a check to the flow of rewards may be much more disturbing, because of the sharpness of the contrast, than a frustration which is only one of many recently experienced. A further important determinant is the comparison between oneself and others judged to be similar in circumstances. If few of one's peers are being thwarted in their efforts, a frustration experience leads to aggression under conditions in which an aggressive response appears effective in carrying out the task in hand, indicating the importance of the person's interpretation of the effectiveness of his response repertoire. In short: frustration is most likely to provoke aggression in individuals who have learned to behave aggressively and for whom aggression has a functional value.

People learn to behave aggressively in certain social settings which provide models for such behaviour and opportunities for copying them successfully. Frustration is only one – and not necessarily the most important – factor affecting the expression of *aggression* (q.v.). It follows that frustration is of some, though probably limited, importance in explaining crimes against the person, such as various types of assault.

J. Dollard, L.W. Doob, N.E. Miller, O.H. Mowrer, R.R. Sears, C.S. Ford, C.I. Hovland and R.T. Sollenberger (New Haven, 1939), *Frustration and Aggression*; A. Bandura (N.Y., 1973), *Aggression: a Social Learning Analysis*.   MPF

G

Gambling Often viewed by the leaders of society as both offensive in itself and as productive of profligacy, corruption, vice and criminality, gambling tends to be restricted in various ways. Proscription by the criminal law of the conduct of gamblers themselves is largely a thing of the past; gambling (the generic term for betting, gaming, lotteries and prize competitions) is now a permissible and highly popular leisure pursuit. Structures in which gambling occurs are, on the other hand, subject to fairly intensive regulation to guard against overdependency in clients, their ignorance as to the odds, and fraud on the part of promoters and others. The *Royal Commission on Gambling* (below) found 'no evidence of any disturbing invasion now, by criminals into gambling'. They had no doubt that the existence of the Gaming Board set up under the *Gaming Act* (1968) was responsible for preventing the invasion, particularly at that time, of casinos by criminals and criminal syndicates. But 'this is not to say that all those concerned can now relax their vigilance.' The Royal Commission perceived that lotteries remained an area of continuing abuse, and legislation is now awaited.

Report of the Royal Commission on Gambling 1976–8 (1978), Cmnd 7200; D. Cornish (1978), *Gambling: a Review of the Literature and its Implications for Policy and Research*, HORS no. 42; D. Downes (1979), 'From raffles to heart-stoppers: the social regulations of gambling', *Brit. J. Law & Society*, 6(2), 235; D. Miers (1981), 'The mismanagement of casino gambling', *BJC*, 21 (1), 79.   ARP

Gang, the Until the work of F.M. Thrasher published as *The Gang* (Chicago, 1927), gangs were merely regarded as loose collections of criminals with limited involvement with each other and were seen as having importance only in relation to acts committed by them (rather than being important in themselves). Thrasher changed this through his pioneering work which involved collecting dossiers on numerous gangs and describing them in their terms. A gang was a street-corner family for the detached, existing in the face of adult indifference to youngsters' needs. Members spent very long hours in the company of their gang, which he defined as 'an interstitial group originally formed spontaneously and then integrated through conflict. Characterised by meeting face to face, milling, movement through space as a unit, conflict and planning.' In short he showed that gang life *in itself* was important and significant for members. The tendency since then has been the too hasty use of the term *sub-culture* (q.v.) in place of that of gang, implying both a permanence and a structural origin which may rather miss the point. Ganging is normal for children and teenagers, but comparatively few gangs are long-lived, criminal or associated with anything other than the desire of teenagers to mix with their own age group.   DPW

Group therapy.   See *Therapy*.

Guardianship Order   A court order which can be made in the same circumstances as those set out in paras 1 and 2 under *Hospital Order* (q.v.), with the effect, however, of committing the offender to the care of the local authority, i.e. its Social Services Department, who thereupon assume all the powers over him exercisable by a father over a child under fourteen. These orders are infrequently made, probably because local authorities have not sufficiently developed the appropriate facilities. The Butler Committee, though, saw the order as a valuable form of disposal and recommended closer liaison between courts and local authorities to improve the arrangements. See Committee on Mentally Abnormal Offenders (1975), *Report*, Cmnd 6244 (Butler Report).   ARP

G

H

Habitual offender, the   With the decline in the use of transportation, public concern mounted in Victorian Britain over the number of criminals who appeared impervious to efforts to reform or deter them, returning repeatedly from prison sentences to continue plying their 'trade' as thieves. From the mid-nineteenth century onwards, there can be traced a series of legislative experiments to control or incapacitate such 'habitual' offenders, all of which ended in failure. Minimum terms of incarceration on a second felony conviction (e.g. *Penal Servitude Act* (1864)), powers of surveillance and imprisonment of ex-convicts unable to prove honest means of support (*Habitual Criminals Act* (1869)), and lengthy terms of preventive detention (*Prevention of Crime Act* (1908), *Criminal Justice Act* (1948)) all foundered on common problems of definition, injustice and unpopularity with the courts.

Habitual offender legislation has been attacked on the grounds that sentences should not be disproportionate to the gravity of the latest crime. It is also criticised as ineffective and wasteful of resources. Confusion over the precise category of offender at whom it is aimed has always led to serious anomalies. While legislators have usually worked with the image of 'professional' thieves living off crime, in practice few of those trapped by special provisions could be so described. For example, West (1963) showed that the majority of those sentenced to preventive detention were ageing, inadequate, petty thieves, a nuisance but not a serious threat to society. Preventive detention was replaced in 1967 (*Criminal Justice Act*) by the *extended sentence* (q.v.) aimed at the 'real menace to society', but judges have rarely used this, having already sufficient powers to pass long deterrent sentences on bank robbers and other major criminals.

In recent years attention has shifted from the habitual thief to those who repeat crimes of violence, and proposals have been put forward for special preventive sentences for 'dangerous' offenders (Butler Committee, 1975; ACPS, 1978). Opponents express concern that the framing of definitions and the identification of those likely to commit serious offences in the future pose intractable problems similar to those experienced in the battle against habitual property offenders.

Advisory Council on the Penal System (1978), *Sentences of Imprisonment: a Review of Maximum Penalties*; Committee on Mentally Abnormal Offenders (1975), *Report*, Cmnd 6244 (Butler Report); W. Hammond and E. Chayen (1963), *Persistent Criminals*; N. Morris (1951), *The Habitual Criminal*; T. Parker (1963), *The Unknown Citizen*; L. Radzinowicz and R. Hood (1980), 'Incapacitating the habitual criminal: the English experience', *Michigan Law Review*, 78(8), 1305; D. West (1963), *The Habitual Prisoner*.   MM

Handicap, mental.   See *Mental impairment*.

Handicap, physical.   See *Physical abnormality*.

Handling stolen goods.   See *Fencing*.

Hard labour   The idea that those who break the criminal law should be set to compulsory work has several aspects which are also relevant to the imposition not merely of compulsory work but of 'hard labour'. Not the least important of these has been the view that the labour of criminals might be beneficial to the social body in terms of tasks completed (such as harbour works at Portland in the 1850s) and might in addition repay the cost of incarceration and make reparation to the offended society. Another attitude which underlies the imposition of all work schemes for criminals is that those who offend against the criminal law are distinguished by slothful laziness, that they frequently refuse to perform the social duty of labour, preferring to live on the easy wages of crime. Thus the proper duty of a penal régime (such as the early House of Correction) must be to compel such internees to work so as to inure the body and train the mind to habits of industry, thereby fitting them for self-maintenance after release. However, the practice of hard labour derives a great deal of its justification from the notion that the labour of criminals ought to be a 'most strict and severe' (1779 Penitentiary Act) process, inflicting physical suffering so as to deter the offender and other potential offenders and to enforce expiation of wrong done by suffering endured. These retributory, deterrent concepts especially underlie hard labour.

During the first half of the nineteenth century one of the major disputes among prison discipline theorists was between those who favoured 'hard, incessant irksome and eternal' labour (Sydney Smith, *Edinburgh Review*, no. 72, February 1822) and those who believed that prisoners ought to be provided with an individualised preparatory training for a skill or trade. This dispute was hard fought and thus in the 1820s, for example, in some prisons labour was dominated by the treadmill; in others industrial and skill-training systems were established.

With the discrediting of reformist prison systems in the 1850s, support shifted decisively towards hard labour which itself received great impetus from laws (such as that of 1822) which enabled courts to make an order for hard labour over and above a sentence of imprisonment.

The 1865 House of Lords Select Committee on the Prison System and the introduction of penal servitude in the 1850s were both important events in the eventual dominion of hard labour over other forms of work in Victorian prisons. The Lords Committee clearly desired the uniform imposition of severe labour by use of the crank, treadmill and shot-drill (see *prison*), while penal servitude subjected prisoners to very severe and arduous public work such as quarrying or dock construction.

In 1898, following the Gladstone Committee report, the pendulum began to swing back to prison work as a training or preparation for self-maintenance, and the treadmill and crank were abolished. However, hard labour continued to be a prominent part of prison discipline and judicial sentencing and consisted, after 1898, of particularly severe kinds of work rather than labour upon specially devised machines. It was finally abolished in 1948.   WJF

Her Majesty's Pleasure   Detention 'at Her Majesty's Pleasure' must be ordered for a child or young person under eighteen found guilty of murder. The period served and the custodial arrangements are determined by the Home Secretary (*Children and Young Persons Act* (1933), s. 53).   ARP

Heredity The impact of heredity on behaviour should be discernible when all environmentally generated inputs have been removed. The difficulty lies in successfully accomplishing this. Early studies of crime (see *constitutional theories*) tended to under-estimate the role of environmental factors in favour of heredity, whereas modern studies under-estimate heredity in favour of environment. Clearly, simple (as opposed to compound) traits and attributes are inheritable, but the effect of such inheritance on the creation of crime (seen as violations of a changing list of socially defined rules) is likely to be negligible. A technique favoured by some researchers is the study of twins reared separately, the difficulty being to find adequate numbers (M.P. Feldman (1977), *Criminal Behaviour*, p. 134). See D. Rosenthal (1975), 'Heredity in criminality', *Criminal Justice and Behaviour*, 2 (1), 3. DPW

Hidden crime The problem of the 'dark number' – the unrecorded percentage of the events being studied – is not unique to criminology: however, it takes on particular significance as the volume of crime is itself an interesting quantity both to the general public and to the penologist wanting to assess the deterrent or corrective efficacy of penal measures. And – according to two different types of study – this 'dark number' is potentially very large.

Thus, studies of self-reporting of delinquency or criminality (from Short and Nye (1957) onwards), where a random sample of respondents are asked whether or not they have ever – or in a fixed period of time – committed a delinquent act, suggest that there is an enormous pool of unrecorded delinquency. The most comprehensive British study is that by Belson (1975). Alternatively, victim studies (from Ennis (1967) onwards) where a sample of the general population are asked whether or not they have ever – or in a fixed period of time – been a victim of crime suggest multiplying factors between 1.3 and 13 according to the type of incident. The most comprehensive British study is reported in Sparks *et al.* (1977). Neither is the problem of the 'dark number' a recent invention: Quetelet (1796–1874), who pioneered the analysis of French criminal statistics in the 1830s and 1840s, said: 'all we possess of statistics of crime . . . would have no utility if we did not assume that there is a nearly invariate relationship between offenders known and adjudicated and the total unknown number of offences committed' (quoted by Sellin and Wolfgang (1964,

p. 25)). But Quetelet, like many subsequent authors, is assuming that there is a 'real' *crime rate* (q.v.) to measure and that the problem becomes one of refining the 'accuracy' of measuring instruments as indices of crimes committed in the community (see for example Hardt and Peterson-Hardt (1977) for self-reporting studies).

More recently, some authors have argued that there is no such 'thing' as a real crime rate and that crimes exist only after they have been categorised as such by the agencies of social control (e.g. Douglas, 1967). Others dispute the potential objective nature of the statistics but agree that 'Both working-class crime and upper-class crime . . . are *real* features of a society' (Taylor, Walton and Young (1975, p. 34)). The debate is dealt with in Carr-Hill and Stern (1979), ch. 3.

However, whichever view is taken of the status of the recorded offence rate an understanding of the process by which actions or omissions are transformed into offences is both important and interesting. There are two sets of factors: (a) those which affect reporting to the police by the public such as their view of the offender, the incident, the likelihood of police action and their attitude to the police; (b) those which affect recording by the police such as their limited resources and the stereotypes they develop of what should count as crime. For amplification of these see Bottomley (1973) and Bottomley and Coleman (1981).

W. A. Belson (1975), *Juvenile Theft: the Causal Factors*; A.K. Bottomley (1973), *Decisions in the Penal Process*; A.K. Bottomley and C. Coleman (1981), *Understanding Crime Rates*; R.A. Carr-Hill and N.H. Stern (1979), *Crime, the Police and Criminal Statistics*; J.D. Douglas (Princeton, 1967), *The Social Meaning of Suicide*; P. Ennis (Chicago, 1967), *Criminal Victimization in the United States: a Report of a National Survey* (National Opinion Research Center, University of Chicago Field Surveys, II); R.H. Hardt and S. Peterson-Hardt (1977), 'On determining the quality of the delinquency self-report method', *J. Res. Crime and Delinquency*, 14 (2), 247; OECD (Paris, 1976), *Data Sources for Social Indicators of Actual Victimisation suffered by Individuals with Special Reference to Victim Surveys*, Social Indicators Development Programme, Special Studies, no. 3; T. Sellin and M.E. Wolfgang (N.Y., 1964), *The Measurement of Delinquency*; J.F. Short and F.I. Nye (1957), 'Reported behaviour as a criterion of deviant behaviour', *Social Problems*, 5 (3), 207; R.F. Sparks, H. Genn and D. Dodd (1977), *Surveying Victims*; I. Taylor, P. Walton and J. Young (1975), *Critical Criminology*.   RAC-H

Hijacking The term 'hijacking' can be applied to the illegal seizure and diversion of any vehicle. Some terrorist groups have hijacked buses. In the Netherlands South Moluccan terrorists have seized passenger trains. However, the predominant form has been aircraft hijacking or 'skyjacking'. The older term 'aerial piracy' does not convey the distinctive character of this modern crime. In many cases the hijackers seek to blackmail governments and win concessions by threatening the lives of the hostage passengers and crew.

It is helpful to classify the main types of hijack in terms of underlying motivations: (i) the refugee escape; (ii) criminal ransom extortion and escape; (iii) political terrorist publicity and blackmail; and (iv) the getaway hijack as part of a larger terrorist operation. The refugee escape was the predominant type in the earliest wave of hijackings, 1945–52. Of the twenty-one cases that occurred in these years all but three were carried out by refugees from communist states. They aroused sympathy rather than hostility in Western countries. From 1968 to 1973 a major epidemic of hijackings occurred, including a high proportion for criminal ransom extortion on flights originating in America and a number of spectacular hijackings by Palestinian terrorists confronting victimised governments with major dilemmas.

The Tokyo Convention on Offences and Certain Other Acts Committed on Board Aircraft (1963) requires contracting states to make every effort to restore control of the aircraft to its lawful commander, and to ensure the prompt onward passage or return of the hijacked aircraft together with its crew, passengers and cargo. The 1970 Hague Convention for the Suppression of the Unlawful Seizure of Aircraft requires contracting states to either extradite or prosecute apprehended hijackers. But these conventions do not have universal adherence, and they lack enforcement sanctions. The 1978 Bonn summit of leaders of the Western industrial nations sought to rectify this by threatening sanctions against states providing sanctuary or other assistance to hijackers. The most effective counter-measures, however, have been the comprehensive body and baggage searches for all passengers pioneered by the USA in 1973. In the USA in 1972 there were twenty-nine hijack attempts of which twelve were successful: in 1973 after

103

the US search procedures were instituted there were only three attempts, none of which succeeded. The recent resurgence of hijackings is mainly due to hijackers discovering ways of circumventing search procedures, and continuing loopholes in boarding-gate security in certain airports.   PW

Home Secretary, the   One of the leading Ministers of the Crown, holding cabinet rank in the government and properly known as the Secretary of State for the Home Department. The Secretary's position as relating distinctly to home affairs dates from 1782 and the revival of full parliamentary government after the failures of George III and the American War of Independence. His functions derive from the prerogative powers of the Crown and from statute, and the most important relate to the following matters: the maintenance of the Queen's Peace; the Royal Prerogative of Mercy; the administration of justice (together with the Lord Chancellor and the Law Officers); treatment of offenders, including parole; probation; prison services; police, fire and civil defence services; law relating to the conduct of parliamentary and local elections; legislation on sex discrimination and racial discrimination policy; immigration and nationality; community relations; co-ordination of government action in relation to voluntary social services; public morals and safety; general questions of broadcasting policy.

In all this, and much else of a residuary nature, the Home Office staff advise and carry out the policies of the government. Special mention must be made of the Home Office Research and Planning Unit dating from 1957 and their many authoritative publications, and the Standing Committee on Criminal Law Reform set up in 1959. The Home Secretary has national responsibility for the Probation and After-Care Service and controls the Prison Service; in the Metropolis he himself is the Police Authority; elsewhere police forces are locally administered, but his influence in their affairs is substantial.

F. Newsam (1954), *The Home Office*; J. Pellew (1982), *The Home Office 1848–1914*; T.S. Lodge (1974), 'The founding of the Home Office Research Unit', in R. Hood, ed., *Crime, Criminology and Public Policy*.

See also *Parole*; *Police*.   ARP

Homicide   The lawful or unlawful killing of a human being. By this definition *abortion* (q.v.) is excluded from the category, which herein includes *child destruction*, *infanticide*, *manslaughter* and *murder*.

See also *Capital punishment*; *Diminished responsibility*; *Driving offences*.   ARP

Homosexuality Denotes the disposition to be erotically attracted to one's own sex; between women often called 'lesbianism'. It may or may not be manifested in homosexual behaviour; if it is, the law's reaction thereto varies in many ways according to the circumstances – reactions which also vary considerably cross-culturally. In the Western world the last decade or so has seen some growth in tolerance towards homosexuals, and they themselves, especially those involved in pressure groups for homosexual equality or 'on the Gay Scene', are far less inhibited.

The law takes little or no exception to homosexual conduct between consenting females. Between consenting males, however, it is legal only if they are over twenty-one and if they are in private. 'Private' means that they should not number more than two and, even if only two, that they should not be together in a lavatory to which the public has access. When their conduct is illegal it will be dealt with as either *buggery* (q.v.) or *gross indecency* (q.v. at indecency). (See also *soliciting*.)

The Criminal Law Revision Committee (1980) recently intimated that the minimum age of twenty-one and the meaning of 'privacy' were both unduly restrictive. Eighteen was thought to be the more appropriate age, and with regard to privacy, they thought that what was required was simply a provision on the lines that privacy would be exceeded only in the case of acts 'likely to be seen by others to whom they would be likely to cause serious offence'.

Committee on Homosexual Offences and Prostitution, *Report* (Cmnd 247, 1957) (Wolfenden Report); Criminal Law Revision Committee (1980), *Working Paper on Sexual Offences*; T. Honoré (1978), *Sex Law*; M. Schofield (1965), *Sociological Aspects of Homosexuality*; D. West (1977), *Homosexuality Re-examined*.   ARP

Hospital Order (1) A court order whereby an offender suffering from mental disorder may be compulsorily detained in an appropriate hospital in lieu of punishment, when the court thinks this the most suitable method of disposing of the case. The offence must be one punishable by imprisonment (other than one for which the sentence is fixed by law, as in murder) and two medical practitioners must present evidence revealing mental disorder amounting to mental illness, severe mental impairment, mental impairment or psychopathic disorder, and of such a nature or degree as to make it appropriate for him to be detained in hospital for medical treatment. Additionally, in the case of mental impairment and psychopathic disorder, the available treatment must be such as is likely to alleviate or prevent a deterioration of his condition. Unless coupled with a *Restriction Order* (q.v.), the Order enables a hospital to detain the patient only for a year in the first instance, but renewably. Discharge lies with the responsible medical officer or the Mental Health Review Tribunal, or may result from absconding and not being re-taken within a specified time.

This is the principal context in which Hospital Orders are made, either on summary conviction or in the Crown Court: there are others, viz:

(2) In summary proceedings, magistrates may make the order without convicting, where they are satisfied the defendant committed the offence, provided the medical evidence reports him to be suffering from mental illness or severe mental impairment.

(3) Where the Crown Court finds the accused to be under mental disability constituting a bar to his being tried ('unfit to plead') or finds him not guilty by reason of insanity, it must make an order that he be admitted to such hospital as may be specified by the Home Secretary. On admission, this Order takes effect as a Hospital Order coupled with a Restriction Order made without limitation of time (*Criminal Procedure (Insanity) Act* (1964)).

(4) The Home Secretary may transfer someone from prison to hospital where two medical practitioners report, as in (1) above, and he may impose restrictions on discharge. The effect is as if the patient had been admitted under a Hospital Order with or without a Restriction Order.

The general statutory framework for the operation of Hospital Orders is to be found in the *Mental Health Act* (1959) as amended by the *Mental Health (Amendment) Act* (1982). See Committee on Mentally Abnormal Offenders (1975), *Report*, Cmnd 6244 (Butler Report).

See also *Forensic psychiatry*.   ARP

Hostels   The main aim of hostels is to provide a bridge between closed or semi-closed institutions and ordinary living in society, or simply to provide some form of accommodation for those without. Each one houses only a small number of men or women and offers short-term stay facilities with low supervision. Inmates work in the community during the day, returning at night and using the hostel as a means of adjusting to ordinary life in outside society. Hostels are provided for a variety of groups; e.g. prison hostels for those nearing the end of long sentences, probation or bail hostels, hostels for alcoholics, ex-mental patients or homeless people. In addition to those officially provided, some are made available by voluntary organisations.   DPW

House of Correction   The House of Correction (which is also very commonly called a Bridewell up to the early nineteenth century) came into existence as a result of legislation passed in the late sixteenth century. Its origin is linked to the emergence of Tudor Vagrancy and Poor Laws in that legislators offered it as an architectural structure within which immoral, recalcitrant, idle or wandering destitute people might be received on an order of magistrates. Thus by a 1597 Act, boroughs and counties were encouraged to erect Houses of Correction for the punishment of rogues, vagabonds and sturdy beggars and a 1607 Act ordered their establishment. This structure constituted a medium severity response to the undeserving destitute who might alternatively merely be whipped and returned to the parish of origin or transported 'beyond the seas' or branded.

H

The early House of Correction appears to have had several distinct objectives. First, it was intended to offer a harsh severe experience so as to deter others from evil ways and the internee himself from future immorality, sloth or bad conduct. Second, it aimed to inure the body to regular, hard, strenuous labour so that after release physical habits thus acquired would be utilised to maintain the individual by work. Third, it was intended to habituate the mind to apprehend the necessity for hard work and obedient behaviour as a basis for living. Fourth, of course, it served as a means whereby moral non-conformists might be stigmatised and segregated.

During the seventeenth and eighteenth centuries the laws about social treatment of paupers and vagrants defined many more pieces of behaviour (such as bearing a bastard child or wandering about with no settled abode) as being punishable in themselves by a term in the House of Correction or as qualifying the actor for punishment in such a place as a rogue and vagabond. In addition the criminal law began to allow certain small crimes to be punished by an order to the House of Correction.

These institutions were thus an early example of an attempt to create an institutional régime which had reformatory as well as retributory and deterrent aspects. And indeed the House of Correction was one of the most important ancestors of the modern prison. Notwithstanding, when reformers and philanthropists explored them in the late eighteenth and early nineteenth centuries they found that their régimes had long since lost any reformatory objectives and the subsequent penal innovations of the nineteenth century were as much the reconstitution of the House of Correction as of the common holding gaol. Indeed, the *Prisons Act* (1865) ended the use of the term House of Correction, and henceforth the law referred to total institutional structures for the compulsory incarceration of people who had collided with the criminal law as 'prisons'.

WJF

Housing It has long been known that poor housing and slums are strongly associated with crime. For example overcrowded housing, as well as providing increased opportunities for observational learning of crime, involves reduced personal territory which entails less privacy, more interference and intrusion and more threats to territory, all of which are potential instigators of crime. Patterns of adaptation to slum existence which include crime (see *gang*, *sub-culture*) show remarkable endurance. T. Ferguson and M.G. Pettigrew in their article, 'A study of 187 slum families rehoused for upwards of ten years', *Glasgow Medical Journal* (August, 1954), showed that crime rates for rehoused juveniles were the same as those obtaining in the slums they came from. (Learnt behaviours were merely transferred to a new physical location.)

See also *Area studies*; *Chicago School*; *Poverty*; *Prevention*, *environmental*.

DPW

Howard League, the. See *Penology*.

Hulks In 1776, as a result of the American Revolution, it was impossible to transport convicts to America. A law was created therefore which had as its objects both the containment of those sentenced to transportation and the setting of them 'to hard labour in the raising of sand, soil and gravel and cleansing the River Thames'. An overseer of this system, appointed by the Middlesex magistrates, was given the task of implementing the legislation, and two disused ships of war were purchased and moored in the Thames. These were the first two prison hulks and in them were placed about 300 convicts.

In 1787 transportation was begun again to the Australian colonies, and floating hulks were retained as a feature of the initial stages of the disposal in that convicts were held in them until arrangements could be made for a convict ship to carry transportees out of England. Thus by 1790, hulks were in existence at Portsmouth, Plymouth and London, and by 1817 ten hulks held about 4,500 transportees.

Prison hulks attracted the vilification of philanthropists, evangelicals and utilitarians from an early stage. It was said that their régimes were corrupting of morals by virtue of over-crowding, deficient classification, lack of measured discipline, absence of religious instruction, and bad medical care, and despite brief attempts to reorganise hulks to satisfy the Howardian reformers they continued to be regarded with deep suspicion by those whose vision of incarceration was one of orderly discipline and reformation. In 1847 one of the inspectors of prisons appointed under the 1835 *Prison Act* examined the hulks at Woolwich and reported that their régimes were wholly unsuitable, being characterised by practices entirely contrary to Howardian basic principles of incarceration. In 1849 Joshua Jebb, the Surveyor General of Prisons, recommended their immediate abolition and replacement by convict prisons and by 1857, they had been discontinued in the British Isles.

WJF

I

Identity Either legally the name of a perpetrator or, in psychology, the answer a person would give himself to the question, 'Who am I?' Identity is a concept describing what it is that the individual most values and sees to be most important about himself. The focus has been on the extent to which (a) an individual doing deviant acts acquires or needs to acquire a deviant identity (H.S. Becker (N.Y., 1963), *Outsiders*; J. Lofland (Englewood Cliffs, N.J., 1969), *Deviance and Identity*) and (b) legal process and incarceration in custodial institutions (see *total institutions*) may (unconstructively) challenge or threaten identities.   DPW

Ideology A belief system promulgated by a power group. It is not necessarily 'right', 'true', accurate or internally consistent, but it purports to provide 'verifiable' answers to questions worrying people. The emphasis has been on the pervasiveness, intrusiveness and power of ideologies generated by the ruling class in defining reality. It has mainly been used to describe situations where a ruling group ideology (a) exists to both control and allay the suspicions of non-ruling-group members and (b) charts how to attain goals which in reality are unobtainable.

See also *Frustration*; *Strain theory*.   DPW

Illness, mental. See *Mental abnormality*.

Illness, physical. See *Physical abnormality*.

Imprisonment A term of judicial sentence available for a convicted offender over the age of twenty-one, involving incarceration in prison for a specified time (except in the case of the indeterminate sentence of *life imprisonment*). See S.

110

McConville, ed. (1975), *The Use of Imprisonment.*
See also *Extended sentence*; *Prison.*   DPW

Incapacitation   As a penal measure, the aim of incapacitation is to ensure that an offender will not offend again. In contemporary Western society some methods would now hardly be contemplated – e.g. the amputation of a limb or castration – though *capital punishment* (q.v.) is still debated. Imprisonment has a similar objective (among others) in 'keeping offenders out of circulation'. Some recent studies have examined its effectiveness from this point of view and in the context also of its other effects and economic considerations. Full references are given in the articles mentioned below.

K. Pease and J. Wolfson (1979), 'Incapacitation studies: a review and commentary', *HJ*, 18(3), 160; P. Ainsworth and K. Pease (1981), 'Incapacitation revisited', *HJ*, 20(3), 160.

See also *Criminology*; *Dangerousness*; *Extended sentence.*
                                                        ARP

Incest   This was made a criminal offence by the *Punishment of Incest Act* (1908); previously it had been a matter for the obsolescent jurisdiction of the ecclesiastical courts. Recent commentators have seen in the enactment an example of a *symbolic crusade* (q.v.) in which the prestige of the proponents of the new law is alleged to have been of more significance than instrumental concerns (Bailey and Blackburn, 1979). The law, however, is straightforward:

> It is an offence for a man to have sexual intercourse with a woman whom he knows to be his grand-daughter, daughter, sister or mother.

> It is an offence for a woman of the age of sixteen or over to permit a man whom she knows to be her grandfather, father, brother or son to have sexual intercourse with her by consent [ss. 10 and 11 of the *Sexual Offences Act* (1956), re-enacting the earlier law].

The conduct of the parties may therefore be consensual and often is, while other offences may be involved should this not be so.

The Criminal Law Revision Committee's *Working Paper on Sexual Offences* (1980) suggests, with qualification, the following rationale for the offence:

INCHOATE CRIME

(1) The genetic risks which seem to be highest where the parties are related in the first degree;

(2) The ill effects of a psychological and social kind on the parties and other members of the family; the capacity, especially of children, to form normal emotional and social relationships may be impaired;

(3) The aversion which many feel to incestuous unions.

About 300 cases per annum come to police notice, with prosecutions (consent of DPP required) following in 80 per cent or more. Most convictions have been for incest with a daughter under sixteen (Walmsley and White, 1979).

J. Bailey and S. Blackburn (1979), 'The Punishment of Incest Act 1908: a case study of law creation', *CLR*, 708; R. Walmsley and K. White (1979), *Sexual Offences, Consent and Sentencing*, HORS no. 54; Criminal Law Revision Committee (1980), *Working Paper on Sexual Offences*.   ARP

Inchoate crime   *Attempt*, *conspiracy* and *incitement* (qq.v.) are known as inchoate because the substantive crime contemplated has not reached completion.   ARP

Incidence   A term referring to the proportion of an age group convicted in one year. *Criminal Statistics* do not give incidence information and little is known concerning it.

See also *Prevalence*.   DPW

Incitement

(1) General   The incitement of a person to commit a crime is itself an offence at common law. Threats or pressure or persuasion all amount to incitement. It matters not that the crime incited is not, or cannot be committed, however if it is then committed, the inciter becomes liable as a party thereto.

(2) Incitement to racial hatred   A substantive offence is committed by one who: (a) publishes or distributes written matter which is threatening, abusive or insulting; or (b) uses in any public place or at any public meeting words which are threatening, abusive or insulting, in a case where, having regard to all the circumstances, hatred is likely to be stirred up against any racial group in Great Britain by the matter or words in question (*Race Relations Act* (1976), s. 70).   ARP

Indecency   Indecent conduct (as distinct from its portrayal, e.g. in books, for which see *obscenity*) is proscribed by the law either when it takes the form of some specific act, as with *indecent assault* (q.v.) or, as with gross indecency, when it occurs in certain specified contexts as follows:

(1) *Between males*The *Sexual Offences Act* (1956) as amended by the *Sexual Offences (Amendment) Act* (1967), penalises gross indecency between males except when there are just two of them over twenty-one in private and mutually consenting. Gross indecency is nowhere expressly defined, although there is no need for actual physical contact. This is the largest category of crime recorded by the police in the area of illegal *homosexuality* (q.v.) and it has been pointed out by Walmsley that following the 1967 Act (which legalised *certain* homosexual acts) the recorded incidence has doubled, the number of persons prosecuted has trebled and the number of persons convicted almost quadrupled.

(2) *With a child under fourteen*The *Indecency with Children Act* (1960) penalises a person who commits an act of gross indecency with or towards a child under fourteen or who incites such an act. This filled a gap in the law, because indecent assault does not cover an invitation to a child to handle someone indecently.

   R. Walmsley (1978), 'Indecency between males and the Sexual Offences Act, 1967', *CLR*, 400; R. Walmsley and K. White (1979), *Sexual Offences, Consent and Sentencing*, HORS no. 54.   ARP

I

Indecent assault   An *assault* (q.v.) committed in circumstances of indecency, the assault being any touching or immediate threat without the other's consent: and where the victim is under sixteen the offence is committed even though there is consent.

   These offences regularly constitute at least a half of the total of serious *sexual offences* (q.v.) recorded annually by the police, and the victims are female about four times more frequently than male. Some of the offenders – but very few – are female. See R. Walmsley and K. White (1979), *Sexual Offences, Consent and Sentencing*, HORS no. 54.   ARP

INDECENT EXPOSURE

Indecent exposure   This can amount to a public nuisance and be indictable at common law, but usually it is dealt with under the *Vagrancy Act* (1824), s. 4, which penalises a man who, 'wilfully, openly, lewdly and obscenely', exposes his penis in any public place or in full view of a public place with intent to insult a female. Such offences (which are probably largely under-reported) are committed by men as a form of sexual gratification or as an insult and appear to be unconnected with other more serious sexual offences. Little is known concerning the origin of this behaviour, beyond the assumption that perpetrators are 'inadequate' and lack necessary social skills required for more conventional forms of sexual relationships.

DPW

Indeterminate sentence   One which will expire only when a decision to that effect is made, as with *life imprisonment* (q.v.): in other sentences the period is fixed in advance, though it may be reduced by *remission* (q.v.) or *parole* (q.v.). What is controversial in the indeterminate sentence is the ability of those responsible to determine the appropriate moment for release, a point that was also raised in connection with proposals for the sentencing of *young adult offenders* (q.v.) and of dangerous offenders, and is also made in relation to parole.

N. Walker (1975), 'Release by executive decision: a defence', *CLR*, 540; R. Hood (1975), 'The case against executive control over time in custody: a rejoinder to Professor Walker's criticisms', *CLR*, 545; L. Radzinowicz and R. Hood (1981), 'Dangerousness and criminal justice: a few reflections', *CLR*, 756.

See also *Criminology*; *Dangerousness*; *Life imprisonment*.

ARP

Index of crime and delinquency

Origin and development   An important problem in counting offences is that they are so varied in nature. This makes comparisons between one area and another and over time very difficult, even if we suspend judgment about the nature of official criminal statistics themselves (see *official statistics*).

The simplest approach has been to count only the more serious offences. But several researchers with a faith in the validity of the basic data have attempted to construct an index by assigning different values to different offences. Early efforts

114

based their weighting system on the sentences that could be imposed for different types of offence – either in terms of the maximum permissible or on the actual sentences. But the one promulgated most seriously is the proposal by Sellin and Wolfgang (1964) to base their weight on the ratings given by a sample to a set of offence descriptions which contained different combinations of injury, theft and/or damage.

Technical problems   There are technical problems associated with developing such an index. Two obvious ones are (i) Who do you sample – policemen, university students and juvenile court judges (as did Sellin and Wolfgang)? – or the inmates of a long-stay prison? And how do you resolve differences in ratings between different groups as reported e.g. by Walker (1978); (ii) What happens with composite offences – can you just add up the scale scores for the elements of each offence? – or does the very multiplicity alter the judgment of seriousness as Wagner and Pease (1978) show? If the latter, there is no way of calculating the value for offences which may or may not have been committed by the same person.

Rationale   The main problem, however, is why have an index at all? Sellin and Wolfgang (1964) argue that it would be a more sensitive measure of the character and trend of delinquency. But the supposed 'gain in usefulness from . . . incorporating a calculation of seriousness as well as for frequency, seems to be more than outweighed by the loss of descriptive information included even in existing criminal statistics based on questionable legal classifications' (Bottomley, 1973, p. 30).

Moreover, useful for what? Or whom? The 'general public' is likely to be concerned with what types of offence are being committed at any one time and in any one country. And, while the decision-maker does confront a problem of lack of knowledge throughout the criminal and penal process this situation requires not encapsulation in an index but more elaborate information which is pertinent to that specific problem. In general, the construction of indicators or indices is appropriate only if there is a clearly delimited and shared social policy concern and we can situate the movements of such an index in a theoretical context (see OECD, 1977).

A.K. Bottomley (1973), *Decisions in the Penal Process*, ch. 1; T. Sellin and M.E. Wolfgang (N.Y., 1964), *The Measurement of Delinquency*; H. Wagner and K. Pease (1978), 'On adding up scores of offence seriousness', *BJC*, 18, 175; M. A. Walker (1978) 'Measuring the seriousness of crimes', *BJC*, 18, 348; OECD (Paris, 1977), *Measuring Social Well-being: a Progress Report on the Development of Social Indicators*, Social Indicators Development Programme, no. 3.   RAC-H

Indictable offence Criminal offences classified with reference to their mode of trial are either *indictable* or *summary* (q.v.) or triable either way. The most serious are triable only on indictment (see *Crown Court*), but other indictable offences may be dealt with that way, should the Magistrates' Court so decide, or summarily. Where the court does not insist on trial on indictment the accused may himself choose it or may agree to summary trial (*Magistrates' Courts Act* (1980), ss. 17–28).

ARP

Infanticide The killing of a child under the age of twelve months by the wilful act or omission of its mother while 'the balance of her mind was disturbed by reason of her not having fully recovered from the effect of giving birth to the child or by reason of the effect of lactation . . . ' (s. 1 of the *Infanticide Act* (1938)). The prosecution may charge the mother with infanticide instead of murder, or she may plead infanticide to a charge of murder. If the mother kills not only her own last-born but another child she cannot benefit from this plea, but usually receives a verdict of *diminished responsibility* (q.v.). A conviction for infanticide means that the sentencing judge has a choice of any disposal, as in cases of *manslaughter* (q.v.). The usual disposal is probation with a requirement of psychiatric treatment: imprisonment is very rare. 'Infanticide' is an anachronism, created in 1922 to save homicidal mothers from a death sentence which was invariably commuted. It seems unnecessary to preserve it alongside diminished responsibility; but the Criminal Law Revision Committee's 14th Report, *Offences against the Person* (Cmnd 7844, 1980), argued for its retention.

NDW

Inmate culture Arises in *institutions* (q.v.) such as hospital and prison in reaction to the existence of staff pressure (see *total institutions*) and to enable the inmates to cope with the inevitable stress of living in such places through developing a separate 'underground' culture characterised by special language, behaviours and technology which essentially aims to soften the impact of physical and social deprivation and to provide meaning, interest and purpose. Hence such culture is very often in diametric opposition to the formal aims of the establishment. Prison inmate culture organised around hostile tough-minded, self-sufficient defensiveness is most evident in training prisons and much less so in local ones where shorter sentences and faster inmate turnover mean that outside behaviours are never wholly replaced by *prisonisation* (q.v.). Similarly, hospital inmate culture is more evident in long-stay units. DPW

Inquest. See *Coroner*.

Institution An organisation (such as a prison, hospital or 'home') set up to achieve a formal purpose, either custodial or treatment-centred, and in which all activity is subservient to this purpose. People may be sent there usually for a fixed period of time for treatment or reform, and while there they spend their entire time leading a formally administered existence of routine. Prolonged exposure to such a regulated existence creates dependence on it, and removes all capacity for independent action, including even the desire to leave when the time comes. The term institutionalisation refers to this state (see also *prisonisation*).

See also *Decarceration*; *Total institution*. DPW

Intelligence Early work tended to show that convicted criminals were of very low intelligence (the derivative issue then becoming the extent to which this intelligence was inherited). Since then it has been realised that test instruments (such as I.Q.) were unfavourably class-biased, and hence would frequently produce misleading results. Further, with the introduction of the concept of *white-collar crime* (q.v.), it was realised that such criminals can be highly intelligent, and finally from *self-report studies* (q.v.) that criminals who are caught are only a fraction of the criminal population; therefore generalising about their intelligence is of limited value, since lower intelligence might be presumed by the fact of capture. It is now accepted that if intelligence is normally distributed among the general population then it will also be so among criminals, some being very dull and some very intelligent. DPW

Intermediate institution. See *Irish system*.

Intermediate Treatment (I.T.)   A new form of treatment for children and young persons made possible by the *Children and Young Persons Act* (1969) with its origins in the Home Secretary's Advisory Council on the Treatment of Offenders Report (1962), *Non-Residential Treatment of Offenders Under Twenty-One*. Previously *Juvenile Courts* (q.v.) had to decide on removing a child from home or not. I.T. provides an intermediate possibility of allowing a child to remain at home while bringing him into contact with a different environment and experiences, the object being to offer new interests and new relationships. Children or young persons are made subject to *Supervision Orders* (q.v.) and are then under the care and guidance of a supervisor (either a local authority or a probation officer). The I.T. requirement may entail two different forms of treatment: either up to three months' residence in an approved place *or* temporary residence, attendance or participation for up to a month per year of the Order, or a mixture of the two. (Approved places and facilities include the full range of educational and recreational facilities available in the community.) Children and young persons subject to I.T. are *not* necessarily offenders and the aim is to involve them in beneficial activities which will carry over into their lives after the treatment is finished.

DHSS (1972), *Intermediate Treatment*; DHSS, Social Work Service, Development Group (1977), *Aspects of Supervision and Intermediate Treatment*; A.L. James (1981), 'Policies into practice: Intermediate Treatment and Community Service compared', *J. Social Policy*, 10 (2), 145; N. Tutt (1979), 'Intermediate Treatment: the integrated approach', *Social Work Service*, 20, 33.   DPW

Introversion.   See *Extraversion*.

Irish system   A system of penal administration founded in 1854 by W.F. Crofton (1815–97), head of the Irish convict prisons. It adopted *remission* (q.v.) early and also used a system of progressive stages. The first stage of imprisonment involved solitary confinement, and in the second a prisoner was transferred to a normal prison with association. There were four grades in this stage, progress from one to another depending upon the number of 'marks' earned within fixed time periods as a result of good conduct and industry; see *marks system* (adopted from Maconochie). The third and final stage used an 'intermediate institution' as a pre-release stage, aiming to break a man from institutionalisation and to accustom him to outside difficulties and temptations, using work similar to that in which he would be employed after his release on 'ticket of leave'. DPW

I

J

Judges. See under the courts where they appear.

Judges' Rules. See *Cautioning*.

Jury, the The very cornerstone of the Anglo-American legal system, and the right to jury trial is regarded as fundamental to all cases which involve serious criminal charges. The jury is, to use Lord Devlin's celebrated phrase, 'the lamp that shows that freedom lives'. Even so, it is important to note that, in England and Wales, no more than one defendant in twenty who is eligible to be tried by jury is actually tried in this way.

In England, juries are composed of twelve lay people drawn from a local community, who sit as an independent tribunal to determine the question of a defendant's guilt. Juries of different sizes are to be found in other jurisdictions (fifteen jurors sit in Scotland, for instance) and the functions served by juries are similarly varied.

Though research on juries is a uniquely difficult undertaking since researchers are not permitted to eavesdrop on juries' deliberations or, in England, even to discuss cases with jurors, researchers have for generations attempted to challenge the inscrutability of juries' verdicts. Hundreds of empirical studies, adopting a variety of sociological and psychological approaches, have been carried out in the present century. Most of this work has been conducted in the USA, and most of it has concerned the accuracy of verdicts, with researchers on the whole avoiding the crucial political and constitutional functions served by juries. In the USA, the massive Chicago Jury Project, started in the 1950s, has produced an impressive (if controversial) series of research findings. In the most important publication arising out of the Project – *The American Jury* – Kalven and Zeisel sought to ascertain whether trial judges across the country generally agreed with the verdicts returned by juries. The authors produced a mass of evidence to support their contention that juries on the whole returned verdicts based on the evidence and verdicts, moreover, with which judges concurred. Other researchers in the USA, using simulated panels of jurors sitting in courtrooms and in laboratories, have presented evidence in support of similar conclusions.

A somewhat different picture has emerged in England and Wales, where research has been conducted on a more limited basis. Most research has focused on the relatively narrow question of the reliability of jury acquittals and has been on a small scale. The exception is the study by Baldwin and McConville (1979), in which the outcomes of some 500 contested trials in Birmingham and 438 in London were analysed. On the basis of views expressed by judges, prosecuting and defence lawyers, and police officers, the authors concluded that juries reached questionable verdicts with some frequency. This conclusion applied not only to jury acquittals but also, more disturbingly, to those cases in which the defendant was convicted.

The passing of the *Contempt of Court Act* (1981), s. 8 of which prohibits any disclosures by jurors of what took place in the jury room, has finally ruled out the possibility of researchers in England involving jurors directly in their studies. This means that English researchers will have to continue to rely on second-best, indirect techniques if they are to strive further to uncover the mysteries of jury trial.

J. Baldwin and M. McConville (1979), *Jury Trials*; H. Kalven and H. Zeisel (Boston, 1966), *The American Jury*.   JB

Justice   In the criminal law and its administration, the word justice tends to refer to the provision actually made for the trial and treatment of offenders: e.g. statutes such as the *Administration of Justice Act* (1970) or the *Criminal Justice Act* (1982). In philosophy it has a more general, more abstract, meaning as a normative ideal; but the links between the two uses of the word are not straightforward.

An important and helpful approach is advocated by Hart (*The Concept of Law*, 1972, p. 156) who sees in the idea of justice 'two parts: a uniform or constant feature, summarized in the precept "Treat like cases alike" and a shifting or varying criterion used in determining when, for any given purpose, cases are alike or different.' This criterion should, then, shift as

J

knowledge and experience, e.g. of psychological states or social effects, themselves change. It may also vary, however, with social morality and here philosophical problems abound.

See also Lord Lloyd (1979), *Introduction to Jurisprudence*, p. 93; A. Ashworth (1979), 'Concepts of criminal justice', *CLR*, 412.   ARP

Justices of the Peace.   See *Magistrate*.

Juvenile, the   One who has attained the age of ten years and is under seventeen. In relation to criminal procedure, therefore, this is the age range (comprising *children* and *young persons* (qq.v.) subject mainly to the *Juvenile Court* (q.v.).   ARP

Juvenile Court   Established as an alternative to the seemingly crimogenic and stigmatising processes of the adult court, the Juvenile Court first developed in the USA in the late nineteenth century (Parsloe, 1978). Recent historical scholarship has begun to question the preponderant benign intentions of those reformers who sought to save children from contamination by adults in this way, claiming that the procedural laxity afforded to the Juvenile Court served to legitimate greater intervention than would be permitted in the case of adults on the basis of pursuing the child's 'best interests' (Platt, 1977). The English Juvenile Court was founded by the *Children Act* (1908), whereby Magistrates' Courts would at special sittings deal with criminal and civil matters involving children and young persons under the age of seventeen by means of summary procedures. Subsequent legislation, most notably the *Children and Young Persons Acts* (1933) and (1969), has placed upon the courts two primary obligations – the protection of the community and the promotion of the welfare of the child – and it is the organisation and execution of these goals which forms the focus of continuing debate surrounding the Juvenile Court (Morris and Giller, 1979).

The current legislation governing the operation of the Juvenile Court, the *Children and Young Persons Act* (1969), in practice gives no clear mandate as to which of these goals should be given predominance. Consequently, wide discretion is given to the Court to determine its own procedures and the application of a range of interventions which variously serve to pursue both welfare and penalty aims. Consistently, therefore, research has demonstrated that a wide variety of procedural styles exist among Juvenile Courts (Anderson, 1978; Parker *et al.*, 1981) with great disparities in the application of available interventions (Priestley *et al.*, 1977). For those who claim to promote the welfare interests of children, the over-concern of Juvenile Courts with the protection of the community has led to the criticism that welfare measures are insufficiently and inefficiently used. Conversely, for those who claim that the Juvenile Court is first and foremost a court of law, the lack of faith in welfare measures to contain and control juveniles is used as a rationale for a continuing and growing use of penalties (House of Commons Expenditure Committee, 1975).

In the policy arena awareness of the contradictory goals of the Juvenile Court has given rise to a variety of attempts to alter the balance between them at different times (see e.g. Committee on Children and Young Persons, 1960). During the ascending of the rehabilitative ethic in the 1960s, for example, (unsuccessful) attempts were made to replace the Juvenile Court with a panel of experts who would decide the form of intervention most likely to further the child's best interests, regardless of the formal grounds of referral (Bottoms, 1974). (A version of this approach was successful in Scotland – see Martin *et al.*, 1981; Morris, 1978.) With the nadir of the rehabilitative ethic greater credence has been given to the idea that there should be limitations placed on the wide discretionary powers of the Juvenile Court which, in the name of promoting the child's welfare, legitimate far greater intervention than could be justified on the basis of the nature of the referral (Morris *et al.*, 1980; Taylor *et al.*, 1980). In the USA this 'lawlessness' in the Juvenile Court led to legal decisions (e.g. In re Gault 387 US 1), and subsequently legislative proposals, fundamentally to shift the balance in favour of tighter legal regulation of the work of the court (Institute of Judicial Administration and American Bar Association, 1977). In England such a thoroughgoing review has yet to be undertaken given the political sensitivity of the subject-matter (cf. Northern Ireland – Children and Young Persons Review Group, 1979), although the recent *Criminal Justice Act* (1982) has introduced sentencing criteria into the Juvenile Court while at the same time giving magistrates greater powers to directly intervene in the lives of juvenile offenders.

R. Anderson (1978), *Representation in the Juvenile Court*; A.E. Bottoms (1974), 'On the decriminalization of the English Juvenile Court', in R. Hood, ed., *Crime, Criminology and*

Public Policy; Children and Young Persons Review Group (HMSO, Belfast, 1979), *Report* (Black Committee); Ingleby Committee on Children and Young Persons (1960), *Report*, Cmnd 1191; House of Commons Expenditure Committee (1975), *Eleventh Report, Children and Young Persons Act* (1969): I, Report; II, Evidence, HC 354, i and ii; Institute of Judicial Administration and American Bar Association (Cambridge, Mass., 1977), *Juvenile Justice Standards Project*, vols 1–24; F. Martin, S. Fox and K. Murray (1981), *Children Out of Court*; A. Morris (1979), *Juvenile Justice?*; A. Morris and H. Giller (1979), 'Juvenile justice and social work in Britain', in H. Parker, ed., *Social Work and the Courts*; A. Morris, H. Giller, E. Szwed and H. Geach (1980), *Justice for Children*; H. Parker, M. Casburn and D. Turnbull (1981), *Receiving Juvenile Justice*; P. Parsloe (1978), *Juvenile Justice in Britain and the United States*; A. Platt (2nd ed., Chicago, 1977), *The Child Savers*; P. Priestley, R. Fuller and D. Fears (1977), *Justice for Juveniles*; L. Taylor, R. Lacey and D. Bracken (1980), *In Whose Best Interests?*. HG

K

Kidnapping The crime of kidnapping is the unlawful seizure and detention of a person or persons by force or fraud against their will. Originally the term 'kidnapping' denoted seizing a person and taking him or her to another country for involuntary servitude, or the impressment of males into military or naval service by force or fraud. Another form of kidnapping is the abduction and sale of women for prostitution or concubinage, though in most legal codes this is treated as a separate offence of abduction. There have been cases where the main motive for kidnapping has been revenge or cruelty, such as the desire to inflict involuntary servitude on the victim, to cause pain and grief to the victim's loved ones, or to commit some further crime against the victim. However, in the overwhelming majority (over 90 per cent) of modern kidnappings the main motive is criminal gain. Most of these crimes are committed by criminal gangs seeking to make a fortune by obtaining a ransom for the safe release of the victim. An epidemic of kidnapping for extortion occurred in the USA in the 1920s and 1930s. A particularly notorious case was the 1932 kidnapping of the US flyer Charles Lindbergh's baby boy. It was partly as a result of outcry over this case that the USA introduced legislation imposing the death penalty for carrying a kidnap victim across State boundaries.

It was only in the late 1960s and early 1970s that politically motivated kidnappings by revolutionary groups seeking publicity and the release of imprisoned guerillas from gaol in addition to ransom payments became a fashionable tactic. For example, in 1969 Brazilian terrorists kidnapped the US Ambassador to Brazil and secured the release of fifteen imprisoned terrorists in return for his freedom. For the release of the German and Swiss Ambassadors kidnapped the following year the price escalated to 40 and 70 prisoners respectively. Among the most notorious

125

KIDNAPPING

recent political kidnappings in Italy, which, next to Latin America, has the highest incidence of this type of crime, was the seizure of the Christian Democrat politician, Signor Aldo Moro in 1978. The Italian authorities stood firm and refused to negotiate political concessions with his captors, the Red Brigades, and the terrorists murdered Signor Moro. In some cases, as in 1982 with the rescue of the kidnapped US General Dozier, the authorities have been fortunate in discovering the terrorists' hideout and securing the release of the kidnap victim unharmed. Nevertheless, kidnapping is an extremely difficult crime to counter. In every country it is regarded as a very serious offence, for which the penalty is either death or lengthy imprisonment. PW

L

Labelling theory   The idea that a man defined in a certain way by authority comes to change both his Self-percept and his behaviour to conform to this definition as a result of social pressure was first developed by Erikson and Erikson (N.Y., 1962) in 'The confirmation of the delinquent', in H.M. Ruitenbeek, ed., *Psychoanalysis and Social Science*. An influential description of the process was T.J. Scheff's (1966) *Being Mentally Ill*, who argued that someone who is categorised as mentally ill must ultimately display 'illness', and then be caught in a trap; i.e. how can he from this position prove his normality once and if it is regained? The same process was seen to apply to captured criminals undergoing a confirmation ritual in a law court, in which they are formally labelled as criminals and as a result of which they are expected to behave as such.

Subsequent recidivism is then explained in terms of the labelling process rather than in terms of a person's individuality. Important as it is, labelling theory does not explain why first offenders offend, or why those who are *not* caught continue to commit crime, nor does it give any insight into how courts, prisons, hospitals and so on can discharge their duties without using categories.

D.P. Farrington (1977), 'The effects of public labelling', *BJC*, 17, 112; W.R. Gove, ed. (1975), *The Labelling of Deviance*: *Evaluating a Perspective*.   DPW

Libel   It is an offence at common law to publish a libel; that is words, normally in some enduring form, which tend to lower a person in the estimation of right-thinking members of society; it is also actionable in civil proceedings for damages. Words merely spoken (except in the public performance of a play, see *Theatres Act* (1968)) do not amount to libel; they may amount to slander, but, as such, are actionable only in civil proceedings.

127

LIFE IMPRISONMENT, LIFE SENTENCE

Private prosecutions are sometimes brought, but the existence of the offence as it stands is thought by some to be an anomaly.

J. Spencer (1977), 'Criminal libel: a skeleton in the cupboard', *CLR*, 383; J. Spencer (1979), 'Criminal libel in action: the snuffing of Mr Wicks', *Cambridge Law Journal*, 38 (I), 60.

ARP

Life imprisonment, Life sentence   Life sentences of imprisonment had existed for various offences before *capital punishment* was abolished, but in 1965 by the *Murder (Abolition of Death Penalty) Act* of that year, they also became the new punishment for all murder and are still available for other serious offences. Such a sentence is indeterminate and the offender is immediately imprisoned for a number of years (average about ten). His case is periodically reviewed and when it is judged that he is no longer a danger to the public he may be released on licence. He normally will progress from a high security training prison to an open prison throughout his period of imprisonment. There are currently about 1,600 people serving such sentences.

A life sentence prisoner or a person detained during *Her Majesty's Pleasure* can be released by the *Home Secretary* if the Parole Board so recommend after consultation with the Lord Chief Justice and the trial judge. A life sentence prisoner is released only after a very detailed and careful consideration of his case and circumstances (including any recommendation made by the original trial judge for a minimum period of imprisonment). Once released and under supervision by a probation officer, a close watch is kept on the man to see how he is settling back into the community. He may be recalled to prison at any time during the rest of his life if his conduct gives rise for concern, either by the Home Secretary if the Parole Board recommend it or by a court.

European Committee on Crime Problems (Strasbourg, 1977), *Treatment of Long-term Prisoners*; R. Short (1979), *The Care of Long-term Prisoners*; D. Smith, C. Brown, J. Worth, R. Sapsford and C. Banks (1979), *Life Sentence Prisoners*, HORS no. 51.

DPW

Local prison   One which serves a local catchment area without specialisation. Such a prison, of which there are about two dozen, accommodates almost every type of prisoner, some for their whole sentence, some from the outset only and some

128

temporary transfers, but mainly short-sentence men. Local prisons are generally unpopular with prisoners because they tend to be the most overcrowded, but they possess the advantages of ease of visits and a rapid turn-over of men. Prior to the *Prison Act* (1952) (and aside from the *Prison Inspectorate Act* (1835) and the *Nationalization Act* (1877)), local prisons were shaped by two main Acts, the *General Gaols Act* (1823) and *The Prison Act* (1865). See R.F. Sparks (1971), *Local Prisons: the Crisis in the English Prison System*.   DPW

Longitudinal research This involves repeated measures of the same people, or of samples from the same population. Its primary use has been to investigate the course of development, the natural history and prevalence of a phenomenon at different ages, how phenomena emerge, or continuities and discontinuities from an earlier age to a later age. It has also been used to study the relationship between earlier and later events, the effects of particular events or life experiences on the course of development, and the transmission of characteristics from one generation to the next. For a review of longitudinal research on crime and delinquency, see D.P. Farrington (1979) in N. Morris and M. Tonry, eds, *Crime and Justice*, vol. 1.

The first major longitudinal studies in criminology were carried out in the United States by S. and E.T. Glueck. They followed up (a) 500 men released from a reformatory, (b) 500 women released from a reformatory, (c) 1,000 juvenile delinquents examined by a clinic, and (d) 500 institutionalised delinquents and 500 matched non-delinquents. These follow-up studies extended up to fifteen years. The longest criminological follow-up is of the Cambridge–Somerville study by J. McCord (1978), in *American Psychologist*, 33, 284, and extends over thirty-five years. Other major American longitudinal surveys have been carried out by L.N. Robins and M.E. Wolfgang.

A major national longitudinal survey in England, Scotland and Wales is the National Survey of Health and Development. This is a follow-up of over 5,000 children born in one week of March 1946, and criminological data from this survey have been summarised by M. Wadsworth in *Roots of Delinquency* (1979). Similar national follow-ups of children born in 1958 and 1970 are also under way, but no information about crime and delinquency has yet been published from them. Another long-lasting English survey is the Cambridge Study in Delinquent Development, described by D.J. West and D.P. Farring-

L

ton in *The Delinquent Way of Life* (1977). This is a twenty-year follow-up of over 400 London boys.

One of the major uses of longitudinal research in criminology is to study criminal careers. Attempts are made to predict the beginning and ending of such careers, to document the incidence of different kinds of offending at different ages, to study the relationship between juvenile delinquency and adult crime, to investigate whether offending is specialised or generalised and to establish the effects of penal treatments and other events such as marriage on offending. Studies which combine frequent interviews with information from official records are the most useful. DPF

Looting (from Hindi *lut*: to rob) Where war or civil disturbance creates a climate of lawlessness and provides apparent justification and opportunity, there will be those ready and able to make away with the property and possessions of others; such is 'looting', and it may be dealt with as *burglary* and *theft* (qq.v.).

See also *Public order*; *Riot*. ARP

M

Mafia, the (also known as 'Cosa Nostra') A deeply-rooted, well-defended, criminal organisation dedicated to money-making. Originating in Sicily, it spread to the USA, where it has been involved in the organisation of illicit supply (gambling, prostitution, narcotics), labour union manipulation and more recently it has infiltrated legitimate industry. It is based on autocratically feudal private enterprise, the key unit being the 'family', consisting of a Boss, Underboss, lieutenants and 'soldiers'. It has been described (Vassalli, 1974) as a 'mentality' which stresses secrecy, honour (respect), loyalty and the ruthless suppression, or efficient corruption, of opponents.

J.L. Albini (1975), 'Mafia as method: a comparison between Great Britain and USA regarding the existence and structure of types of organised crime', *Int. J. Criminology & Penology*, 3 (3), 295; V. Teresa and T. Renner (N.Y., 1973), *My Life in the Mafia*; G. Vassalli (1974), 'An Italian enquiry concerning the Mafia', in R. Hood, ed., *Crime, Criminology and Public Policy*.

DPW

Magistrate, the

> Magistrate is the common denomination under which are included all those who are entrusted, whether by commission or appointment, or by virtue of their office, with the conservation of the peace and the hearing and determination of charges in respect of offences against it (*Halsbury's Laws of England*, vol. 29, para. 201).

However, it was as 'keepers' and then 'justices' of the peace that these officers were first introduced into the counties of fourteenth-century England, and the *Justices of the Peace Act* (1361) is still in force. Over the centuries their involvement in local government waxed and then waned, so that now their functions are mainly judicial, exercised in *Magistrates' Courts* (q.v.). 'JP' and 'Magistrate' are more or less synonyms, though the full-time legally qualified stipendiary magistrate of some large cities is not ordinarily spoken of as a JP. Elsewhere in the country the magistrates are lay justices appointed by the Lord Chancellor with the advice of local committees on which the political parties are represented. The basic law relating to magistrates is now to be found in the consolidating *Justices of the Peace Act* (1979).

See also *Crown Court*; *Magistrates' Court*.   ARP

Magistrates' Court   'Any justice or justice of the peace acting under any enactment or by virtue of his or their commission or under the common law' (*Magistrates' Courts Act* (1980) s. 148). Excepting stipendiary magistrates, who may sit alone, a Magistrates' Court must be composed of at least two justices of the peace and not more than seven, though a single justice may conduct committal proceedings in the case of an indictable offence. Summary trial in a Magistrates' Court is initiated either on an arrest without warrant, when permissible, or by information laid before it followed by summons or arrest on warrant. It is estimated that around 98 per cent of all prosecutions are dealt with summarily, leaving only the more serious indictable cases for trial on indictment in the *Crown Court* (q.v.) before a jury. The basic law relating to the subject is now to be found in the consolidating *Magistrates' Courts Act* (1980).

See also *Crown Court*; *Magistrate*.   ARP

Manic-depression.   See *Mental abnormality*.

Manslaughter   Homicide committed either:

(1) With the malice aforethought of murder, but with certain mitigating factors reducing it to manslaughter (viz. *diminished responsibility* (q.v.) or when it is the result of a suicide pact or provocation: see *Homicide Act* (1957)).

(2) Without the malice aforethought of murder but with a degree of blameworthiness sufficient in the eyes of the law to constitute the offence. Unfortunately the law is unclear and quite impossible to summarise: it is, in G. William's words, 'the common law at its worst', *Textbook of Criminal Law* (1979, p. 223). The Criminal Law Revision Committee (1980) recom-

mend that this form of manslaughter be statutorily defined simply as causing 'death with intent to cause serious injury, or being reckless as to death or serious injury' (14th Report, *Offences against the Person*).   ARP

Marks system   One of the reforms invented by A. Maconochie (1787–1860), when appointed Superintendent of Norfolk Island penal colony, off the east coast of Australia, in 1840. When each prisoner arrived he was debited with marks according to the seriousness of his offence. These were redeemable through work and good behaviour, and when all were cancelled the prisoner was considered for conditional release on 'ticket of leave'. The aim was to give a man an inducement to reform by making it possible for him to shorten his sentence. See J.V. Barry (Melbourne, 1958), *Alexander Maconochie of Norfolk Island: a Study of a Pioneer in Penal Reform*.   DPW

Maternal deprivation.   See *Deprivation*.

Maturity/Maturation   It has been suggested (Roper, 1951) that most criminals are immature, and that immaturity and criminality are much the same thing, which both assumes a clear definition of 'maturity' and ignores the phenomenon of 'late-starters' in crime. S. and E. Glueck (1937) further argued that most criminals mature out of crime by the age of thirty-five and recommended (1940) the establishment of a 'maturation quotient' (M.Q.) to measure the degree of deviation from the 'maturation norm'. The opposite view is given by Frey (1951), who asserts that an early start in crime (as a child) leads to the creation of hardened adult criminals who do *not* mature out of crime. However only a small proportion of all early starters continue as persistent adult criminals. The small number of known late-starters (at above the age of forty, say) are conventionally seen as becoming involved through ideological shift, 'mid-life crisis', 'disappointments' or unshareable problems (Cressey, 1953), but such a view largely ignores the phenomenon of *white-collar crime* (q.v.). Crime, especially violent crime, is mostly associated with youthfulness, and ageing appears to reduce much known conventional criminal activity, so the bulk of criminals might be said to 'mature' out of it (although not necessarily at any arbitrary age); however, all

M

133

such assessments are derived from official records and have to presume that there is no failure to detect crime.

D.R. Cressey (N.Y., 1953), *Other Peoples' Money*; E. Frey (Basle, 1951), *Criminalité précoce et récidivisme*; S. and E. Glueck (N.Y., 1937), *Later Criminal Careers*; S. and E. Glueck (N.Y., 1940), *Juvenile Delinquents Grown Up*; W.F. Roper (1951), 'A comparative survey of the Wakefield prison population in 1948 and 1949: Part II', *BJD*, I (4), 243.　　　DPW

Measurement of crime/delinquency　The variety of behaviour classified as criminal is almost as wide as the variety of behaviour in general. The only common factor between, for example, a prostitute soliciting potential clients and someone breaking into someone else's house is that the state disapproves of the behaviour enough to proscribe it. Although, as the British Prime Minister recently said in referring to IRA activities, 'A crime is a crime is a crime', distinctions between crime are usually made in published criminal statistics. The most pervasive distinction in criminal statistics is that between more and less 'serious' crimes. In published statistics the distinction is most often made through the type of court procedure to which the crime might lead. In England and Wales, published statistics of Offences recorded by the Police are limited to the more serious, now known as Notifiable Offences (i.e. those which were triable as *indictable offences* (q.v.) before the *Criminal Law Act* (1977)). Elsewhere, the classification of crime into felony and misdemeanour serves the same essential purpose. Such divisions, while useful for some routine statistical purposes, do not do justice to the central role which offence seriousness plays in decisions in the criminal justice process. People disapprove of crimes to varying extents. The only defining characteristic of crime is that it is behaviour so disapproved as to be forbidden. Thus the extent of the disapproval is, not surprisingly, the central dimension considered by the police (see e.g. Farrington and Bennett, 1981), the courts (Thomas, 1979) and the paroling authorities (Nuttall *et al.*, 1977). For this reason, crime and delinquency measurement is usually synonymous with the measurement of offence seriousness: for example the classic work of Sellin and Wolfgang (1964), entitled *The Measurement of Delinquency*, dealt exclusively with judgments of offence seriousness. A sophisticated scale of offence seriousness has been something of a Holy Grail for criminologists. Such a scale would have many uses, from serving as an aid to optimal police deployment, to detecting changes in criminal careers. The typically impressive amount of public consensus about offence seriousness (see Walker, 1978) would seem to make such a scale achievable in principle. However, although scales have been developed for specific purposes (the guidelines movement relies on one such scale – see Wilkins, 1981), the best-known general purpose scale, developed from the work of Sellin and Wolfgang (1964), is inadequate for the judgment of complex offences (see for example Gottfredson *et al.*, 1980).

Attempts to measure crime and delinquency in terms of the dimension of offence seriousness will continue as long as retribution underpins penal practice.

D. Farrington and T. Bennett (1981), 'Police cautioning of juveniles', *BJC*, 21, 123; S.D. Gottfredson, K.L. Young and W.S. Laufer (1980), 'Additivity and interaction in offence seriousness scales', *J. Res. Crime Del.*, 17, 26; C.P. Nuttall *et al.* (1977), *Parole in England and Wales*, HORS no. 38; T. Sellin and M. Wolfgang (N.Y. 1964), *The Measurement of Delinquency*; D.A. Thomas (2nd ed., 1979), *Principles of Sentencing*; M. Walker (1978), 'Measuring the seriousness of crime', *BJC*, 18, 348; L.T. Wilkins (Washington, 1981), *The Principles of Guidelines for Sentencing*, US Dept of Justice Monograph.

See also *Index of crime*. KP

Media The term 'mass media' was invented by M. Young (1958) in *The Rise of the Meritocracy* as a shorthand to describe television, radio and newspapers. Interest has centred on three largely unproven accusations levelled at the media. They have been accused of (a) irresponsibility, in the sense of stating as facts things for which there is no real evidence and in the sense of informing people exactly how crime is committed (and hence possibly generating emulative crime), (b) manufacturing artificial 'news' which is either untrue or of no interest, and (c) creating and enforcing *moral panics* (q.v.) by their selective reporting and block concentration on fashionable *social problems* (q.v.). And see S. Cohen and J. Young, eds (1973), *The Manufacture of News*.

See also *Television, effects of*. DPW

Mediation An example of diversion from the criminal justice process which may occur at any stage from the moment it is first alleged that an offence has been committed through to

M

135

appearance of an accused before the court. It may also be used as part of a sentence, though that is comparatively rare. Participation depends upon the consent of both parties.

Derived from the models of the African tribal moot and extrajudicial dispute resolution in certain ethnic communities in the USA, this procedure brings complainant and alleged offender together, preferably in a neutral place and at a time convenient to both, in the presence of an impartial third party (a mediator). His principal function is to encourage and assist the parties to listen to each other's account of the event and its background, and then with a fuller understanding of each other's viewpoint by discussion to reach a mutually satisfactory settlement of their differences. If empowered to do so by prior agreement of the parties involved, the mediator may impose his solution if they are unable to arrive at a solution of their own. This further process is known as arbitration. The incident which led to the mediation taking place may be part of a wider pattern of behaviour by one or both of them, and far from apportioning blame the mediator will ideally enable them to explore the underlying causes and to negotiate an agreement which seeks to regulate their future conduct as well as dealing with the trouble of the past.

Both parties therefore have their say, and there are none of the restrictive rules of evidence which in the adversary style of Anglo-American criminal proceedings typically prevent the parties from mentioning background events which to them are of great significance and often serve to explain the incident itself. A sentencer has a limited range of options, but there are no standard restrictions upon the contents of parties' own agreements.

The greatest proliferation of formal experiments based upon this concept has taken place in the USA, beginning with the Night Prosecutor Program in Columbus, Ohio, in 1971. Since then approximately a hundred schemes (widely known as citizen dispute resolution centres) have been established in the United States, sponsored variously by some component of the criminal justice system (e.g. courts, prosecutors), by private non-profit-making organisations (principally the American Arbitration Association and the Institute of Mediation and Conflict Resolution), or local government. Publication of a US Department of Justice review by D. McGillis and J. Mullen (1977), entitled *Neighborhood Justice Centers: an Analysis of Potential Models*, was followed by a Federally-funded field test, whose results appeared in 1980 (R.F. Cook, J.A. Roehl and D.I. Sheppard, *Neighborhood Justice Centers Field Test: Final Evaluation Report*).

There is a wide variety of approach and practice. Most centres concentrate upon incidents involving people who were previously known to each other (e.g. spouses, relatives, friends, neighbours, fellow employees, landlords and tenants). Typically such persons must learn to coexist peaceably and are least willing to follow a prosecution through to the bitter end. Some schemes undertake 'stranger' cases as well. Most prefer to deal, at least at first, with lesser offences, but some are prepared to deal with potentially serious offences (see e.g. R.C. Davis *et al.* (1980), *Mediation and Arbitration as Alternatives to Prosecution in Felony Arrest Cases: an Evaluation of the Brooklyn Dispute Resolution Center*, Vera Institute, N.Y.).

One of the biggest differences concerns the identity of mediators. Some are lay people (in some instances with an attempt to recruit a representative sample of the local community), others are professionals, such as lawyers, psychologists and social workers. For most of them, this is a spare-time activity for which they receive a modest stipend to cover their expenses. After intensive initial training, much depends thereafter upon individual and shared experiences.

Some schemes retain the option for a prosecution to proceed if a mediated agreement rapidly breaks down, but further misbehaviour is likely to constitute fresh grounds for prosecution in any event. Fulfilment of agreements largely depends upon the goodwill of participants, though most schemes make provision for follow-up by their own staff to check progress and, where appropriate, to persuade the recalcitrant to co-operate.

RG & KW

Mens rea The legal expression for such attitude of mind on the part of an offender at the time of his offence as renders him responsible for it in law. *Mens rea* (literally 'guilty mind') involves intention or recklessness in his conduct, without which it cannot be said that he has committed a crime, however serious the outcome. But see *Strict liability*.

See also *Responsibility*. ARP

Mental abnormality Madness has been recognised throughout history, the disputes being about causes and cures. Promising

137

MENTAL ABNORMALITY

Graeco-Roman beginnings gave way in Europe to the perverted theologies of (demoniacal) possession and witchcraft and their attendant 'treatments'. Science and social reform flickered into life in the eighteenth century and have been battling ever since with varying degrees of success. Nineteenth-century optimism that mental illness was the behavioural expression of brain disease faltered, and psychoanalysis arose giving rise in turn to many varieties of psychotherapy. The biological–social psychological dichotomy has continued to the present, sometimes diverging at other times converging. The current psycho-biological ethos is an example of the latter and is probably a healthy trend away from the doctrinaire. It has been furthered considerably by the development of successful physical treatments for some disorders.

By the mid-nineteenth century the medical profession had control of the care of the institutionalised mentally ill person and there ensued a period of detailed descriptions of psychiatric syndromes. 'To classify is as inevitable as death' (G.A. Foulds *et al.* (1965), *Personality and Personal Illness*, ch. 4), and today's systems (*International Classification of Diseases*, 9th revision, Geneva, 1975; *Glossary of Mental Disorders*, Geneva, 1978) owe much to work done a hundred years ago. There are three groups of mental disorders:

(1) Psychoses.

(2) Neuroses, personality disorders and other non-psychotic disorders.

(3) *Mental impairment* (q.v.).

The psychoses are described as non-understandable or morbid states, the implication being that they are manifestations of underlying brain disease. In the case of the organic psychoses such as the dementias and toxic states, this is certain and it is probably true of the 'functional' psychoses, e.g. schizophrenia.

The non-psychotic disorders are considered to be understandable, albeit abnormal, reactions or developments. The experiences are familiar, but their degree and/or the ease with which they are precipitated are maladaptive. Brain disease is not involved in the cause, but rather social and psychological influences over the period of development from childhood rendering the individual more susceptible to everyday stresses and life-events. Neurotic symptoms are often differentiated from personality traits, the former being more circumscribed and of more recent onset, whereas the latter are of long-standing and more fundamental to the individual's make-up.

All classifications depend upon an understanding of mechanisms and it is clear that there is a serious lack of objective data concerning the 'pathology' of most mental disorders. Until such data are available we must fall back on clinical descriptions with references to course and apparent causes, whether these be psychological, pathological or genetic. It is said by some that such classifications are worthless, being the imposition of an unnatural order upon inevitably intangible issues. Certainly classification can be taken to absurd lengths, whether it be of a biological medical kind or founded on unconfirmed schemas of psychodynamic mechanisms. Foulds's remark nevertheless remains true, but the present system is unable to satisfy the basic requirements of a classification. Categories overlap, disorders share symptoms, specialists disagree about diagnosis and many terms are not well differentiated.

There are numerous classifications, but the most widely used and most generally useful is the International Classification of Diseases, which is really a dictionary of operational definitions of clinical syndromes which serve as diagnostic categories until something better comes along.

Organic psychoses   Conditions in which there is impairment of intellectual function and orientation, and possible altered mood, clouding of consciousness with hallucinations and deterioration in social standards. These may be acute as in toxic states (e.g. alcoholic delirium), injury, generalised metabolic disorders like diabetic coma and epilepsy, or chronic such as the dementias and Korsakoff's alcoholic psychosis. The former group either recover or die, although a few may lapse into chronicity. They need urgent medical attention. The dementias, usually occurring in the elderly, are long-drawn-out degenerative states which are a burden for the individual sufferer, the relatives and society. There is an increasing incidence because there is an ageing population.

There are other organic disorders which as well as having disturbances of memory and intellect, also and sometimes only, show themselves as neurotic symptoms such as irritability and asthenia or personality change with behavioural disorder. The organic basis of these conditions such as frontal lobe syndrome and post-concussional syndrome is often not recognised, which leads to considerable difficulty and often injustice to the sufferer.

Non-organic (functional) psychoses

Schizophrenia – Symptoms include disturbances of thinking (pressure, poverty, distorted form with incomprehensibility, broadcasting, insertion, withdrawal and delusion); affect or mood (elation, depression, anxiety, perplexity, inappropriateness, giggling, shallowness, coldness); perception (hallucinations of hearing, vision and touch), volition or will (controlled movements, negativity, posturing, apathy, stupor, overactivity and excitement). There are several sub-types such as simple, hebephrenic, catatonic and paranoid which comprise various combinations of this wide range of symptoms. The disorder can lead to severe disruption of personality and day-to-day functioning, bringing unemployability, isolation, alienation and extreme sensitivity to stress. Acute varieties can have a very good prognosis, but those of more insidious onset tend towards chronicity and permanent personality damage. Insight is usually limited and may be absent.

Causes are unknown, but there seems to be a genetic vulnerability which can be exposed by aspects of upbringing and stress. Biochemical disturbances underlie the symptoms. Onset is typically in the mid-teens, more boys than girls, but the paranoid type is more common in older adults, particularly women. Treatment consists of a combination of physical (ECT, drugs), psychological (behavioural) and social (suitable employment, appropriate rehousing).

Affective psychoses – Severe disturbances of mood accompanied by upset biological functions (loss of appetite, weight and libido, constipation, dryness of the mouth, amenorrhoea, disturbed sleep, especially early morning wakening and diurnal variation of mood). Depression is the commoner mood change, with slowness of thinking and of movement, reduced concentration and interest, occasional hallucinatory voices, feelings of unworthiness, guilt and failure (which may be delusion) and loss of desire to live, with possibilities of suicide.

The opposite mood is mania, a state of excitement, elation, joy of living, grandiosity, enhanced energy, fleeting but numerous interests, omnipotence and reduced judgment, both social and financial.

Individuals may suffer only depression or only mania (unipolar) or have recurrences of both types (bipolar/circular

manic depressive psychosis). Sex distribution is about equal
with onset in the middle twenties and increasing incidence
especially of depression into late middle age (involutional
melancholia). Again, causes are unknown but there are genetic
influences and underlying biochemical changes with social
stresses and life changes precipitating mood alterations in
vulnerable people. Treatment is a combination of physical and
psycho-social (psychotherapy, environmental changes).

Non-Psychotic Disorders

Neuroses – Disorders without apparent primary underlying
organic basis, albeit often manifesting physical experiences and
symptoms. Sufferers have insight, and do not confuse internal
experience with external reality.

A tendency to neuroticism may show itself early on, and lead
to maladaptive attitudes and ways of coping from adolescence
onwards. It is sometimes difficult to differentiate neurotic
symptoms from personality characteristics, but the former are
less ingrained and may not appear except under marked stress.
Many of the symptoms occur in most people at some time, but
in neuroses they become extreme and disabling.

Anxiety states – Combinations of physical and mental
experiences such as palpitations, sweating, dry mouth, stomach
and bowel disturbances, tremor, tension and apprehension.
May be persistent or episodic, sometimes amounting to panic.
Related conditions are the:

Phobic/(anxiety) states – in which anxiety is more circumscribed and relates to specific objects or situations which would
not normally induce anxiety, or if so only to a minor or useful
extent. Dread can be of animals, heights, open spaces, crowds
and social occasions.

Hysteria – Restricted field of consciousness (dissociation) or
disturbances of motor or sensory function (conversion) occurring usually in response to stress, and in which it has been
assumed there is unconscious motivation producing advantage
('secondary gain' – 'primary gain' is the reduction of anxiety).
There may be selective amnesia, transient personality changes
with fugue states, paralyses, seizures or naïve mimicry of
psychosis.

Obsessive-compulsive disorders – Feelings of subjective
compulsion to carry out some action, dwell on an idea or
philosophical question. The intrusive ruminative thoughts and

M

urges are recognised as being nonsensical and are resisted. Actions may be ritualistic in an apparent attempt to keep anxiety at bay, which, however, is increased by resistance, e.g. hand-washing, counting.

Depressive neuroses – More akin than psychotic depression to everyday unhappiness. The reaction to circumstance may be understandable but is probably disproportionate in intensity or duration. Symptomatology is also less specific, anxiety is often prominent, possibly as a personality characteristic. Depression may be profound and prolonged in vulnerable people and can lead to suicide. Acute episodes of depressive distress account for much para-suicidal behaviour.

Other conditions – For example, neurasthenia (nervous debility), depersonalisation (disturbance of perception of surroundings or body) and hypochondriasis (excessive preoccupation with health and bodily functions) which also often occur as features of other mental disorders. Probably best included in the neuroses are a range of conditions including the so-called 'psychosomatic' disorders, such as asthma, eczema, colitis and hypertension, and conditions such as anorexia nervosa, stammering, tics, sleep disturbances, bed-wetting and soiling and psychogenic pain, all of which can be symptoms of underlying organic disorder and care is needed in labelling them as psychogenic. In addition there are such conditions as alcohol and drug dependence, drug abuse and varieties of sexual deviation and difficulty.

Personality disorders – Deeply ingrained patterns of behaviour, recognisable early in life and continuing throughout life with some mitigation later on. The individual may have a totally disorganised personality or more commonly be abnormal in certain aspects of expression. There are some characteristics related to neuroses and psychoses; for example cyclothymic, paranoid, schizoid, obsessional, hysterical or asthenic. However, a wide range is possible, which may be abnormal in the statistical sense of outside the usual or exaggerated, for example explosiveness, aggressiveness, passivity (see also *psychopath*).

Treatment will comprise a mixture of psychotherapies, behaviour modification, relaxation, social skills training, institutional training and occasional use of physical methods, including rarely psycho-surgery, for severe intractable neurosis.

GDPW

Mental impairment Previously known as retardation, handicap, (severe) subnormality, it means subnormal intellectual functioning. There are a variety of causes (e.g. following infections and intoxications, with disorders of metabolism, growth or nutrition, associated with brain disease, due to psycho-social deprivation) and while until recently the majority of those so afflicted have been cared for in hospital, the current trend is towards an extensive supportive network of community care. DPW

Mental testing. See *Intelligence*.

Missing persons Although thousands of people are reported missing to the police every year, the term 'missing person' only has any legal force behind it if a crime is suspected (such as murder) or the person who has disappeared belongs to one of the specially vulnerable categories of the young, the disabled, the old or the imprisoned. Because there is, with the exception of the cases previously noted, no central agency concerned with missing persons in England and Wales, the majority of those who go missing are not regarded as a cause for public concern. In that technical sense there is no official missing persons problem in Britain or in any other Western country.

Analyses and explanations of the act of going missing, and becoming a missing person, reflect the anxieties and difficulties of the particular agencies concerned as in the case of police responsibility for an escaped prisoner, a missing child or an old person who has apparently wandered from a geriatric ward. When there are reasonable grounds for assuming an individual who is defined as legally responsible has made a voluntary decision to leave home, there is unlikely to be any sustained official search. Relatives and friends, if they wish to pursue the matter, must seek the services of unofficial agencies such as the Salvation Army (whose work is well documented in R. Williams (1969), *Missing*) and private detectives.

It is the act of voluntary disappearance, so difficult to research, which has been of most interest to sociologists in England and Wales and the USA. Major contributions from Lenore Weitzman (1970, 'Social Suicide', New York, Columbia University PhD thesis) and M. Featherstone and M. Hepworth (1974, 'Persons believed missing', in P. Rock and M. McIntosh, eds, *Deviance and Social Control*) draw attention to the theoretical significance of voluntary social disengagement for a

M

143

symbolic interactionist approach to personal identity in adult life. In particular, they stress the importance of taking the missing person's point of view into account when constructing explanations of various acts of physical disappearance. Conventional explanations reflect the perspective of those who have been left behind and the agencies whose duty it is, under specific circumstances, to take action, and consequently suffer from significant limitations.   MH

Modelling The adoption or use of previously witnessed behaviours displayed by an observed model. This has been shown (M.P. Feldman (1977), *Criminal Behaviour*, p. 85) to have particular applicability in relation to *aggression* (q.v.), and undoubtedly modelling is of importance in crime generally. Studies indicate that publicising offences is highly unlikely to decrease their frequency.

See also *Crime wave*; *Television, effects of*.   DPW

Moral crusade. See *Symbolic crusade*.

Moral entrepreneur One who, involved in the enterprise of legislating and law enforcement, adopts a moral stance to his subject-matter, which it becomes important for him to uphold for symbolic as well as instrumental ends. See H. Becker (N.Y., 1963), *Outsiders*, ch. 8.

See also *Symbolic crusade*.   ARP

Moral panic The term given by S. Cohen (1972) in *Moral Panics and Folk Devils* to a process of collective over-reaction to a form of apparently widespread deviance. The *media* (q.v.) initially 'identify' the 'crisis' and the inevitable societal reaction is to demand greater control through greater policing and more retributive law.   DPW

Motive The intended, but not necessarily realised, consequence of a course of criminal action as assessed by the offender; i.e. what induces him to act in the first place. Specifying motive suffers from the same difficulties as isolating *cause* (q.v.), in that (a) there is always the danger of an assessor from a position of power inserting his judgment as to what the motive *must* have been (often based on a wrongful assumption that the act was complete, a 'success' and turned out as expected), even though the offender's assessment, had it been solicited, might not tally; (b) the theoretical range of motives is very great, and (c) multiple motives may be operating together. Lists of motives for crimes are conspicuous by their absence.

See also *Typology*.   DPW

Motor vehicles (offences relating thereto). See *Driving offences*; *'SUS' law*; *Taking conveyances*.

MUFTI (Minimum Use of Force Tactical Intervention) A form of riot control introduced into prisons in 1978. The aim of MUFTI is to ensure the maintenance of control in the establishment by staff, using the minimum amount of force necessary to do so. (Authority and limitation of use of force in prison is specified in Rule 44 (1) and (2) of the *Prison Rules* (1964).) Officers on MUFTI duty carry protective shields and light staves and wear protective clothing and a helmet.

DPW

Murder Unlawfully, and with malice aforethought, causing the death of a human in being, the death following within a year and a day. The definition is derived from the common law though the punishment is now fixed by the *Murder (Abolition of Death Penalty) Act* (1965). (Life imprisonment is mandatory. The court may also declare the period which it recommends to the Home Secretary as the minimum period which in its opinion should elapse before release on licence.)

What is crucial in the definition is the meaning of 'malice aforethought': the following is taken from the 14th Report of the Criminal Law Revision Committee (1980), *Offences against the Person*:

> it is murder if a person kills by doing an act – (i) intending to kill; or (ii) intending to cause serious bodily harm; or (iii) knowing that death is a [highly] probable result of the act; or (iv) knowing that serious bodily harm is a [highly] probable result of the act [provided that the act is 'aimed at' someone] (para. 17).

(The words in square brackets may not be necessary elements of the definition; they are the outcome of some uncertainty as to a recent House of Lords Decision (Hyam v. DDP (1975) AC 55.) The Committee's principal recommended definition is that it should be murder only: (a) if a person, with intent to kill, causes death, and (b) if a person causes death by an unlawful act intended to cause serious injury and known to him to involve a risk of causing death (para. 31). This form of words should, in their view, distinguish the crime more effectively from that of *manslaughter* (q.v.). See especially the regular chapter on Homicide in *Criminal Statistics*.

See also *Capital punishment*; *Diminished responsibility*; *Her Majesty's Pleasure*; *Life imprisonment*.   ARP

N

NACRO   The National Association for the Care and Resettlement of Offenders is a national charitable organisation founded in 1966 to replace the National Association of Discharged Prisoners' Aid Societies (created 1936). Its aim is to 'stimulate, co-ordinate and service' voluntary effort in relation to prison welfare work, the after-care of offenders and crime prevention. As such, it is a powerful pressure group for *penal reform* (q.v.).

DPW

Natural crime   R. Garofalo (1852–1934) introduced the term in 1885 in his *Criminology* (the first book to be so called). Natural crimes involve behaviours which run counter to the natural human sentiments; two criteria invariably being associated with such crime, the violation of feelings of pity (producing crimes of violence) and probity (producing crimes against property).

DPW

Naturalism   It comes as a surprise to some students embarking upon criminology that some researchers seek neither to explain crime nor to prevent its occurrence: their emphasis is upon description. But description is a literally superficial term for the work of certain writers, especially David Matza. Abstraction, classification and generalisation yield description and this through a distinctive cultural ethos. It is necessary to 'unwrap' these layers to get at, to understand, to *appreciate* the phenomena which make up 'crime'. 'The vision of naturalism strives to illuminate the world as it is' (Matza, 1969). It is a vision which others share and they are not without their following. But more sceptical readers of their work have asked, 'Where does it lead us?', and the more critical have revealed an unsound epistemology.

H. Becker (N.Y., 1963), 'Becoming a marihuana user', in

147

Outsiders, p. 41; D. Matza (Englewood Cliffs, N.J., 1969), *Becoming Deviant*; D. Beyleveld and P. Wiles (1975), 'Man and method in David Matza's "Becoming Deviant"', *BJC*, 15 (2), 111; G. Pearson (1975), *The Deviant Imagination*, esp. ch. 3.

ARP

Neurosis/otic. See *Mental abnormality*.

Neuroticism A dimension of personality linked, in the view of H.J. Eysenck, to the *extravert*-introvert dimension (q.v.) of his theory of crime and personality. When the tendency is towards both excessive extraversion and neuroticism, criminality will be the outcome. The extreme of neuroticism is characterised by emotionality and instability, being either melancholic moodiness, including depression and anxiety, or excitability and aggression. In later work he added the further dimension of *psychoticism* (q.v.), and suggested that a typology of crime might be constructed with reference to the three-dimensional theory. Empirical support, however, remains equivocal.

H. Eysenck (3rd ed., 1977), *Crime and Personality*; D. West (1982), *Delinquency: its Roots, Careers and Prospects*.

ARP

Neutralisation The name given to the process originally described by G.M. Sykes and D. Matza (1957), in 'Techniques of neutralisation: a theory of delinquency', *ASR*, 22, 664, and then in D. Matza, *Delinquency and Drift* (N.Y., 1964), by which an individual who *knows* that an act is morally wrong is still able to do it by unconsciously or consciously refusing to accept that the moral proscription applies to him at the time, while still accepting that it applies to others. DPW

O

Obscenity Conduct which is in itself obscene may well come within the ambit of particular criminal offences (e.g. *indecent exposure* (q.v.)), but the term 'obscenity' is generally reserved for portrayals of such conduct in publications and other representations. Various laws have sought to regulate this ever-contentious matter, ranging from out-and-out prohibition through systems of censorship to local by-laws, and the present position (but without reference to video-tapes) was fully reviewed by the Home Office Committee on Obscenity and Film Censorship (1979). In all such discussion freedom of expression, varying from that of hard pornography to work of artistic or scientific merit, has contended with the effects, psychological or social, it is thought to have. Of particular interest is the research of Kutchinsky (1978) indicating that the availability of pornography may have some beneficial social consequences in reducing the rates of some sexual offences. Here the criminal law currently regulates obscenity as follows:

(1) It is an offence (a) to publish an obscene article whether for gain or not; (b) to own, possess or control an obscene article for publication or for gain; (c) to present or direct an obscene performance of a play. In these contexts 'obscene' means tending to deprave and corrupt and 'publish' means to distribute, etc., or to show, play or project something (broadcasting and television are exempted; query video systems). It is a defence that it was in the public interest and expert testimony may be admitted to show this (*Obscene Publications Acts* (1959) and (1964), as amended by the *Criminal Law Act* (1977); *Theatres Act* (1968)).

(2) It is an offence to take, distribute or possess with a view to distribution any indecent photograph of a child under sixteen (*Protection of Children Act* (1978)).

(3) It is an offence to post any indecent or obscene matter;

meaning matter offending against the recognised standards of propriety, indecent being at the lower end of the scale and obscene at the upper end of the scale (*Post Office Act* (1953) as judicially interpreted).

(4) Customs officers may prevent the importation of indecent and obscene matter which then becomes liable to forfeiture (*Customs Consolidation Act* (1876)).

B. Kutchinsky (1978), *Law, Pornography and Crime*: *the Danish Experience*; Home Office, Committee on Obscenity and Film Censorship (1979), *Report* Cmnd 7772; G. Robertson (1979), *Obscenity*; G. Robertson (1980), 'The future of film censorship', *Brit. J. Law & Society*, 7 (1), 78; J. Smith and B. Hogan (1978), *Criminal Law*, p. 691.   ARP

Official statistics

Origin and development The first annual publication of criminal statistics was in 1827 in France. They were designed to 'assist in determining the circumstances which co-operate in increasing or diminishing the number of crimes' (quoted in Sellin and Wolfgang (1964), p. 8). Other European countries quickly followed suit, the first regular publication for England and Wales being in 1837 (with the present series of *Criminal Statistics, England & Wales*, starting in 1857).

What is presently available The two main publications are:

(i) *Criminal Statistics, England & Wales,* which give annual statistics on crime and court proceedings for the whole country and for Crown Courts (prior to 1 January 1972, the Assizes and Quarter Sessions) and Magistrates' Courts separately of the number proceeded against for each offence, by sex, age and result of proceedings. More detailed breakdowns appear in the *Supplementary Criminal Statistics* as well as tabulation of the numbers of offences known to the police by police district. For Scotland, the publication *Criminal Statistics, Scotland* also includes the police district data.

(ii) *Report on the Work of the Prison Department*: *Statistical Tables* (also annual) consists of tables relating to *receptions* into prison analysed by the nature of offence, length of sentence, previous offences and sentences, and by reason for committal; relating to the *numbers* in prisons and other institutions in terms of both the daily average population and the numbers serving sentence during the year; and relating to *recidivism* measured by reconvictions within a period of three years from discharge. The comparison volume for Scotland contains less detail.

Other official publications contain statistical material on specific offences (*Offences Relating to Motor Vehicles* and *Offences of Drunkenness*) and on the police and their activities (*Report of H.M. Chief Inspector of Constabulary* and *Report of the Commissioner of Police for the Metropolis*). More detailed accounts are available in Edwards (1974) and Walker (1971); the major official report is that of the Perks Committee (Home Office, 1967).

Current interpretations The view that criminal statistics are basically a valid reflection of a real state of crime held sway for over a century. But the successive attempts to refine the measuring instruments and especially the problem of assessing the 'dark figure' of unrecorded crime opened the door for questioning the social processes by which events – or non-events – become recorded as crimes (see Bottomley and Coleman, 1981). Most authors would now agree that a wide variety of factors enter into the process by which criminal statistics are generated: a typical list follows:

(a) the type of society and the legal definitions employed

(b) the way in which legal rules are applied and interpreted within a given social structure

(c) the procedures and routines of police practices which lead to the formation of stereotypes

(d) the way in which police resources and time are allocated

(e) the public interest in reporting incidents as offences

(f) the determinants of individual behaviour (Carr-Hill and Stern (1979), p. 259).

A.K. Bottomley and C. Coleman (1981), *Understanding Crime Rates*, ch. 1; R.A. Carr-Hill and N.H. Stern (1979), *Crime, the Police and Criminal Statistics*; B. Edwards (1974), *Sources of Social Statistics*, ch. 7; Home Office (1967), *Report of the Departmental Committee on Criminal Statistics* (Perks Committee), Cmnd 3448; T. Sellin and M.E. Wolfgang (N.Y., 1964), *The Measurement of Delinquency*; N.D. Walker (1971), *Crimes, Courts and Figures: an Introduction to Criminal Statistics*.

See also *Hidden crime*.   RAC-H

OPEN PRISON

Open prison There are about thirteen in England and Wales, and are so called because of the considerable freedom given to inmates in such establishments to move around without restriction. They emerged largely as a result of the work of Paterson (see *prison*), and the first to be built was New Hall in 1936. It is essential that the inmates held in open prisons who are able to 'escape' at any time, because the security is deliberately low-key, constitute no risk to the general public. Accordingly, only category 'D' men (see *prison classification*) are eligible to be sent there. See H. Jones and P. Cornes, assisted by R. Stockford (1971), *Open Prisons*.

See also *Escapes from custodial establishments*.   DPW

Opportunity The term has been used in two main ways. Both Merton (1957) and Cloward and Ohlin (1961) have written on access to socio-economic opportunities and to criminal opportunity systems, emphasising the lack of access of most of a community to legitimate systems of opportunity and the ease of access to criminal ones. Attention has recently turned to specific opportunities for the criminal which function as a stimulus to action. Mayhew *et al.* (1976) point out that opportunity as an inducement or trigger is modified by perceived risk, anticipated consequences and the actor's past experience of linked costs and rewards, and it is *both* the occasion for crime and the temptation. Mayhew classifies opportunities as (a) those that attach to people (the actors' varied opportunities; victims' differential generation of opportunity; opportunities emerging from patterns of daily activity) and (b) those relating to the objects involved in crime (abundance of goods; physical security issues; surveillance and supervision). Much crime undoubtedly is opportunist and to discourage it Mayhew argues that more attention should be given to opportunity reduction, via for example *target hardening* (q.v.) (cf. Clarke and Mayhew (1980)).

R.V.G. Clarke and P. Mayhew (1980), *Designing Out Crime*; R.A. Cloward and L.E. Ohlin (Chicago, 1961), *Delinquency and Opportunity*; P. Mayhew, R.V.G. Clarke, A. Sturman and J.M. Hough (1976), *Crime as Opportunity*, HORS no. 34; R.K. Merton (N.Y., 1957), *Social Theory and Social Structure*.

See also *Displacement*; *Prevention, environmental*.   DPW

Organised crime Groups of varying size may be established for the principal purpose of engaging in criminal activities for the benefit of their members, thus raising the question of whether those involved are 'professional' criminals (McIntosh (1975)). The extent to which such activities are organised has been graphically described in the context of the Mafia (Ianni (1972); Cressey (1972)). As size and complexity increase, an important feature which seems to emerge is the need for a system of internal security and the development of trustworthy contacts with the state, particularly with personnel concerned with law enforcement. Where such criminal organisations flourish, therefore, one would expect a degree of corruption among state officials in order to secure protection from investigation and prosecution, and institutions within the organisation to emerge to maintain discipline. In addition, studies have depicted the development of specialist skills and responsibilities on the part of members for various aspects of the organisation's activities.

Hobsbawm has shown how some groups using violence against persons or property may be perceived by the state as wholly criminal in purpose but by others, politically alienated from the state, as folk heroes or revolutionaries (Hobsbawm (1972); Hobsbawm and Rudé (1969)). The contrast which one seeks to draw then is between a group which, while operating illegally, is not in political conflict with the state, and a group which is; in the latter case one is then referring to 'social bandits' who are viewed by parts of the community as noble robbers, avengers or primitive resistance fighters.

A third type of organised criminality appears to be linked with *white-collar crime* (q.v.), which Sutherland (1949) argued was organised crime. Here, one is dealing with organisations which, while founded ostensibly for legitimate purposes, are used for crime. D.R. Cressey (1972), *Criminal Organisation*; E.J. Hobsbawm (1972), *Bandits*; E.J. Hobsbawm and G. Rudé (1969), *Captain Swing*; A.J. Ianni and E.R. Ianni (1972), *A Family Business*; M. McIntosh (1975), *The Organisation of Crime*; E.H. Sutherland (N.Y., 1949), *White Collar Crime*.

MB

Overcrowding.   See *Housing*.

P

Parental deprivation. See *Deprivation*.

Parole Short-term temporary leave from a custodial establishment on compassionate grounds (e.g. for funerals or weddings), although called parole, is to be distinguished from selective early release from prison followed by supervision. This latter was first suggested in the White Paper *The Adult Offender*, (Cmnd 2852, 1965), the object being to release men from prison at a 'peak in their training at which they may respond to generous treatment, but after which, if kept in prison, they may go downhill.' Parole was implemented by the *Criminal Justice Act* (1967), ss. 59–64, which allows for the release on licence of men who have served at least one-third of their sentence or twelve months, whichever is the longer. It applies only to prisoners with sentences of more than eighteen months and is seen as a privilege and a favour, rather than a right. If further crime is committed while on parole, the parolee is liable to recall. This Act established the legislative framework of local review committees (LRCs) which vet cases and refer them to the Home Office Parole Unit who in turn refer them to the Parole Board, with the Home Secretary having a final right of veto. The practical operation is that a man sentenced to six years' imprisonment is entitled to good conduct *remission* of one-third of his sentence (two years) and he is able to earn parole of up to one-third of his sentence. He could then be released after serving two years of his sentence. His next two years are spent on licence under supervision (by a probation officer) and his last two at liberty, no longer liable to recall.

K. Bottomley (1972), 'Reports of the Parole Board, 1968–70', *BJC*, 12, 89; P. Morris, F. Beverly and J. Vennard (1975), *On Licence: a Study of Parole*; C.P. Nuttall *et al.* (1977), *Parole in England and Wales*, HORS no. 38; D.J. West

154

(1972), *The Future of Parole*; *Reports of the Parole Board* (annual). DPW

Part-time crime   A relatively recent sociological concept. As an organisational generic, it refers to those thefts which persons can freely and even regularly indulge in while retaining both a personally-held and other-defined identity as an honest person. Part-time crimes include various (English slang and argot) roles as 'pilfering' and '*fiddling*' (q.v.), tax-'evasion', public transport fare-'dodging', social security benefit-'scrounging', shop-'lifting', etc. The key characteristic of such activities, in so far as they may be called part-time crimes, is that their practitioners refuse to define themselves as criminals.

The first known coining of the concept is in J. Ditton (1977), *Part-Time Crime: an Ethnography of Fiddling and Pilferage*, where it is explored and developed in particular in pp. 89–115 and 179–84. While the concept is nowhere there explicitly defined, it is nevertheless clear that it is a partially rhetorical, inverted and paired development of an earlier generic, that of full-time crime. The latter had been coined by J.A. Mack ((1964), 'Full-time miscreants, delinquent neighbourhoods and criminal networks', *BJS*, 12, 38) to refer to the identities of, through a discussion of the activities of, stereotypical burglars, bank-robbers and other types of thief of the sort usually believed to typify and exhaust theft itself.

Part-time crime was a concept originally applied to, yet not directly derived from, the felonious activities of English bread-salesmen who regularly steal small sums of money in transactions with both employer and customer. Obvious parallels exist in other similar service occupations, yet no other uses of the term are known.

Part-time crime, however, was rapidly superseded by the rather better structural concept 'the hidden economy' (see S. Henry (1978), *The Hidden Economy*). In turn, and more recently, the originally Italian term 'the black economy' has attracted wider attention (see A. Heertje *et al*. (1982), *The Black Economy*) as a popular generic, and has subsequently expanded its originally restricted semantic application from tax-evasion to cover all those activities originally, but briefly, known as part-time crimes. JD

Partly suspended sentence   Similar in concept to the *suspended sentence* (q.v.), but there is an important practical difference

155

because the offender first serves a portion of his prison sentence; thereafter the remainder of the term is 'held in suspense' in the usual manner. This measure was introduced into English law by the *Criminal Law Act* (1977), s. 47, but remained dormant until 1982, when the Conservative government first implemented the 1977 section, then widened its scope in the *Criminal Justice Act* (1982). Several other countries (but not Scotland) have similar provisions. See further: Advisory Council on the Penal System (1978), *Sentences of Imprisonment*, ch. 13.   AEB

Paternal deprivation.   See *Deprivation*.

Pathology/Pathological   An early organicist concept referring to the diseased or malformed parts of society (crime, mental illness, slums, divorce, etc.), implying the need for excision or suppression, and a search for psychological causes in the mind of the criminal. Durkheim (1858–1917) alone was able to see crime as normal, and appreciate that yesterday's 'pathology' is today's 'normality'. ('How many times, indeed, it [crime] is only an anticipation of future morality – a step toward what will be' (*The Rules of Sociological Method* (1950, p. 71)). The term is now obsolete, the last serious use being by E.M. Lemert, in *Social Pathology* (N.Y., 1951).

See also *Social disorganisation*; *Social problems*.   DPW

Penal colony.   See *Transportation*.

Penal reform   Attempts made sometimes officially and frequently by voluntary agencies (e.g. The Howard League (see *penology* and *NACRO* (qq.v.)) to change or improve the theory or practice of punishment. Beginning with Howard (see *prison*) and Romilly (1757–1818), pressure for improvement continues to be exerted from both within and without the system. A most dramatic and historic step was the movement for the abolition of *capital punishment* (q.v.).

G. Rose (1961), *The Struggle for Penal Reform*; L. Blom-Cooper, ed. (1974), *Progress in Penal Reform*.

See also *Prisoners' unions*.   DPW

Penal servitude   It became clear by the late 1840s that transportation was becoming difficult to continue. In addition, evangelical and utilitarian prison theorists had promoted a belief, which had its roots deep in economic and social changes since 1770, that the Howardian and post-Howardian total institutional prison might reclaim the mind of a criminal or at least recast his conduct by behavioural strategies. It happened that, as an alternative to transportation of offenders, the state created a sentence of imprisonment at home which would hold those previously sent abroad. This new sentence was called penal servitude, and was constructed in two Acts of Parliament passed in 1853 and 1857. It was mainly carried out in the new convict prisons and at first was inflicted upon those who had been sentenced to transportation by now faced with very great difficulties. Later it was ordered by courts as a sentence in its own right, and it was finally abolished in 1948.

The essential feature of penal servitude in the nineteenth century was that it involved graduation from severe stages of incarceration to less severe, and ultimately to conditional liberty (a characteristic that it shared with transportation). Another feature of it was that it was a substantial sentence (for example not less than five years by an 1864 Act). Its intention was to deprive the offender of the opportunity to commit crimes for a moderately long time, but it also had other aims. First, penal servitude was strongly retributory in that its régime was severe and irksome (for example its dependence on hard labour and insistence that the first nine months be spent in separate confinement). Second, it was intended to alter future conduct by promoting a permanent mental attitude in the offender that by obedient and industrious behaviour the conditions of his life would improve. Finally, it was deterrent and demonstrative, illustrating unambiguously the inevitable power of the state over the individual offender and others who contemplated like actions.

Thus by the late nineteenth century the internee would serve his first nine months out of sight and hearing of other convicts, and his next period in classified associated hard labour on public works and in total silence, with marks being awarded for good conduct. These marks would obtain privileges for the prisoner (such as a mattress, less arduous labour, early release). Finally, therefore, he might win release under police supervision and must comply with the conditions of a licence requiring non-association with known criminals, notification of address and an honest industrious life – his so-called 'ticket of leave'. By the same token, those who did not conform to the requirements of the régime of each stage would fail to advance and would lose

157

the opportunity of early release. In the twentieth century certain administrative aspects of this system changed, but the basic principles remained the same.   WJF

Penology The term, which derives from the Greek for punishment, was first used in the nineteenth century to refer to the 'science of punishment'. Later usage is usually with reference to one of the main areas of criminology, the use of sanctions against offenders.

Penology has three central and inter-connected strands: the construction of penal codes, the sentencing of offenders and the administration of penal sanctions.

New penal codes were developed by several European countries throughout the nineteenth century following widespread criticism of criminal law arrangements as being capricious and cruel. Beccaria's (1764) *On Crimes and Punishments* (Eng. trans. 1768) had a particularly significant impact, with the emphasis of the new codes on deterrence as the primary purpose of penal sanctions but with the severity of the offence determining the degree of the penalty imposed. Excessive punishment was eschewed and the new codes sought to place a ceiling on the state's powers. In England, while Beccaria's influence was important, there was powerful and sustained resistance to codification, and reform of criminal law proceeded in an *ad hoc* rather than a comprehensive fashion.

Sentencing principles began to emerge towards the end of the nineteenth century. The impetus, in part, arose from public disquiet as to disparities in the length of prison sentences following the repeal of most capital offences and the elimination of transportation. The higher judiciary developed their own sentencing tariff in 1901, but more important was the setting up of the Court of Criminal Appeal in 1907. Parliament greatly added to the range of sanctions throughout the twentieth century. In particular Probation Orders were introduced in 1907, the availability of fines was extended by the *Criminal Justice Act* (1948), the suspended sentence was introduced in 1967 and the Community Service Order in 1972. Although there has been some legislative effort to structure sentencing discretion (e.g. *Criminal Justice Act* (1948) that imprisonment in certain cases be imposed only if no other method is appropriate), sentencers have retained considerable discretion and have resisted suggestion that this be curbed. In the early 1980s sentencers complained that the 'penal credibility gap' had widened, referring to the difference between the length of imposed and served custodial sentence as a consequence of remission, parole and other decisions of executive government. The training of sentencers has remained at a rudimentary stage, in part because of jealously guarded judicial independence.

Penology is often used with reference to the third strand, the administration of punishment. Attention has mainly been directed to imprisonment, for both remanded and sentenced prisoners, and in particular to conditions within prisons. Howard's *The State of Prisons in England and Wales* . . . (1777) was a monumental and pioneering catalogue of prison conditions in England and some European countries. Howard was one of the first commentators to draw attention to the slow, uneven and sometimes regressive nature of penal practice. Penology encompasses both practice and efforts at reform. The term is less commonly used in the USA, where 'criminal justice', covering a rather broader set of issues, is more evident. From the mid-nineteenth century various penal reform groups, such as the Howard Association founded in England in 1866 (becoming in 1921 the Howard League for Penal Reform), were established. On the continent of Europe penology has a more powerful tradition (see e.g., M. Ancel (1974), 'The relationship between criminology and "politique criminelle"', in R. Hood, ed., *Crime, Criminology and Public Policy*), stressing a multi-disciplinary approach to both crime prevention and dealing with offenders.

The difficulties in formulating basic principles were illustrated in the winding up of the Royal Commission on the Penal System in 1966, two years after it had been set up and before it had produced a report. The sense of optimism displayed in the White Paper, *Penal Practice in a Changing Society* (1959), was not sustained and by the mid-1970s a more cautious mood existed, exemplified by, e.g., Home Office (1977), *A Review of the Criminal Justice Policy, 1976* and S.R. Brody (1977), *The Effectiveness of Sentencing*.

International collaboration on penal issues dates from the International Prison Congress (1872), and every five years there is a United Nations Congress on the Prevention of Crime and the Treatment of Offenders. From these activities have emerged minimum standards; e.g. the United Nations Standard Minimum Rules for the Treatment of Prisoners and the Council of Europe's European Standard Minimum Rules (1973).

PERJURY

See generally, M. Grünhut (1948), *Penal Reform*; S. McConville (1981), *A History of English Prison Administration*, vol. 1; A.K. Bottomley (1973), *Decisions in the Penal Process*.

AR

Perjury In proceedings where evidence is given on oath (including 'affirmations' or 'declarations' in lieu of oaths) it is an offence wilfully to make a false statement knowing it to be false or not believing it to be true (*Perjury Act* (1911)). In a variety of other official contexts – some involving oaths, others not – it is also an offence, though not actually 'perjury', to make false statements, e.g. on registration of births and deaths. Law Commission (1979), *Offences Relating to Interference with the Course of Justice*, Report no. 96.

ARP

Physical abnormality The link between physical abnormality and crime is complex and has been neglected in recent years. (Since early naïve attempts to relate physique and crime have been discredited (see *constitutional theories*), there has been a reluctance to attempt further generalisations.) The link could operate in at least four main ways as follows (but in none of these would the affected group be anything other than a minute proportion of convicted criminals):

(1) Certain disorders, particularly in the early stages of onset before treatment is sought, may result in a clouding of consciousness, such that crime commission becomes more likely in direct proportion to the number and complexity of applicable social rules, e.g. diabetes mellitus in a state of hyperglycaemia, cerebral arteriosclerosis, Huntington's Chorea. For the special case of epilepsy, see Gunn (1977).

(2) Some *mental impairment* (q.v.) may involve physical difference. Any associated crime is of course best appraised in terms of the impairment.

(3) Where physical handicap or disfigurement is present and severe, social rejection by others on this account (see *stigmatisation*) may lead to such bitterness and *frustration* (q.v.) that crime may occur. Ogden (1959) was able to demonstrate that removal of disfigurements from a Borstal sample reduced recidivism and resulted in improved social integration.

(4) Chromosome abnormalities (see *XYY chromosomes*).

In general there seem few grounds for connecting physical abnormality of any sort with crime.

J. Gunn (1977), *Epileptics in Prison*; D.A. Ogden (1959),

'Use of surgical rehabilitation in young delinquents', *Brit. Med. J.*, 2, 432.

See also *Tattooing*.   DPW

Physical disfigurement.   See *Physical Abnormality*.

Pickpocketing/Pocketpicking   Pickpockets steal items from a victim's person in full view. They favour crowded places and although they may operate alone usually do so in a group. The 'cannon' bumps into the victim to distract him, the 'picker' then steals the item and (so that he is 'innocent' if searched) passes it immediately to the 'runner', who runs away keeping the item, but throwing any bags or wallets used to contain it into the nearest bin. Common throughout the nineteenth century, this form of craft-crime still continues episodically. See D.W. Maurer (New Haven, 1955, reptd 1964), *The Whiz Mob*.

DPW

Plea bargaining   An imprecise term which refers to agreements that are struck in the criminal courts under which a defendant who agrees to plead guilty will receive a more lenient sentence than he would receive were he to be convicted after contesting the case. Such bargains take different forms and assume varying degrees of formality. They may involve, for instance, offers of a reduction in the number or level of charges or simply direct promises of a particular sentence. Several writers distinguish between 'explicit' and 'implicit' plea bargaining, the former encompassing out-of-court negotiations before trial between prosecution and defence lawyers (and maybe even trial judges), the latter referring to the substantial reduction in sentence offered virtually as a matter of course to those who plead guilty.

In England, plea bargaining is a highly controversial subject. It is regulated by the rules laid down in 1970 in the key case of *Turner*, which did not actually prohibit pre-trial discussions with trial judges, but restricted the judge's freedom to comment on the sentence he was minded to impose. It was claimed that, as a result of these rules, plea bargaining had all but been eliminated in England. Little empirical research has been conducted on the subject in England (unlike the USA), though the studies undertaken by McCabe and Purves (1972) and by Baldwin and McConville (1977, 1979) demonstrate that back-stairs discussions between judges and barristers still take place

161

PLEAD, FITNESS TO

in the Crown Court with some frequency. Other research conducted by Dell (1971), Bottoms and McClean (1976) and Seifman (1980) suggests that plea negotiation also occurs in the Magistrates' Courts. This evidence shows that the arrangements in the lower courts are less structured and more informal than at the Crown Court, that the magistrates themselves are not involved in pre-trial discussions, and that solicitors and police officers assume a dominant role.

It is curious that, though the Court of Appeal has outlawed explicit forms of judicial plea bargaining (save in wholly exceptional circumstances), several judges and senior members of the Bar continue to assert that it forms a useful part of English criminal justice. Some judges have publicly acknowledged that it is still widely practised. The existence of plea bargaining in the USA (and in other jurisdictions) has never been denied. Indeed it is conceded that, without it, the criminal courts would rapidly become submerged by the sheer volume of contested trials. In England, the practice of plea bargaining remains covert, and it awaits proper supervision and regulation.

J. Baldwin and M. McConville (1977), *Negotiated Justice*; J. Baldwin and M. McConville (1979), 'Plea bargaining and the Court of Appeal', *Brit. J. Law & Society*, 6, 200; A.E. Bottoms and J.D. McClean (1976), *Defendants in the Criminal Process*; S. Dell (1971), *Silent in Court*; S. McCabe and R. Purves (1972), *By-passing the Jury*; R.D. Seifman (Lexington, Mass., 1980), 'Plea bargaining in England', in W.F. McDonald and J.A. Cramer, eds, *Plea-Bargaining*; *Turner* (1970), 54 Cr. App. R. 352.   JB

Plead, fitness to.   See *Hospital Order*.

Poisoning   Administering poisons so as to endanger life or with intent to injure are all offences under the *Offences Against the Person Act* (1861) ss. 23, 24. The sale of poisons is governed by the *Poisons Act* (1972) and by the *Misuse of Drugs Act* (1971). There are no unknown poisons and the technology of identification is very advanced. Police specialists involved in dealing with the very few cases of (detected) poisoning which occur are the pathologist and the chemist. C. Polson and R.M. Tattersall (1969), *Clinical Toxicology*, is a useful work and there is an excellent collectanea of poisons in F.E. Camps and J.M. Cameron (1971), *Practical Forensic Medicine*.

See also *Drug abuse*; *Drug trafficking*.   DPW

Police, the   In its original meaning the term 'police' stands for the good government of a community through civil administration, enforcement of laws and regulations and the maintenance of the health, cleanliness and the public order generally. In the eighteenth and nineteenth centuries the concept and usage of the term began to take on a narrower form. More and more it is found being used to describe the civil force to which is entrusted the task of maintaining public order and enforcement of law for the prevention and punishment of its breaches and detecting crime.

P

The English model   Those police systems based on the English or common law traditions do not have dual military/ civil organisations. Such common law systems can trace their origins back to the idea of communal responsibility for maintaining order and suppressing crime. The duty placed on the groups of families by the king carried with it collective fines for failure to uphold the law and maintain order. In the English kingdom of Wessex, King Alfred (871–99) developed the idea of social responsibility for maintaining the King's Peace and this tradition, considerably strengthened by the Norman administration, influenced the local system of policing which marks its difference from other European systems. As recently as 1962 The Royal Commission on the Police (England & Wales) stressed the social and constitutional importance of the local character of the English model. Although the system was originally based on the ancient office of constable (*comes stabuli* of Roman origins) the *Metropolitan* (*London*) *Police Act* (1829), introduced by Sir Robert Peel, established the modern use of professional police.

Styles of policing   An examination of the nature of policing will reveal considerable variations in styles.

Informal policing   Among the most successful checks on crime in a society are those stemming from traditional and informal social controls. Superstition, taboos, religions, customs, shared values and moral standards in one way or another have preceded the laws upon which the more formal policing arrangements of an advanced society are developed. Where a society retains the cohesion and stability of family units it is likely that the behaviour of the members of that unit will be controlled and that each and every other family unit will be likewise adding up to a cohesive and stable society.

163

POLICE, THE

Passive policing Passive policing is characterised by police whose main purpose is to provide a presence, a 'scarecrow', and to achieve their aim of maintaining order through informal means. Passive police are reluctant to activate the law save in serious crimes or in blatant cases of public disorder where there is little alternative.

There are some advantages for a community in the passive style of policing since it permits a good deal of self-regulation, avoids petty scandal and generally makes for a live-and-let-live atmosphere in which recourse to remedies through the criminal courts is kept to a minimum. On the other hand, one has to look below the surface of passive policing. It may be that the passivity is an indication of incompetence or even of corruption.

Punitive policing Punitive policing has been described as 'policing by suspended terror'. It works on the assumption that, provided the penalties for crimes are sufficiently horrible, people will be deterred from committing them. It presupposes (a) that sufficient people will be caught to render it plausible and (b) that sufficient potential offenders will anticipate that they too might be caught. Both these presuppositions are considerably undermined in practice. Certainly without an effective police to back up the draconian code its effect is likely to be considerably reduced.

As a society becomes more gentle in its attitudes and manners, which usually coincides with higher knowledge and civilisation, it is less likely to permit inhuman penalties. Under totalitarian or despotic régimes the law may have better chances of being enforced severely and implacably by virtue of the monopoly of power to convict, sentence and punish. It can also survive in religious form as in some Islamic countries.

Preventive policing Of all the strategies of policing, it is the preventive one which is superior. It is superior in the ethical sense since by preventing crime it saves people from their follies and the moral obloquy which confrontation with the criminal justice system brings. It marks the concern of society in reducing criminality which victimises both the perpetrator and the person who is the object of the crime. In this way a dual purpose is served. Prevention is not only ethically superior as a strategy but its utility is greater since it reduces the cost as well as the suffering of crime. The diminution of crime eases pressure on all facets of the system of criminal justice and should be a primary police aim. There are three identifiable levels of preventive policing which represent the antithesis to reactive policing.

Pro-active policing describes any lawful form of human activity which accrues to a diminution of conduct forbidden by the criminal law. It embraces activities to influence the community in a multitude of ways in order to attract behaviour away from illegality and towards legality. Unlike its counterpart, reactive policing, its style envisages a more persuasive effect for it involves carrying anticipatory initiatives into practice to head off criminality.

Pro-active policing seeks to strengthen that greatest of all prevention – social discipline and mutual trust in communities. Its methods will therefore vary according to community mores and culture.

Pro-active policing envisages a high degree of co-operation with other agencies of government, both local and central. It needs to be passed down from the strategic policy level to the tactical ground working level and into action. It requires an approach to social problems adumbrating crime, disorder or social agitation of one kind or another together with social services, health, welfare, probation, employment, social security, housing, planning and other statutory and voluntary services. Removing or foiling criminogenic social conditions is its purpose.

Having a broad and long-term strategic characteristic, it has a substantial and meaningful commitment in the field of education at all its levels and must therefore commend itself to education authorities, teaching staff, parents and pupils. In the educational setting it offers for the police an important non-conflict contact point in which a meaningful human relationship can be achieved on issues affecting youth and the police.

Pro-active policing should lead to the lowering of barriers between various agencies from which increased trust and better combined operation can flow to stem criminality and its trail of suffering for victim and sometimes offender and offenders' families and friends. As the future will demand that resources are to be used to the maximum advantage, the existence of rigid professional demarcations between different agencies is inimical to the public good. This is particularly so when it is seen that a number of agencies are all working towards the same ultimate goal, namely the welfare of society.

The police seek to strengthen trust in communities or where

it is lacking to create it, and from this position they, together with other agencies, stimulate the community itself towards self-policing.

Secondary prevention is a term which might be used to cover those activities which are normally associated with the narrower and better understood police function. Preventive policing by the presence of foot and mobile patrols is that part of policing which is heavily dependent on manpower, communications and mobility for its success. Foot patrols have a greater deterrent potential when skilfully deployed, though the response capability is naturally much less than mobile patrols. The latter, however, have less deterrent effect and do not impress themselves on the public. The ideal is clearly a combination of the two in a form of two-tier preventive policing.

Tertiary prevention might be used to describe the detective aspects of the police function, coupled with the correctional work of many other agencies. The belief that detection and conviction are the best deterrents is true at least in this context, but unless detection has a high degree of certainty its deterrent effect is rendered less; if the certainty of conviction is not high, further erosion of the principle takes place. Tertiary prevention also includes a meaningful penal policy.

Reactive policing Police have to be capable of reacting to emergencies which rate high priority in public estimation. They not only have to possess the necessary mobility and communication to do this but they have to be deployed in such a way that other matters such as bad geographical distribution will not impede their adequate response. The time taken from receipt of a call to arrival at the scene, known as 'response time', is regarded as a key measurement of police efficiency. Any police system which cannot keep pace with public demands for quick response in emergencies is in danger of losing its reputation.

The impact of science and technology on police has been very considerable. Just as the same issue has raised questions for medical ethics, for broadcasting and, above all, for war, it has had a profound effect on police methods, the public image and reputation, to say nothing of police psychology. The police have been helped considerably, even crucially, by technology, though in some ways they have been seduced by its brilliance. Stemming from the universal introduction of personal pocket radios some twelve years ago, together with the availability of cheap motor-vehicles and, later on, expensive computerised command and control systems, what was basically a preventive foot patrolling force can become a basically reactive mobile patrolling force. The police have been considerable losers as well as gainers from these changes. The loss of non-conflict contact with the public has severely curtailed police understanding of their public. Policing under these conditions becomes a matter of mobility (motor-vehicles), communications (radio), and information (computers). The gulf that can arise from these conditions can open up as police drift further into their own reactive style. A gulf which can lead to misunderstanding, suspicions, even to hostility. But however much one may deplore the loss, the gain is considerable, for the police could not now deliver the services they do and cope with the workloads they carry.

This seductive power of technology has resulted in a false assumption that it, together with the legal powers, provides the essence of policing. This is a profound mistake. A superior democratic police knows that the essence of policing lies in human care, understanding and education, resulting in a deep attachment of police to public and *vice versa*. Getting this wrong can have lasting deleterious effects on policing.

In their necessary authoritarian role as controllers of public order it is likely that the police will have greater confidence and feel less threatened by hostile publics, and the publics on their part will view the police in their total role with greater understanding and sympathy if they, the police, have opportunities on a day-to-day basis to be guide, philosopher and friend. This is of crucial importance where policing of nervous minorities renders purely reactive policing as quite dangerous.

Repressive police   Rulers or governments lacking in popular support may rely on repressive police to maintain them in power. In such circumstances the police, inevitably supported by the military, have to be endowed with considerable emergency powers of search, arrest and detention. To maintain their reputation they will have to act firmly when required to do so. It is a style of policing which generally, though not exclusively, tends to alienation of police from the community and this can be further compounded by living in barracks apart from the community. Such police are almost invariably likely to be armed and of a quasi-military nature since disciplinary control, fire-power, and military training are necessary for success.

J. Alderson (1979), *Policing Freedom*; B. Chapman (1971), *Police State*; T.A. Critchley (1978), *A History of Police in*

POLICE SCIENCE

England and Wales; *Report of the Royal Commission on the Police, 1960–2*, (Cmnd 1728, 1962); P.J. Stead (N.Y., 1977), *Pioneers in Policing*.
See also *Community policing*.   JCA

Police science   Police scientists may be called upon to assess, analyse and compare materials and objects connected, or thought to be connected, with crimes committed. The main types of specialist available (together with their principal concerns) are: bacteriologists (disease cultures); ballistics experts (ammunition and firearms); biologists (hair, fibres, dust, plant life, pollens, organic stains, paper, etc.); chemists and toxicologists (inorganic stains, poisons, drugs, explosives, paints, metals, oils, etc.; see also *poisoning*); fingerprint experts; handwriting experts (hand- and type-writing, inks, writing instruments); physicists (tool marks, tracks and impressions, glass, etc.); pathologists (the cause and manner of death or injury; see also *forensic medicine*). Local experts in other topics are, in addition, at times asked for advice.   DPW

Political crime/terrorism   The concept of *political crime* can be applied to both states and individuals. It is *par excellence* a feature of one-party states and other dictatorships. For example, in the Soviet régime thousands have been killed or have suffered long incarceration for holding beliefs or opinions considered dangerous or undesirable by the authorities. In many cases, as in Stalin's purges, people were victimised merely on the suspicion of holding ideas unacceptable to the dictator. A hallmark of modern tyrannies is that the judicial process becomes an obedient instrument of political persecution, or is dispensed with completely in the course of general repression. For example, in Argentina and other Latin American military dictatorships, thousands have been 'disappeared' (i.e. secretly rounded up and murdered) by the secret police, army and paramilitary groups.

In liberal democracies the notion of political crime has much narrower relevance, for in a rule of law system there are no political prisoners because no person can be convicted and punished merely on grounds of his or her political beliefs or opinions. The only persons liable for punishment in rule of law societies are those who have been convicted after due process of law for an offence under the criminal code. Political crime in the sense explained above should not be confused with the relatively rare group of offences against the state (such as *treason* (q.v.) or endangering national security) even though the latter are obviously political in implications and frequently (though not invariably) in motive.

The notion of *political offence exception* is a controversial one in international law. Many Western legal systems (e.g. USA, France, Sweden) make provision for persons who successfully establish political motivation for allegedly committed serious offences in a foreign country to be exempt from any extradition requirement. However, a growing trend in Western legal systems recently has been towards a more restrictive use of the political offence exception. For example, in the recent US extradition case of Abu Eain, decided February 1981, the court found that the exception was not intended to prevent extradition of a person suspected of random indiscriminate bombing of the civilian population. And a recent international agreement, the Council of Europe Convention on the Suppression of Terrorism, seeks to remove certain serious crimes of violence, including assassination, hijacking and bombing, from the protection of the political offence exception. The Convention seeks to count them as common crimes and places the *aut dedere aut punire* obligation on Contracting Parties in such cases.

Terrorism is a mode of violence involving the systematic use or threatened use of murder, injury and destruction to intimidate or shock a target group wider than the immediate victims, or to create a climate of terror. Some régimes use mass terror as a routine method of control. Not surprisingly such régimes often label any political opponent or dissident a 'terrorist'. Another misuse of the term is a pejorative for guerrilla war in general. Many guerrilla and partisan leaders have rejected terrorism because it inevitably involves taking innocent life. The terrorism which has increased so rapidly in Western cities in the years since 1970 typically takes place without any accompaniment of guerrilla war or general insurrection. Terrorism is characteristically a weapon of the weak pretending to be strong. Among the extremist groups who have used terrorism against democracies in recent years are nationalists, neo-Marxist revolutionaries, fascists and religious fanatics. Modern terrorism has also become increasingly internationalised, frequently involving attacks on foreign targets across international frontiers, often with the support of pro-terrorist régimes and foreign movements. Terrorists believe that their

169

end justifies the means, and so they are willing to violate human rights to achieve certain tactical objectives which terrorism appears to be able to bring, such as publicity, ransom, the release of imprisoned terrorists, and the intimidation of communities. PW

Pornography The term given to a drawn, written, printed or multiply-reproducible medium (book, picture, film, video, etc.) by which *obscenity* (q.v.) may be expressed. DPW

Positivism The use of the scientific method to study and explain crime and criminal behaviour. Attempts began with anthropometric measurement (see *criminal type*) and somato-typing, continuing with mental testing and cartographic studies, and are most easily identified by schemes of classification, hypothesis testing and the search for the *causes* (q.v.) of crime. Positivism has been widely criticised, notably by I. Taylor, P. Walton and J. Young in *The New Criminology* (1973), chs. 1 and 2, who argue that positivistic points of departure (terms such as 'criminal' and those used for different types of crime and punishment and their associated statistics) are *not* scientific facts, nor are they proper material for scientific study but are value-laden codes (relative and not absolute) covering phe-nomena which change as society (and in turn law) changes. Hence, although through the use of the scientific method 'answers' can be obtained, these are of spurious validity inasmuch as they do not take into account numerous factors which crucially affect crime (see *social class*). A pro-positivist account is N. Walker, *Behaviour and Misbehaviour: Explanations and Non-explanations* (1977). DPW

Poverty The obvious assumption is that poverty leads to crime (and *strain theory* (q.v.) would support this), but much depends on the circumstances of its occurrence (rapidity of onset). Lack of clarity of definition is a major stumbling block; the difference between being poor and a self-perception of being poor. Certainly the poor may be more vulnerable to detection and capture than wealthier people (arrest figures show a higher proportion of the poor and unemployed than in the general population, but self-report studies disclose little difference in the offending behaviour of the poor and the not-poor). It would be prudent to assume a low causal role for poverty specifically, since although many criminals may see themselves as 'in need' there is no evidence that the majority of the poor regularly engage in crime.

See also *Unemployment*.   DPW

Prediction A criminological prediction study might be defined as a study in which one or more criterion measures of delinquent or criminal behaviour are related to one or more measures of other factors (predictors) operating at an earlier time. The most commonly used criterion variable is re-conviction within a specified time period, although some studies attempt to predict convictions within groups of unconvicted people. In most studies, a sub-set of the predictor variables is selected and combined in some way to produce a composite measure. This often takes the form of a prediction table (also called an experience table or a base expectancy table) which divides the sample into categories with different probabilities of re-conviction.

In the USA, one of the earliest and most influential studies was carried out in the 1920s by E.W. Burgess. Like much later prediction research, it was designed to predict success or failure on parole. A prediction table was derived very simply, by giving each factor a weighting of 1 or 0. Another American study which became famous (or infamous) was *Unravelling Juvenile Delinquency* by S. and E.T. Glueck (N.Y., 1950). This appeared to show that juvenile delinquency could be predicted very accurately from an early age. However, this conclusion was unjustified, partly because this research was retrospective rather than prospective, partly because extreme groups of institutionalised delinquents and well-behaved non-delinquents were used, and partly because the Gluecks did not have separate construction and validation samples. It is desirable to construct a prediction technique with one sample and investigate its accuracy with another, to avoid capitalising on chance.

The most influential prediction research in England was by H. Mannheim and L.T. Wilkins, *Prediction Methods in Relation to Borstal Training* (1955). This attempted to predict re-convictions of borstal boys. The research of F.H. Simon, *Prediction Methods in Criminology* (1971), is also important in showing that, with criminological data, different statistical methods of selecting and combining predictor variables work about equally well.

The most extensive use of prediction techniques in this country was by the Home Office in connection with parole (see

PREVALENCE

C.P. Nuttall *et al.* (1977), *Parole in England and Wales*, HORS no. 38). The probability of re-conviction of released prisoners was calculated on the basis of the offender's previous criminal history (e.g. the kind of offence he had committed, his number of previous convictions, his age at first conviction) and also his age, marital status, living arrangements and employment history. Re-conviction probabilities were linearly related to prediction scores in construction and validation samples. The prediction scores were used by the Parole Board in deciding whether to grant parole to prisoners. The scores also determined whether a prisoner was considered by the Parole Board after being rejected for parole by the Local Review Committee. Prediction scores were also used in evaluating the effectiveness of parole, by comparing actual and expected re-conviction rates.   DPF

Prevalence The prevalence of arrests or convictions refers to the proportion of a cohort who are arrested or convicted up to a certain age. In contrast, the incidence of arrests or convictions refers to the proportion arrested or convicted during a specified time period, such as one year. Basically, prevalence is cumulative incidence. These terms are most commonly used in this technical sense in epidemiology, for example in discussing the incidence and prevalence of disease.

The annual Home Office *Criminal Statistics* typically provide no information about incidence or prevalence. They show the number of persons convicted each year per 100,000 in each age group, but this is not the number of different persons. For example, Table 5.19 of the 1980 *Criminal Statistics* shows that the peak age for convictions for indictable offences was eighteen for males, with about 7.4 convictions per 100 persons at that age, and seventeen for females, with about 1.0 convictions per 100. Thirty years ago, these figures were much smaller, and criminologists concluded from them that crime was restricted to a tiny deviant minority of the population. There was a tendency to draw conclusions about prevalence from figures which did not even reflect incidence.

The first prevalence estimates in England and Wales were calculated by A. Little (1965), *ASR*, 30, 260, based on arrests for indictable offences in London. These estimates can be obtained either longitudinally or cross-sectionally. Little's longitudinal estimate was obtained by adding first arrests of eight-year-olds in 1950, nine-year-olds in 1951, and so on up to first arrests of twenty-year-olds in 1962. He estimated that 20 per cent of males and 2.5 per cent of females born in 1942 were arrested up to their twenty-first birthdays. His cross-sectional estimate was obtained by adding first arrests of eight-year-olds in 1962, nine-year-olds in 1962, and so on up to twenty-year-olds in 1962. This produced an estimate that 23 per cent of males and 2.6 per cent of females were arrested up to their twenty-first birthdays.

Similar estimates are provided by longitudinal surveys. M. Wadsworth, *Roots of Delinquency* (1979), calculated that 18 per cent of males and 2.5 per cent of females born in 1946 were convicted or officially cautioned by their twenty-first birthdays. In a London sample of boys born about 1953, D.J. West and D.P. Farrington, in *The Delinquent Way of Life* (1977), found that 31 per cent were convicted of offences normally recorded in the Criminal Record Office by their twenty-first birthdays. In the most famous American longitudinal survey, M.E. Wolfgang, R.M. Figlio and T. Sellin (Chicago, 1972), *Delinquency in a Birth Cohort*, reported that 35 per cent of a cohort of Philadelphia males born in 1945 were arrested by age eighteen.

F.H. McClintock and N.H. Avison (1968) published in *Crime in England and Wales* national prevalence estimates for England and Wales obtained by cross-sectional means in 1965. These showed that 31 per cent of males and 8 per cent of females would be convicted for standard list offences at some time during their lives. D.P. Farrington (1981), *BJC*, 21, 173, was able to repeat this calculation later, and estimated that (at 1977 rates of conviction for non-motoring standard list offences) 44 per cent of males and 15 per cent of females in England and Wales would be convicted at some time during their lives. He forecast that, if present trends continue, the time is near when the majority of males will be convicted at some time during their lives.   DPF

Prevention, environmental A school of thought emerging from the realisation that it is easier to prevent crime through a literal rearrangement or restructuring of the physical arenas in which it takes place, so as to block it, displace it or make its occurrence unnecessary or impossible, than it is to regulate the behaviour of would-be individual perpetrators at source. Its application is of course limited, since special (and alterable) environmental features are not necessary to promote or facilitate the commission of many types of offences. Newman

(1973) drew attention to the way in which architectural design can affect crime rates, arguing that the absence of 'defensible space' in architecture may encourage delinquency and vandalism. Areas of territory which both promote a sense of ownership and are readily surveillable by their inhabitants should attract much lower rates. The other thrust apart from the architectural has been in relation to *target hardening* (q.v.) predicated upon the assumption that criminals would prefer soft targets with fewer locks, bars and alarms.

R.V.G. Clarke and P. Mayhew (1980), *Designing out Crime*; O. Newman (1973), *Defensible Space: Crime Prevention through Urban Design*.

See also *Area studies*; *Displacement*.   DPW

Preventive detention   As a special form of imprisonment, it was introduced by the *Prevention of Crime Act* (1908), modified by the *Criminal Justice Act* (1948), and repealed by the *Criminal Justice Act* (1967) s. 37 (1). It was intended to apply to mature, 'hardened' recidivists guilty of serious offences and its aim was to protect society from the activities of these people by segregating them in prison for long periods of time. The sentence of PD was awarded in addition to the sentence for the specific offence in question (the so-called 'double-track' system). It could be used where it was felt to be expedient for the protection of the public that a man should be held for a long period of time, if the offender was not less than thirty years old (normally about forty), had been convicted of an offence punishable with at least two years' imprisonment and had been similarly convicted on at least three occasions with similar sentences (since the age of seventeen), on at least two being sentenced to borstal or prison. The length of sentence (between five and fourteen years with seven as a normal minimum) was indeterminate and related more to the offender's past crimes than to his present one. After 1963, offenders received one third remission. The first stage of the sentence, lasting for up to two years, was served in a local prison and the second in a special wing in a central prison. In view of the length of sentence, conditions were more relaxed than for ordinary offenders and included extra privileges. A prisoner was released on licence to the supervision of a probation officer, the licence being for the period of the sentence which remained unexpired at the time of the prisoner's release. Any breach of imposed conditions led to recall to prison. Progressively PD became applied in actuality more to petty nuisance offenders with long records of crime than to those for whom it was intended, persistent offenders who posed a serious threat to society. In no sense was it a deterrent. In 1963 the Report of the Advisory Council on the Treatment of Offenders, *Preventive Detention*, recommended abolition and in 1965 the White Paper *The Adult Offender* (Cmnd 2852) supported this, mentioning that there were at the time about 500 men serving such sentences and in 1964 forty sentences of PD had been awarded. PD's successor is the *extended sentence* (q.v.).   DPW

P

Primary deviance The primary and secondary distinction was first used by E.M. Lemert in *Social Pathology* (N.Y., 1951, p. 75) and elaborated in his *Human Deviance, Social Problems and Social Control* (N.Y., 1972). Primary deviance involves actors who engage in deviant acts, but occupy a conventional status. The self-concept is not involved and the deviance is seen as part of a socially accepted role by the actor. Whereas secondary (or career) deviance is the term for the actions of those who are committed to deviance, where it *has* affected the self-concept and where a deviant role is being consciously acted out. Secondary deviance develops when the deviant role is reinforced through increasing involvement with other more committed deviants (through for example membership of *sub-cultures* (q.v.)) and often through the effects of *labelling* (q.v.).   DPW

Prison A place of incarceration. Conditions in early prisons were quite simply appalling as a result more of indifference and neglect than positive cruelty. They only slowly began to be changed as a result of John Howard's (1726–1790) philanthropic work from 1770 onwards. Gaolers were unpaid and obtained their livelihood from prisoners' fees, which amongst other abuses meant that people had to stay in prison purely because they had arrears of fees. After Howard gave evidence to a House of Commons Committee in 1774 two Acts were passed, the first immediately released every prisoner against whom a grand jury failed to find a true bill, giving gaolers a sum from the county rate in lieu of abolished fees and the second required JPs to see that prison interiors were whitewashed once a year, that rooms were cleaned and ventilated, that hospitals existed in prison with proper medical advice, that the naked should be clothed and that underground dungeons should be used as little as possible. Howard's book *The State of the Prisons in England and Wales with preliminary Observations and an Account of Some Foreign Prisons* (1777) and its appendix (1780) was a landmark.

Prisons at this time showed great variation, but broadly consisted of open rooms in which inmates spent their entire time without employment, privacy or separation of the sexes. Elizabeth Fry (1780–1845) was so disgusted by conditions among the female prisoners at Newgate in 1813 that she founded in 1817 the association for the Improvement of the Female Prisoners in Newgate, which aimed to separate men and women prisoners, to classify female prisoners, to provide female staff for female prisoners and to give the prisoners religious and educational instruction and work. These improvements were adopted for females.

In the 1830s two rival systems of positive penal administration began to emerge (with their origins in American experiments), to replace the erstwhile ramshackle *ad hoc* local arrangements, the *silent system* and the *separate system* (qq.v.). (See S. McConville (1981), *A History of English Prison Administration*; vol. 1, 1750–1877, and M. Ignatieff (1978), *A Just Measure of Pain: the Penitentiary in the Industrial Revolution 1750–1850*.) At this time Joshua Jebb's (1793–1863) prison-building programme began. In 1837 Jebb was appointed technical adviser to the Home Office. He designed and built the new model convict prison at Pentonville (opened 1842) and in the six years following fifty-four new prisons were built on this model. In 1844 he was appointed the first Surveyor General of Prisons, and when in 1850 the Directorate of Convict Prisons was established, he was appointed chairman, remaining in post until his death. His building programme very largely constrained and directed the subsequent form of penal administration and still does do so.

With *transportation* (q.v.) coming to an end, the separate system gained ascendency in Jebb's new cellular prisons, and in 1863 Edmond DuCane (1830–1903) was appointed to the Directorate of Convict Prisons (becoming chairman in 1869). In 1877 when prisons were 'nationalised', DuCane became the first chairman of the Prison Commission. A strict disciplinarian, his over-riding aim was to make prisons deter prisoners from recidivating. The means to achieve this he variously described as 'hard fare, hard labour and a hard bed' and, 'the punishment of hard, dull, useless, uninteresting, monotonous labour'.

This was accomplished very largely with the use of the crank, the treadmill and shot-drill (and see *hard labour*). Shot-drill involved compulsory 'drill' with cannon-balls weighing 24 or 32 lb, and the crank was a machine with a heavy handle which had to be turned for so many revolutions by the prisoner. (The handle was extremely hard to turn through being attached to a wheel revolving in a trough containing gravel to provide resistance.) The treadmill was a large cylindrical machine provided with steps. Men held onto a rail and the wheel revolved by the pressure of their weight, their feet being kept in continual motion walking 'up' the steps as the wheel turned.

DuCane succeeded in fusing together a large number of small, varied prisons into one unified system, a major achievement. In each prison the deterrent system was carried out without variation and no prisoner was treated as an individual (see also *stage system*). His whole approach was attacked by William Morrison (1852–1943), however, who as Wandsworth prison chaplain demonstrated that there had been an increase in crime as a result of the DuCane régime, not a decrease as was claimed. Morrison's attack directly led to the setting up of the Gladstone Committee in 1895, created to examine DuCane's work. The Committee disproved DuCane's claim that the deterrent character of prison life under his rule had reduced crime. It further regarded non-productive labour and separate confinement as unsuitable, and particularly condemned his refusal to treat prisoners as individuals.

In 1895 DuCane retired and was succeeded by Evelyn Ruggles-Brise (1857–1935), chairman of the Prison Commission 1895–1921. Ruggles-Brise accepted that deterrence and retribution were the basis of the prison system, but in addition he saw it as both reformatory and paternalistic, boasting of its uniformity. His main preoccupations were the abolition of DuCane's hard labour machines and making improvements in classification of prisoners, their education and moral training, diet, medical care and sanitation, discharge aid and officer training. His particular ambition was to improve the conditions of young prisoners, and he founded *borstals* (q.v.) for this purpose. Further relaxation of severity was provided by Alexander Paterson (1884–1947) who, from 1922 to 1947, was Director of Convict Prisons and a Prison Commissioner. Paterson was renowned for the vigour and ingenuity with which he attempted to reshape prisons as more open and meaningful institutions after the harshness of the DuCane régime. He stated, 'Men come to prison as a punishment, not for punishment', and pressed for a new approach, emphasizing training for prisoners intended to fit them for a law-abiding life. He also introduced *open prisons* (q.v.), stressing that 'you cannot train men for freedom in a condition of captivity' (see S.K. Ruck (1951), *Paterson on Prisons*).

Having shifted from a hotch-potch of local lock-ups and horrific dungeons, experimented with several systems of administration inspired by religion, and become a single system dedicated to deterrence and purposeless labour, prison gradually emerged as an institution, but what could it in fact realistically accomplish? As a result of the historical legacy, physical constraints, lack of finance and investment, the modern prison system (dating from the *Prison Act* (1952)) suffered severe difficulties from the start. The greatest single difficulty, however, has been lack of clarity of objective. So long as prison mixes retribution and reform, 'success' cannot occur, but the very definition of success is signally unclear. In the absence of public consensus as to what prisons are 'for', the prison service has been notably efficient in achieving one of the few undisputed objectives – containment.

See M. Fitzgerald and J. Sim (1982), *British Prisons*; R. Giallombardo (N.Y., 1966), *Society of Women: a Study of a Woman's Prison*; T.P. and P. Morris (1963), *Pentonville*; D.A. Ward and G.G. Kassebaum (Philadelphia, 1972), 'Women in prison', in R.M. Carter, D. Glaser and L.T. Wilkins, eds., *Correctional Institutions*.

See also *Convict prison*; *Escapes*; *Prison classification*; *Prison discipline*; *Prison labour*; *Prison officer*; *Prison security*; *Prison uniform*.   DPW

Prison classification The (1823) Gaol Act recognised (as a result of Howard's work) the need to separate prisoners to prevent them from 'contaminating' each other, and since then the prison system has been preoccupied with classification, aiming both to simplify and to rationalise administration and to avoid '*contagion*' (q.v.). The current general principle (*Prison Rules* (1964), Rule 3) is that men shall be classified, 'having regard to their age, temperament and record and with a view to maintaining good order and facilitating training.' Apart from temporary separation for punishment (see *prison discipline*), the main ways in which inmates are classified are: male and female; length of sentence; convicted and unconvicted; adults and young prisoners; and, since 1967, the prime way of classifying is by security category. Security categories are:

A Prisoners whose escape would be highly dangerous to the public or the police or to the security of the state.

B Prisoners for whom the very highest conditions of security are not necessary, but for whom escape must be made very difficult.

C Prisoners who cannot be trusted in open conditions, but who do not have the ability or resources to make a determined escape attempt.

D Those who can reasonably be trusted to serve their sentences in open conditions (Mountbatten Report, *Report of the Inquiry into Prison Escapes and Security* (Cmnd 3175, 1966), para. 217).

Depending upon security category, men are located in open, medium security or maximum security prisons. Mental condition and resistance to authority are additional ways of classifying depending upon availability of accommodation, and more elaborate schemes are used in young offenders' establishments. Each prison may hold only prisoners in a single category, or, more usually, each is subdivided to enable men in different categories to be separately held in the same prison. In the past those sentenced to death, *corrective training* or *preventive detention* were separately confined from other men. From 1879 onward, classification was used to keep criminally sophisticated men ('ordinaries'), away from first offenders ('stars'). This system was modified by the *Prison Act* (1898), which introduced a scheme whereby prisoners were classified (originally by the courts) into one of three groups according to degree and character of offence. (The groups were ordinary, habitual and long sentence and each in turn was further subdivided into star, intermediate and recidivist.) The division between stars and ordinaries is still in existence.

See also *Prison security*. DPW

Prison discipline For a closed institution to function there has to be a high standard of conformity, and in addition prisons aim to raise the standard of conduct of prisoners. Rule 47 of the *Prison Rules* (1964) lists twenty-one activities which constitute offences against discipline. When an offence has occurred the charge is laid as soon as possible, it is enquired into, and the prisoner is kept separate (since there is little privacy in prison, the problem of identifying culprits is minimised). The Governor then carries out an adjudication upon the offender and may, if the offence is proven, caution, cause privileges to be forfeited or postponed, exclude from associated work, stop earnings, place in cellular confinement or cause loss of remission (Rule 50). For more serious offences a *Board of Visitors* (q.v.) adjudication is held which may punish in a similar way, but can do so for longer terms (Rules 51 and 52). Proceedings in both these adjudications are inquisitorial rather than adversarial. Governors may also, to ensure the smooth running of their prison, place a man temporarily in solitary confinement (Rule 43) for the maintenance of good order and discipline (used mainly against men suspected of bullying others). (Prisoners who are fearful of being attacked by others (as a result of the type of offence they have committed) can apply to be removed from association and go on Rule 43 at their own request, for their own protection, but this has nothing to do with discipline.) After 24 hours an authority must be obtained from a member of the Board of Visitors for a man to continue in solitary confinement for any reason. This may be given for up to a month and may be renewed thereafter. For information on numbers of men punished see annual *Report on the Work of the Prison Department*.

See also *Segregation unit*.   DPW

Prison labour   Rule 28 of the *Prison Rules* (1964) states: 'A convicted prisoner shall be required to do useful work for not more than ten hours a day, and arrangement shall be made to allow prisoners to work, where possible, outside the cells and in association with one another.' Unconvicted prisoners are not required to work unless they wish to. Prison labour flourished in the early congregate prisons and even under prisons operating the *silent system* (q.v.). The demise of normal productive work arose with the development of the *separate system* (q.v.). The effects of this régime were to last until well into the present century. Only with the passing of the *Criminal Justice Act* (1948) did it really become possible to begin to make ordinary work available to prisoners. (Paid piecework was introduced for the first time in all prisons in 1933 and the present flat-rate system of pay was introduced to replace piecework in 1959.) Factors which regulate what sort of work may be carried out in prison include the attitude of trades unions; availability of staff, both discipline and instructors, to supervise; possible civil opposition to prisoners being given normal work; security considerations (in relation to use of materials in assault or escape attempts); overcrowding and space and money for plant and equipment. Available work includes building and maintenance work, domestic services, work on prison farms, and vocational training courses. Little plant-related employment exists; there is some contract labour, but most men are involved in permanent routine work, frequently making articles for use in prison, or for use by the Department of the Environment or the Post Office. A few men under hostel schemes work outside prison, returning at night. The average prisoner in a local prison earns about £1 a week.   DPW

Prison officer, the   A member of staff in a prison (similar staff work in remand centres, borstals and detention centres). From an early history of corruption and stark brutality the image of the officer has only recently begun to be rehabilitated (not without some hiccups caused by allegations of brutality, especially in relation to riot control), but, because of its associations, the work is still seen by many people as low status. Most staff are ordinary discipline officers administering the routine round of inmate life; above them are Senior Officers (introduced in 1968), Principal Officers and Chief Officers. In addition there are specialist hospital, trades, catering and night patrol officers and physical education instructors. Their union, the Prison Officers' Association (POA), was founded in 1938.

See J.E. Thomas (1972), *The Prison Officer since 1850*; *Committee of Inquiry into the U.K. Prison Services, 1979* (1979) May Report, Cmnd 7673.   DPW

Prison security   In the broad sense this means the creation and maintenance of safe and stable conditions of living and working for prison inmates, and this of course specifically includes the eradication of opportunities for escaping, facilitating an escape, doing injury to another prisoner, a member of staff or attempting suicide. Although the term is accepted and applied in its broadest sense, it is in the specific sense that security is most in evidence. Both the spate of *escapes* (q.v.) in the 1960s resulting in the Mountbatten Report, *Report of the Inquiry into Prison Escapes and Security* (Cmnd 3175, 1966) and the riots abroad (e.g. Attica 1971, New Mexico State prison 1979) and those at home (e.g. Dartmoor 1932, Parkhurst 1969, Albany 1972, Hull 1976, and Gartree 1972 and 1978) have intensified demand for this. Originally prisons operated on cell security,

PRISON UNIFORM

where each man was confined to his cell for most of his time and periodic lock and window-bar checks and spot cell searches were all that was necessary. The policy now is where possible to allow men freer movement in prison and to keep obvious 'security' limited to the perimeter. Perimeter security is maintained with such things as unclimbable wire fences, wall and fence alarms, 'S' wire, searchlights, cameras with all-round vision, dog patrols and check points. All data from patrols, alarms and cameras are fed into the continuously manned control room, which, in the event of any incident, becomes the nerve-centre for directing operations. In the prison itself, since workshops may facilitate theft or manufacture of weapons or escape articles, care is taken to count and check items such as tools, and on leaving a shop men are subject to a body search. Although the general intention is for this form of security to be as low key and unrestricting as possible, in local prisons in particular where pure perimeter security is not always feasible it is very much in evidence. Such an inevitable emphasis on physical security (necessitated by the public's fear of escapees very largely) of course drastically limits attempts to reform and rehabilitate. Level of security provision is directly related to the security classification of the men involved (see *prison classification*). DPW

Prison uniform Men in prison are issued with a variety of clothing and footwear. Uniform generally consists of black shoes or slippers, a blue and white striped shirt and a jacket and trousers, usually of denim. Unconvicted men wear brown jacket and trousers and convicted either blue or grey. There are no special markings to indicate security classification, but specially privileged and trusted prisoners, 'redbands', wear an armlet of red cloth and prisoners who are an escape risk wear yellow 'patches' (see *escapes*). Wearing clothes stamped with the broad arrow was discontinued in 1948. DPW

Prison Visitor, the Men and women voluntary workers appointed by the Home Office on the recommendation of the Governor of a particular prison whose task is to visit prisoners there and keep them in touch with the community. Introduced into prisons for men in 1922, Prison Visitors had already been officially accepted for female prisoners as early as the 1890s (Elizabeth Fry's 'Ladies' Prison Committees' being their forerunners). The work of Prison Visitors is co-ordinated by the National Association of Prison Visitors.   DPW

Prisoners' rights Since the nineteenth century, the British Prison Rules laid down the conditions under which prisoners are confined. Such 'rights' as visits, letters, association, home leave, parole, etc., are in fact privileges, which may be withheld or removed for bad behaviour. Prison discipline and control were held to require that the governor and his Board of Visitors had this degree of authority over prisoners. However, since the upsurge in *prisoners' unions* (q.v.) in the late 1960s in the USA, Continental Europe and Britain, attempts have been made to establish greater access for prisoners to legal advice and representation in disciplinary hearings. A decision of the High Court in 1979 (concerning five prisoners involved in the Hull riot) set aside a Board of Visitors' decision on the ground that they had not had a fair hearing. In 1972 a prisoner gained access to the European Commission on Human Rights over alleged medical negligence, and a settlement was made before the Commission could hear the case. Since then, freer correspondence with lawyers and access to independent medical opinion have been allowed. In 1975 the European Court of Human Rights ruled that the Home Office had been in breach of the European Convention by denying a prisoner the opportunity to bring an action against a prison officer. Since then prisoners can seek advice about civil proceedings without first petitioning the Secretary of State. In 1979 another decision of the Commission over censorship of letters went against the Home Office. Disputes between prisoners, prison reformers and the Home Office continue over the status of decisions over parole, the use of drugs in prisons, and confinement in segregation units.

                                                                  WJOJ

Prisoners' unions The idea of unions for prisoners was a product of the libertarian era of protest in the late 1960s. The first such union was in Sweden in 1966, and was closely followed by similar organisations in Norway, Finland and Denmark. The Swedish union had some success in stopping the expansion of high-security prisons. In Britain, a union called PROP (Preservation of the Rights of Prisoners) was set up in 1972. About 5,000 prisoners were involved in protests called by the union soon afterwards, about 1,000 of whom were punished. The Home Secretary refused to recognise the union. PROP deman-

P

ded parole as a right, appeal against refusal of parole, the opening of prisons to the public and press, implementation of training and rehabilitation, and the allocation of prisoners to gaols in their home areas. PROP espoused a political framework for its campaign, which was broadly Marxist. Subsequent campaigns have focused on the use of drugs by prison authorities, and on violence by prison staff (see also *prisoners' rights*). WJOJ

Prisonisation A term used by T.P. Morris in *Pentonville*, (1963) to refer to the behaviours used by an individual in prison to help him to adjust to life there. Elaborated by the inmate social system, these behaviours enable a person to appear to be complying with régime requirements while inwardly rejecting them, at the same time as softening the impact of the sentence through involvement with the inmate social system. Unlike *institutionalisation* (q.v.), behaviours involved in prisonisation are shed at the end of a sentence.

See also *Total institution*. DPW

Probation Probation Orders are a form of binding over of offenders, subject to conditions of supervision by a probation officer. These orders arose, more or less simultaneously, in Boston, USA, and in England in the 1880s, when religiously motivated citizens stood as sureties for the good behaviour of certain offenders, usually in cases involving alcohol. The Probation Service was put on an official footing in Britain with the *Probation of Offenders Act* (1907). Before the Second World War the number of Probation Orders, for juvenile and adult offenders, grew only slowly. Rapid growth in the use of probation by courts did not occur until after the *Criminal Justice Act* (1948). Under this Act, probation officers were charged with the task of 'advising, assisting and befriending' those placed under supervision, and between then and the late 1960s probation was the main alternative to imprisonment in more serious cases. Following the Streatfeild Report of 1961, probation officers (in addition to preparing background social reports on many defendants) increasingly made recommendations on sentencing to the higher courts, as well as to Magistrates' Courts.

Since the late 1960s, alternative measures allowing conditional liberty – such as suspended sentences, deferred sentences and Community Service Orders – have been available to the courts.

Since the *Children and Young Persons Act* (1969) was partially implemented, the Probation Service has been less involved in reports on and supervision of juvenile delinquents. Probation Orders as a proportion of all sentences on adult offenders fell sharply from 1970 onwards, in both higher and lower courts.

Meanwhile, probation officers have become increasingly involved in the after-care of discharged prisoners, dealing with both parole and voluntary cases. They have also increasingly contributed reports on the welfare of children in divorce cases, and supervised access and custody arrangements. Most recent-ly, the Probation Service has provided day care for offenders – mainly the unemployed. There is continued debate about whether the Service should develop as part of the penal system, as part of the courts system, or as a separate social work service.

J.F.S. King (1969), *The Probation and After-care Service*; D. Haxley (1978), *Probation: a Changing Service*; A.E. Bottoms and W. McWilliams (1979), 'A non-treatment paradigm for probation practice', *Brit. J. Social Work* (9), 2; Interdepart-mental Committee on the Business of the Criminal Courts (Streatfeild Committee), *Report*, Cmnd 1289, 1961.   WJOJ

Probation hostel. See *Hostels*.

Procuration The *Sexual Offences Act* (1956), s. 23 makes it an offence for anyone to procure (implying persuasion or induce-ment) a woman under twenty-one to have unlawful sexual intercourse with a third person. 'The wording of the law suggests that the original object of this law was to stop the recruitment of prostitutes, but the effect is much wider' (Honoré (1978), *Sex Law*, p. 57); s. 22 makes it an offence for anyone to procure a woman of any age to become a prostitute.

It is also an offence for a man to procure another man to commit buggery with a third man or to commit an act of gross indecency with a third man. This is so even though the acts of buggery and gross indecency themselves may be committed legally.   ARP

Professionalism Serious criminological research into the phe-nomenon of professional crime was pioneered in 1937 by Edwin Sutherland. In his classic study of 'Chic Conwell', he showed that the activities of a small proportion of people involved in predatory crimes against property – mainly burglary, robbery, theft or fraud – could be understood as the exercise of a skilled

PROFESSIONALISM

craft with its own traditions, rules and values. He isolated a number of factors which distinguished the 'professional' from the 'amateur' thief, helping the former to make a substantial living from stealing while avoiding excessive imprisonment. These were, chiefly, specialisation, skill, wit and tutelage from and recognition by other professionals.

Sutherland's approach was adopted or adapted in several subsequent descriptive studies, notably Maurer's (1964) work on professional pickpockets, Einstadter's (1969) study of armed robbers and Jackson's *A Thief's Primer* (1969). His definition of professionalism was also largely accepted by Clinard and Quinney in their ambitious typology of criminal behaviour systems (1967).

However, some modern criminologists have found the term 'professional' ambiguous and unhelpful, and have argued that its use should be abandoned entirely. Cressey (1972), who claims that Sutherland's thief is a disappearing breed, criticises the indiscriminate application of the term 'to almost all criminals believed by the police to have intelligence levels something above that of idiots'. Attention should be focused, he argues, less upon individual qualities and more upon the *nature and level of organisation* achieved by criminal groups. In this he is supported by the Scottish criminologist, John Mack, who stresses the importance of 'background operators' – suppliers, receivers, organisers and patrons – without whom few 'front-line' thieves can prosper. Mack also points out further confusions in the frequently-made distinction between 'professional' ('Bill-Sikes-type') and 'organised' ('Mafia-type') crime.

The value of an 'organisation'-oriented approach has been demonstrated by McIntosh (1975), using historical material, but there is a surprising dearth of recent descriptive evidence about professional crime, however defined. Letkemann (1973) has analysed theft within the framework of occupational theory, using interviews with offenders, and the world of 'good' or 'high-level' burglars has been briefly examined by Shover (1972) and Maguire (1982). However, the difficulties of penetrating a secretive area, where most evidence comprises hearsay from criminal informants or policemen, have deterred the main body of researchers from tackling this important branch of criminology.

M.B. Clinard and R. Quinney (N.Y., 1967), *Criminal Behaviour Systems*; D.R. Cressey (1972), *Criminal Organisa-*

tion; W.J. Einstadter (1969), 'The social organisation of armed robbery', *Social Problems*, 17, 64; P. Letkemann (Englewood Cliffs, N.J., 1973), *Crime as Work*; M. McIntosh (1975), *The Organisation of Crime*; J.A. Mack (1975), *The Crime Industry*; E.M.W. Maguire (1982), *Burglary in a Dwelling: the Offence, the Offender and the Victim*; D.W. Maurer (New Haven, 1964, first published 1955), *Whiz Mob*; N. Shover (1972), 'Structures and careers in burglary', *JCLCPS*, 63, 540; E.H. Sutherland (Chicago, 1937), *The Professional Thief.*   MM

PROP. See *Prisoners' unions*.

Prosecution The initiation and carrying on of criminal proceedings before a court of law. In general it may be said that in England and Wales the decision whether or not to initiate a prosecution lies with the police: private prosecutions are possible but rare; also some prosecutions need the consent of the Attorney General or the Director of Public Prosecutions. It may also be said that the police have complete discretion in making their decision, but in fact this discretion normally operates within limits, though they are not legally binding or easily discernible. The first and basic question is, do the police have a *'prima facie* case', that is 'enough admissible evidence to prove all the necessary elements of the offence and evidence that does not appear to be so manifestly unreliable that no reasonable tribunal could safely convict upon it' (*Royal Commission on Criminal Procedure*, p. 128). The police may have advice from qualified lawyers (their own Prosecuting Solicitors' Departments or local firms), but not always; and they need not follow it. But by no means all *prima facie* cases go to prosecution. For some offences juveniles are regularly dealt with by *caution* (q.v.) instead, and older offenders, too, for compassionate reasons. The 'public interest', e.g. the burden of business upon the courts, may also inhibit proceedings. The *Royal Commission on Criminal Procedure* found the discretionary process – as have other commentators – a grey area where the issues were not clear cut and no firm answers forthcoming. But they concluded that 'the ability of any prosecution system to take account of these considerations of humanity and of other elements of public interest is a hallmark of its fairness, provided that such criteria are applied consistently' (ibid., p. 129).

Fairness, openness and accountability, and efficiency were

the Commissioners' standards of evaluation. Their critical deliberations led them on the one hand to the view that there should be agreed and consistent criteria for the exercise of the discretion to prosecute, but that it should continue to be exercised by the local police forces; on the other hand they felt that there should be a statutorily-based prosecution service in every police force area to conduct prosecutions from this point on, and to advise the police. See *Report of the Royal Commission on Criminal Procedure, 1978–81* (Cmnd 8092, 1981), Pt II. ARP

Prostitution A form of activity in which women known as prostitutes sell their sexual services for a limited time to any man who will pay the price agreed. May (1934) defines it as sexual intercourse characterised by barter, promiscuity and emotional indifference. It does not constitute a crime, but *soliciting*, i.e. attempting to make such bargains in public, does (*Street Offences Act* (1959)). There are also male prostitutes who sell their services to other males (cf. Caukins, 1976); those who do so to females being known as gigolos. Literature on prostitutes and their activities is vast, but inconclusive as to precipitants or participants, due to the difficulty of obtaining representative samples. An excellent history is Henriques (1961).

S.E. Caukins *et al.* (1976), 'The psychodynamics of male prostitution', *Amer. J. Psychotherapy*, 30 (3), 441; F. Henriques (1961), *Stews and Strumpets: a Survey of Prostitution*; G. May (N.Y., 1934), 'Prostitution', *Encyclopedia of Social Sciences*. DPW

Psychological factors. See *Aggression*; *Behaviour modification*; *Conditionability*; *Deprivation*; *Extraversion*; *Forensic psychiatry*; *Frustration*; *Heredity*; *Identity*; *Intelligence*; *Mental abnormality*; *Modelling*; *Motive*; *Physical abnormality*; *Psychopath*; *Violence*.

Psychopath, the This term exemplifies the problems of psychiatric diagnosis. The difficulty has been to clearly define those people with a 'life long propensity to behaviour which falls midway between normality and psychosis' (Lewis, 1974). Over-confident assertions that the psychopath is easy to recognise but difficult to describe have led to much harm being done.

There is disagreement about the historical roots of the concept of psychopathy. The belief that Pinel's 'madness without delusions' and Prichard's 'moral insanity' were forerunners has been questioned. Many cases quoted were clearly of recent and unexpected onset, albeit frequently exhibiting violence. Medicine's reflection of current social mores makes difficult nineteenth-century writings with their moralistic and judgmental tones. Nevertheless, ideas such as modified responsibility and defective rearing contrast favourably with such notions as heritable evil and the 'born delinquent'. While intellectual defect was originally thought important, the person of high intelligence with serious moral deficiencies ('the creative psychopath') was recognised. Medico-legally it was important to demonstrate defect of reason (delusion) for a plea of insanity to be successful. 'Moral insanity' was difficult to distinguish from 'ordinary depravity'.

The present approach is to take the concept of abnormal personality and attempt to describe various sub-types. All such classifications have serious faults and lack heuristic or clinical value. There are recognisable types such as the obsessional, cyclothymic, but the antisocial or explosive personalities are unconvincing.

Whether it is the individual concerned or society that mainly suffers can be practically useful. Traditionally the psychopath is seen as someone with undesirable characteristics and ways of behaving. The *Mental Health Act* (1959) describes psychopathy as 'a persistent disorder or disability of mind . . . which results in abnormally aggressive or seriously irresponsible conduct'. The generally agreed chief features are – inability to profit from experience, poor control over impulses, antisocial behaviour, no sense of responsibility, emotional immaturity, unresponsiveness to punishment, defective relationships, lack of guilt feelings and clear objectives, egocentricity, lying and aggressiveness. From this cluster emerge two opposite types, the affectionless aggressive, who may commit unpleasant crimes, and the non-aggressive feckless drifter.

There is probably a small but important genetic/constitutional component with the superimposition of a large element of faulty early training.

Management and its results are uncertain. The idea that psychopaths settle with age has not been confirmed, there being a high incidence of recidivism, alcoholism and depression. The more emotionally intact can benefit from a therapeutic community approach but the aggressive paranoid individual probably does best in an authoritarian directive régime.

W. Davies and P. Feldman (1981), 'The diagnosis of psychopathy by forensic specialists', *Brit. J. Psychiatry*, 138, 329; A. Lewis (1974), 'Psychopathic personality: a most elusive category', *Psychological Med.*, 4, 133; P. Pinel (Paris, 1801), *Traité médico-philosophique sur l'aliénation mentale ou la manie*; J.C. Prichard (1835), *A Treatise on Insanity*.

GDPW

Psychosis/otic. See *Mental abnormality*.

Psychoticism To extend his two-dimensional system for the study of crime and personality (see *extraversion*–introversion and *neuroticism*), H.J. Eysenck added a further dimension which he called 'psychoticism'. He claims that it is 'a dimension of personality which leads from outright psychosis through psychopathy to normality'. It is allegedly characterised by various traits: solitary/troublesome/cruel/lacking feeling/sensation-seeking/hostility/liking oddity/disregard for danger/upsetting and making fools of others. S. and H. Eysenck (1970), 'Crime and personality: an empirical study of the three-factor theory', *BJC*, 10 (3), 225; H. Eysenck (3rd ed., 1977) *Crime and Personality*. ARP

Public order The maintenance of public order relies on preventive regulation as well as punitive sanction, all contained in an amalgam of common law and statute, complex and often uncertain in scope. Both aspects are being reviewed, the former at the instigation of the Home Secretary (see the Green Paper: *Review of the Public Order Act (1936) and Related Legislation* (Cmnd 7891, 1980), the latter as part of the Law Commission's programme of codification of the criminal law of England and Wales (see *Offences against Public Order*, Working Paper no. 82, 1982). Reference should also be made to Lord Scarman's analysis in his report, *The Brixton Disorders* (Cmnd 8427, 1981). The Law Commission considers 'rout' to be obsolete.

See also *Affray*; *Riot*; *Unlawful assembly*. ARP

Punishment, dates of use of some obsolete forms Beheading, 1076–1747 (last use); boiling of murderers to death, 1530–47; branding, from Saxon times until 1829; brank (scolding-bridle), never legalised, not used before the seventeenth century, last use 1856; burning to death, anciently until 1790 (last use 1789); stool of repentance (cucking-stool), Saxon times until the early seventeenth century; drawing and quartering, 1284–1870 (sentence last passed 1867); drowning, Saxon times until c. 1623 (Scotland, 1685); ducking-stool, early seventeenth to early nineteenth centuries (last use 1817); gibbeting in chains or irons, 1752–1834 (last use 1791); mutilation (ears, eyes, limbs, testicles), from before 1016, termination uncertain, instances up to 1637; outlawry, Saxon times until 1879 (abolition in civil proceedings) and 1938 (abolition in criminal proceedings); pillory, from before 1266 until 1816, retained until 1837 for perjury and subornation (last use 1830); stocks, Saxon times until early nineteenth century, never abolished (last use 1865); torture, never legalised in common law, but widely used extra-judicially, c. 1422–1640. For other forms, see relevant entries.   DPW

Punishment, theories of. See *Compensation*; *Deterrence*; *Incapacitation*; *Reformation*; *Rehabilitation*; *Restitution*; *Retribution*.

Punishment types, modern. See *Attendance centres*; *Borstal*; *Binding over*; *Care Order*; *Cautioning*; *Community homes*; *Community Service Orders*; *Compensation*; *Deferred sentence*; *Detention centres*; *Discharge*; *Exemplary sentence*; *Extended sentence*; *Fine*; *Guardianship Order*; *Hospital Order*; *Hostels*; *Imprisonment*; *Indeterminate sentence*; *Intermediate Treatment*; *Life imprisonment*; *Local prison*; *Parole*; *Prison*; *Probation*; *Royal prerogative*; *Segregation unit*; *Sentencing*; *Special hospitals*; *Supervision Order*; *Suspended sentence*; *Youth custody*.

Punishment types, obsolete. See *Capital punishment*; *Convict prison*; *Corporal punishment*; *Corrective training*; *Hard labour*; *House of Correction*; *Hulks*; *Penal servitude*; *Preventive detention*; *Transportation*.

R

Race. See *Ethnicity*.

Rackets/Racketeering. See *Organised crime*.

Radical criminology A school of thought which rejects *positivism* (q.v.) and 'correctionally oriented' criminology and, arguing that the basis for *deviance* (q.v.) is reaction to economic pressure, rejects the narrow definition of crime in favour of a general theory of deviance. Such a theory is concerned with the behavioural implications of the co-existence of numerous diverse value systems in one society, and with the individual's reaction to the maze of structures used to regulate behaviour. See I. Taylor, P. Walton and J. Young (1975), *Critical Criminology*, ch. 1.   DPW

Radzinowicz, Sir Leon (1906–) A Polish criminologist, resident in England since 1946, who must rank as the individual most responsible for establishing scientific criminology in the UK. In 1946 he became Assistant Director of Research at Cambridge University, and from 1949 to 1959 he was Director of the Department of Criminal Science there. In 1959 he became the first Wolfson Professor of Criminology and in 1960 the first Director of the Institute of Criminology at Cambridge. In 1963 he was further appointed first chairman of the Criminological Council of the Council of Europe and in 1970 he was knighted. He has held numerous advisory and consultative posts in addition to being a prolific writer. His principal published works are: *History of English Criminal Law* (4 vols, 1948–68), *In Search of Criminology* (1961), *The Need for Criminology* (1965), *Ideology and Crime* (1966), *Crime and Justice* (co-edited with M.E. Wolfgang), 3 vols. (1971). He has also been co-editor and editor of fifty volumes in the Cambridge

Studies in Criminology series. For a full bibliography see R. Hood, ed. (1974), *Crime, Criminology and Public Policy*.

DPW

Rape   A man commits rape if:

(1) he has unlawful sexual intercourse with a woman who at the time of the intercourse does not consent to it; and at that time he knows that she does not consent to the intercourse or he is reckless as to whether she consents to it; or

(2) he induces a married woman to have sexual intercourse with him by impersonating her husband.

These forms of the offence are explicitly defined by statute, but other forms in which consent is nullified (this being the point in (2) above) may also arise by implication (*Sexual Offences Act* (1956), s. 1 and *Sexual Offences (Amendment) Act* (1976), s. 1).

The recent history of the law has been concerned with the matter of consent and an accused person's attitude to its absence; and with the protection of women from unsympathetic investigation, unfair questioning and harmful publicity while still safeguarding the rights of the accused. In these respects, as Honoré comments in *Sex Law* (1978), p. 58, 'rape is a battlefield between men and women.'

Rape amounts to around 5 per cent of the totality of serious *sexual offences* (q.v.) recorded annually by the police. The *Criminal Statistics* (1980) comments that the increase (of the order of 20 per cent) in the recorded level after 1977 'may have been due in part to a growing willingness of victims to report offences', the 1976 Act (above) having enabled them to remain anonymous in reports of court proceedings.

The following features (among others) emerge from the Home Office Research Study (1979):

(1) Age of offender: of those convicted of rape, one in ten was under seventeen, four in ten were seventeen to twenty and half were over twenty-one, though only a handful over forty.

(2) Single and multiple rape; 40 per cent of all convictions were for multiple rape, but fewer than one in five victims was the victim of such.

(3) Relationship; 50 per cent were strangers to their victims, 27 per cent were casual acquaintances, 23 per cent were well known to each other. See R. Walmsley and K. White (1979), *Sexual Offences, Consent and Sentencing*, HORS no. 54.

ARP

193

Receiving. A term now replaced by 'Handling stolen goods'. See *Fencing*.

Recidivism. See *Habitual offender*; *Re-conviction*.

Re-conviction The conviction for subsequent offences of a person already convicted of a crime or crimes. However, published information generally offers a rate of re-conviction for an identified group of offenders. Obviously the establishment of re-conviction rates rests on a reliable method of recording information about offenders' previous criminal careers. In England and Wales the systematic provision of nationwide re-conviction rates dates from the establishment of Police and Prison Returns in 1857 under the stewardship of Samuel Redgrave, the Criminal Registrar. It was recognised at the time that the information on re-conviction provided by both the Police and Prison Returns could only be broadly relied on. The police in particular were known to vary in their efficiency and knowledge from district to district. They had also an axe to grind, as re-conviction rates were used by them to demonstrate the size of the 'criminal class', which became a nineteenth-century criminological obsession. With the later use of photography and fingerprinting, and with the 'nationalisation' of the prisons in 1877, both Police and Prison Returns came to provide more reliable measures of re-conviction.

In the twentieth century studies of re-conviction have largely been used to measure the 'effectiveness' of different forms of punishment or treatment: relative 'success' or 'failure' being judged by the size of the re-conviction rate. Also, prediction studies have been conducted which estimate the probability of re-conviction for different groups of offenders by identifying background indicators which discriminate between success and failure. However, such judgments are fraught with difficulty. Which re-convictions should be regarded as relevant? It would seem bizarre to regard a conviction for reckless driving on the part of a former armed bank robber as a re-conviction. To some extent this problem can be dealt with by constructing an index of offences, rating them according to their presumed seriousness. What time scale or follow-up period should be used? Research has varied in the time scale adopted, although there is strong evidence that the vast majority of re-convictions occur within five years and a large majority within two. Are re-conviction rates a reliable measure of subsequent criminality? They may be more a measure of vulnerability to arrest and successful prosecution than of the commission of crime. Evidence regarding the variable detection rate for different types of crime must reduce our confidence in re-conviction rates as a measure of criminality and therefore as a measure of the effectiveness of different penal measures.

Despite the caveats made above, studies of re-conviction will continue undoubtedly to be the primary method whereby the effectiveness of different penal measures can be compared.

S.R. Brody (1976), *The Effectiveness of Sentencing*, HORS no. 35; A.E. Bottoms and F.H. McClintock (1973), *Criminals Coming of Age*; G.A. and R.A. Carr-Hill (1972), 'Reconviction as a Process', *BJC*, 12, 35; V.A.C. Gatrell and T.B. Hadden (1972), 'Criminal statistics and their interpretation', in E.A. Wrigley, ed., *Nineteenth Century Society: Essays in the Use of Quantitative Methods for the Study of Social Data*; D. Glaser (Indianapolis, 1964), *The Effectiveness of a Prison and Parole System*; H. Mannheim and L.T. Wilkins (1955), *Prediction Methods in Relation to Borstal Training*.

See also *Career, criminal role*; *Habitual offender*; *Prediction*.

MNS

Reductivism   That aim of a criminal justice system which seeks to reduce the frequency of the types of behaviour prohibited by the criminal law.

N. Walker (1969), *Sentencing in a Rational Society*, esp. ch. 3, 'The techniques of crime-reduction'; N. Walker (1980), *Punishment, Danger and Stigma*.   ARP

Reform/Reformation   By reform is really meant to 'improve'. There have been reform schools and reformatories and one of the implicit objects of prison has been to reform inmates. The concept in relation to the treatment of individuals includes an assumption that there is something 'wrong' or 'bad' in a criminal, which under properly regulated treatment can be corrected, reformed or re-shaped and, with improved behaviour learnt in the institution, the individual will then remain free of crime. Reformation in custodial institutions has usually been attempted through either religion alone (cf. the *solitary system*), or through a 'reformative régime' of exercise, work, hygiene, discipline, education and religion. In practice reformation proves a remarkably elusive goal, due to institutional constraints and limited resources; conflict between ethical systems (when one person is subjected to a compulsory training course in another person's conception of Goodness), and to ethical problems involved in drastic *behaviour modification* (q.v.) which might be necessary were reformation to succeed. The softer, more limited, less ambitious but ethically more acceptable option is *rehabilitation* (q.v.). Spontaneous reformation (not invariably pro-social, cf. *contagion*) among offenders is likely to arise, if at all, as a result of either ageing or abrupt changes in personal circumstances (e.g. bereavement).

See also *Maturation*. DPW

Rehabilitation As a punishment objective as defined by Allen (1959), this assumes that behaviour is the product of antecedent causes which can be discovered; that knowledge of these causes permits the scientific control of behaviour and that measures used to treat offenders based on this knowledge should serve a therapeutic function. Opposition to the practicability of rehabilitation emerged with the realisation that such positivist criminology was not supplying the requisite knowledge and particularly with a survey of penal evaluation studies which concluded that rehabilitative efforts had had no appreciable effect on recidivism (Martinson, 1974). See Bottomley (1979, ch. 4).

F.A. Allen (1959), 'Criminal justice, legal values and the rehabilitative ideal', *JCLCPS*, 50, 226; A.K. Bottomley (1979), *Criminology in Focus*; R. Martinson (1974), 'What works? – questions and answers about prison reform', *The Public Interest*, spring, 22. DPW

Remand The legal expression for a court's decision to commit a defendant to custody or release him on bail pending the next stage of criminal proceedings (see *bail*). The proceedings are thereupon adjourned and the defendant is said to be 'on remand'. A remand in custody may not usually be for longer than eight days if before conviction or three weeks if after conviction: but the court may make further remands (*Magistrates' Courts Act* (1980), ss. 128–31). The defendant will normally be held in *prison* or in a *remand centre* (qq.v.), occasionally in a police station. ARP

Remand centre Either a wing of a local prison, quite separate from the main prison, or a separate prison-like institution set aside to receive people on *remand* (q.v.). There are about a dozen such centres, and the length of time spent by a person awaiting trial in them may be considerable and has been adversely commented on by A.K. Bottomley (1970), *Prison Before Trial: a Study of Remand Decisions in Magistrates' Courts*; and R.D. King and R. Morgan (1976), *A Taste of Prison*. DPW

Remand homes These were *institutions* (q.v.) designed to cater for children up to the age of seventeen and mainly intended to ensure that children due to make a court appearance were readily available. However, children could also be sent there for a month's detention as a punishment, and children in need of care and protection could be sent there as 'a place of safety'. Institutions mixing such different types of case were both difficult to run and of necessity unsatisfactory. They were originally provided by local police forces, but in 1932 the responsibility for running them was transferred to local authorities. The *Children and Young Persons Act* (1969), s. 46, provided for their progressive discontinuance and replacement by *community homes* (q.v.). DPW

Remission Under Rule 5 of the *Prison Rules* (1964) as amended by the *Prison* (*Amendment*) *Rules* (1968) and (1972), a portion of a sentence of imprisonment (one-third) need not be served if the offender has been of good behaviour throughout the first two-thirds of his sentence. This is termed remission, it is not available for those sentenced to *life imprisonment*, only applies to sentences of more than a month and does not permit reduction of the actual term served to less than thirty-one days. Remission can be forfeited as a result of disciplinary proceedings. It was not formally introduced in England and Wales until the *Prison Act* (1898), although prior to this portions of sentences had often been remitted by local administrators very much on an *ad hoc* basis.

See also *Parole*. DPW

Reparation. See *Compensation*.

Reporting Since Lodge's (1953) article it has been accepted that sometimes what was reported as a crime may not have been one, that changes in methods of recording and classifying crimes mean that comparisons over time (and between countries) are unreliable, that the police may not record all crimes reported to them, and that persons affected do not always report crime. The under-reporting of crime witnessed occurs for example as a result of poor observation, indifference, fear or not wishing to 'get involved'. Just how much crime was not reported was not clear until *self-report studies* and *victim surveys* (qq.v.) began. For example, Sparks (1977) estimated that at least two-thirds of the crimes mentioned by the victims in his sample were not reported to the police, and this applied to serious as well as to nuisance offences. Additional support for the view that massive under-reporting of crime is typical (and hence what *is* reported is in some sense 'special') comes from responses to recent victimisation questions included in the (OPCS) *General Household Survey*, 1972 onwards.

T.S. Lodge (1953), 'Criminal statistics', *J. Roy. Stat. Soc.*, Series A (General), CXVI, pt. III, 283; R. Sparks, H. Genn and D. Dodd (1977), *Surveying Victims*.

See also *Moral panic*; *Visibility*.   DPW

Responsibility Whether one believes that penalties are justified by the good they do or because they are deserved, it is usual to accept the principle that people should not be penalised for conduct for which they are not 'responsible'. The word, however, has several meanings. It can be used in a causal sense: e.g. 'earthquakes are responsible for great damage to houses' – in this sense it can be applied to things or people. In another, proprietary, sense it can be used to identify a person who can be called to account for the behaviour of a person other than himself, or of an animal or inanimate possession: e.g. 'he is responsible for the injury inflicted by his child (dog, bonfire, etc.)' or simply 'he is responsible for the child'.

The most interesting sense, however, is what we mean when we say 'he was not responsible for what *he* (not someone or something else) did'. We say this of sleepwalkers, epileptics who have just had fits, and sometimes of people who have done harm by accidents not due to their negligence. Our reason in such cases seems to be that the act was not willed. Sometimes we say it when the act was willed but excusable – e.g. violence under duress, or in those rare cases labelled 'necessity' – but it is better simply to call such acts 'excusable' than stretch the meaning of 'non-responsible' in this way. More interesting are cases in which we apply the term to people who act under such fear, provocation or other emotion that we feel they were somehow not in control of themselves. English law recognises self-defence in certain circumstances, or actions under threats of death, as grounds for an acquittal; but provocation is merely accepted as reducing, not abolishing culpability. In England and Wales the McNaghten Rules provide a special acquittal (but hospitalisation) for someone whose disease of the mind caused him to be mistaken as to 'the nature and quality of his act' (e.g. to think he was the owner of someone else's property, and therefore not stealing it) or not to realise that his act would be criminal (e.g. to think that mercy killing is permitted by law). In some jurisdictions a disordered person who acts in the belief that he is morally right but legally wrong is regarded as excusable. In the American Law Institute's Model Penal Code, 'disease of the mind' which renders the person unable to conform his conduct to the law also entitles him to an acquittal. What is common to all these situations is that the circumstances or the person's state of mind make us feel that he should not be morally blamed for what he did. The reasons for this feeling, however, are varied. There have been attempts to identify something which they have in common (such as absence of rationality), but a sounder view seems to be that responsibility is one of those notions which are such that we can say when they are not applicable, but not define them.

In the eyes of many determinists, people can be responsible in the causal sense or the proprietary sense, but not in the moral sense, since even an action which is willed with deliberation and in full appreciation of its nature is the outcome of a causal chain, so that the person could do only what he did. On such a view moral blame would be merely an emotional reaction, equally determined, but not the reflection of any genuine distinction between actions for which the actors were and were not responsible.

See also *Diminished responsibility*; *Infanticide*; *Punishment, theories of*.   NDW

Restitution May be ordered by the court when property has been obtained by stealing, deception or blackmail against a person convicted of any offence relating thereto: the property or its proceeds must then be restored or payment made of a sum not greater than its value out of money found on him on apprehension (*Theft Act* (1968), s. 28).   ARP

Restriction Order A court order which may be coupled with a *Hospital Order* (q.v.) – it cannot be made on its own – to the effect that the patient can be discharged from hospital only with the consent of the Home Secretary or on the direction of a Mental Health Review Tribunal. The period of restriction may be fixed or indefinite. Used where the court thinks the public needs protection, many offenders thereupon go to a secure *special hospital* (q.v.), but this is a matter for administrative arrangement. Only the Crown Court can make this Order, but magistrates may also refer an appropriate case to it. *Mental Health Act* (1959) as amended by the *Mental Health (Amendment) Act* (1982).   ARP

Retribution A form of punishment philosophy in which the focus is on the criminal act that has been committed, rather than on the offender, his personal circumstances or the pressures he was confronted with. Once a criminal act has been committed then it is punished by an award of pain *at least equal* to that created by the crime, to redress the imbalance created by it, to deter both the offender from committing a similar act again and also others who might be contemplating similar acts. Although formally codified by Bentham's philosophy of utilitarianism, this form of societal revenge has been practised throughout history from the Old Testament *lex talionis* (eye for eye, tooth for tooth, Exodus 21:24) onwards and formed a justification for *capital punishment*, *hard labour*, *corporal punishment*, *penal servitude*, etc. Retribution still forms a basis for judicial decisions.

   See also *Criminology*; *Deterrence*; *Tariff*.   DPW

Reverse record check A term used by Sparks in *Surveying Victims* (1977) to refer to a procedure for checking on the victim's recall of offences in *victim surveys* (q.v.). It involves collecting data from a sample of those who have reported an incident to the police involving an alleged offence and then interviewing them subsequently to see how many mention the incidents and how accurately they are described.   DPW

Riot A common law offence with five necessary elements: '(1) a number of persons, three at least; (2) a common purpose; (3) execution or inception of the common purpose; (4) an intent to help one another by force if necessary against any person who may oppose them in the execution of their common purpose; (5) force or violence not merely used in (and about the common purpose) but displayed in such a manner as to alarm at least one person of reasonable firmness and courage' (Field *v*. Receiver of Metropolitan Police (1907), 2 K.B. 853, 860). (Punishment at court's discretion.) Prosecutions are not frequent. Claims for compensation from the police rate may be made, even if there is no prosecution, where a 'tumultuous' riot causes loss relating to property (*Riot (Damages) Act* (1886)). The Law Commission's Working Paper no. 82, *Offences against Public Order* (1982) suggests there should be a new statutory definition of the offence. ARP

Robbery

> A person is guilty of robbery if he steals, and immediately before or at the time of doing so, and in order to do so, he uses force on any person or puts or seeks to put any person in fear of being then and there subjected to force (*Theft Act* (1968), s. 8(1)).

For the meaning of 'steals' see *theft*. The combination of stealing with some degree of violence or apprehended violence is what has always characterised robbery; it also indicates the wide variety of activity which is encompassed. As 'mugging' (street robbery of personal property), it has constantly invited the attention of the *media* (q.v.) in recent years. Robbery regularly amounts to fewer than 1 per cent of all serious offences recorded by the police per annum in England and Wales, though the average annual rate of increase 1970–80 was about 9 per cent compared with 5 per cent or so for all serious offences together.

Home Office (1981), *Criminal Statistics, 1980*; F. McClintock and E. Gibson (1961), *Robbery in London*. ARP

Role careers. See *Careers*, *criminal role*.

Royal prerogative In constitutional theory, the residue of power inherent in the sovereign, following processes of subtraction in the development of democratic institutions. In practice, in the criminal justice systems of Great Britain, this means that the sovereign (by convention on the advice of a Home Secretary) may exercise the royal prerogative to pardon offenders or to commute their sentences. In this way sentence of death was not infrequently commuted to one of life imprisonment. ARP

S

Scapegoat, the An individual or group selected out for retributive punishment by the rest of society in the absence of being able to identify, capture or punish the real perpetrators of a crime or series of them. Choosing a scapegoat satisfies public desire to 'see something done' and to restore an equilibrium disturbed by crime.

See also *Stereotype*.   DPW

Schizophrenia. See *Mental abnormality*.

Science, police. See *Police science*.

Secondary deviance. See *Primary deviance*.

Secure units Such units for children in community homes perform two functions. They are used as a remand location for those under the age of sixteen awaiting court appearance who are charged with serious offences, and also they provide a comprehensive assessment period for children who have re-peatedly disrupted the life of open residential establishments as well as for those who are suicidal or a danger to others around them through violence. They arose as a result of a riot at Carlton School (an approved school) in 1959, which led to the initial establishment of three secure units as a crisis measure. (The first to be built was Kingswood, in 1964, the others being Redhill, in 1965 and Redbank School in 1966.) Their numbers are now rapidly growing. They are run by the DHSS, and their operation is governed by the Community Homes Regulations (1972). They are effectively miniature children's prisons, with varying levels of security and a high staff:inmate ratio. Secure units are expensive to operate and their main achievement in this very difficult area is *incapacitation* (q.v.)

See P. Cawson and M. Martell (1979), *Children Referred to Closed Units*, DHSS Statistics & Research Division, Research Report no. 5; M. Hoġhughi (1978), *Troubled and Troublesome*; Howard League Working Party (1977), *'Unruly' Children in a Human Context: Types, Costs and Effects of Security*; S. Millham, R. Bullock and K. Hosie (1978), *Locking Up Children*.   DPW

Security.   See *Prison security*.

Sedition   A vague common law offence which

embraces all those practices, whether by word, deed or writing, which are calculated to disturb the tranquility of the State, and lead ignorant persons to endeavour to subvert the Government and the laws of the Empire. The objects of sedition generally are to induce discontent and insurrection and to stir up opposition to the Government, and bring the administration of justice into contempt; and the very tendency of sedition is to incite the people to insurrection and rebellion (R. v. Sullivan, 1868, quoted by the Law Commission (1977), *Treason, Sedition and Allied Offences*, Working Paper no. 72, p. 4).

Prosecutions for sedition have been very rare in modern times and the Law Commission's provisional view is that there is no need for a separate category for this crime, as there is already a sufficient range of offences in the law.   ARP

Segregation units   Separate confinement in prison for violent and refractory inmates has always existed in some form and is not new, but the Mountbatten Report *Report of the Inquiry into Prison Escapes and Security* (Cmnd 3175, 1966) (see *prison security*) gave it that appearance when it proposed that 'segregation units' should be introduced for inmates who pose a special problem. These units essentially are a means of isolating subversive or disruptive men from others.

See also *Control units*.   DPW

Self-mutilation   This self-injury through cutting, burning (with cigarette ends) and *tattooing* (q.v.) is relatively common amongst inmates and patients of both custodial institutions and mental hospitals. It may be related to boredom, to pre-existing mental illness or to suicidal attempts (e.g. wrist- or stomach-slashing).

See R. Johnson (1977), *Culture and Conflict in Confinement*; H.M. Cookson (1977), 'A survey of self-injury in a closed prison for women', *BJC*, 17, 332.   DPW

Self-report studies   Thirty years ago, the extent of criminal and delinquent behaviour was almost invariably measured using official criminal statistics. However, increasing dissatisfaction with the accuracy of these statistics led to the development of alternative methods of measuring such behaviour, and one of the most popular of these is the self-report questionnaire. Typically, people are presented with descriptions of delinquent or fringe-delinquent acts (often on cards), and are asked to say how often they have committed each within a specified period (e.g. the last year).

This method was popularised in the United States by F.I. Nye and J.F. Short (1957), in *ASR*, 22, 56. It was first used in England with young males in the 1960s by W.A. Belson, H.B. Gibson and H.D. Willcock. It has since been used with young females in England by A. Campbell and others, and it is now being used with older people.

The method typically suggests that the criminal or delinquent acts which are recorded in the official statistics are the tip of a large iceberg of unrecorded crime. For example, D.J. West and D.P. Farrington (1977), in *The Delinquent Way of Life*, found that only 13 per cent of admitted burglaries led to convictions, and only about 6 per cent of admitted offences of taking motor vehicles. These figures were much less than the police 'clear-up' rates for these offences at that time, which were about 36 per cent, because many offences admitted in self-report question-naires never appear in any official record.

While the proportion of offences leading to an official record was very low, the proportion of offenders who were convicted sooner or later was relatively high. West and Farrington found that 62 per cent of youths who admitted burglary had been convicted of it, and 38 per cent of youths who admitted taking vehicles. Self-report studies suggest that, while official records seem to be very inaccurate as a measure of the incidence of *offending*, they are more valid if used to identify *offenders*.

In some of the early American research, it seemed that key variables which were strongly related to official delinquency (e.g. sex, race and social class) were much less related to self-reported delinquency. This led to suggestions that there were systematic biases in the official processing of offenders. The most recent exhaustive review of the literature by M.J. Hindelang, T. Hirschi and J.G. Weis (Beverley Hills, 1981), in *Measuring Delinquency*, concludes that there are few discrepancies between results obtained with the two measures, and that the existing minor discrepancies do not reflect official biases.

A crucial question is the extent to which self-reports of offending are valid. An earlier review of this by D.P. Farrington (1973), *JCLC*, 64, 99, and the book by M.J. Hindelang *et al.* both conclude that they are, with young white males. There are suggestions in current research that this may not be true of older people, blacks or females.   DPF

S

Sentence In its widest meaning – and as normally used – the word refers to all methods of dealing with convicted offenders. The courts' powers are many and varied, and are described herein under specific headings. In general it should be noted that a *Magistrates' Court* (q.v.) cannot normally sentence an offender to more than six months' imprisonment, though it may commit him for sentence to the fuller jurisdiction of the Crown Court, if it has convicted him of an *indictable offence* (q.v.).

ARP

Sentencing The practice of sentencing involves the application of legal rules in a process which, though largely discretionary, features many principles formulated on the appellate review of sentences. A judge before whom an offender has been convicted does not have to give reasons for his sentence, but must act within the law and in accordance with principle. The work of the Court of Appeal (Criminal Division) has been fully analysed and described by D. Thomas (2nd ed., 1979), *Principles of Sentencing*, and R. Cross and A. Ashworth (3rd ed., 1981), *The English Sentencing System*.

See also *Punishment, theories of*; *Punishment types, modern*.

ARP

Separate system A system of prison administration emerging in the 1830s and gaining ascendancy in the 1850s. It was derived from the *solitary system* (q.v.), and under it men remained in their cells, eating and working there under a rule of silence, but communication was allowed with the chaplain and with officers.

SEXUAL OFFENCES

Total separation from other prisoners was insisted upon, and during exercise hoods were worn. The emphasis was on deterrence and useless and pointless forms of work. By 1877, the *stage system* (q.v.) became superimposed on the basic outline of the separate system, which was finally abandoned during the First World War. See W.J. Forsythe (1980), 'The aims and methods of the separate system', *Social Policy and Administration*, 14 (3), 249.   DPW

Sexual offences   English law penalises a wide variety of sexual activity, some of it for no other reason than that it is thought to be immoral. Without denying the validity of this point of view, there is also much support for the rather different view that the function of the law in this area is

> to preserve public order and decency, to protect the citizen from what is offensive or injurious, and to provide sufficient safeguards against exploitation and corruption of others, particularly those who are specially vulnerable because they are young, weak in body or mind, inexperienced, or in a state of special physical, official or economic dependence (Wolfenden Report, 1957).

In 1980 the Criminal Law Revision Committee *Working Paper on Sexual Offences* took the same approach. The offences dealt with herein are the principal ones listed under the heading 'Serious Sexual Offences' in the *Criminal Statistics*. The number of such offences recorded annually by the police has, for many years, been a very small proportion (around 1 per cent) of all recorded serious crime.

Committee on Homosexual Offences and Prostitution, *Report* (Cmnd 247, 1957) (Wolfenden Report); Criminal Law Revision Committee (1980), *Working Paper on Sexual Offences*.

See also *Abduction*; *Bigamy*; *Buggery*; *Child molestation*; *Defilement*; *Homosexuality*; *Incest*; *Indecency*; *Indecent assault*; *Indecent exposure*; *Procuration*; *Prostitution*; *Rape*; *Soliciting*; *Unlawful sexual intercourse*.   ARP

Shoplifting   The slang term for a form of theft in which retail goods are stolen from shops during opening hours. The crime has been known to exist since 1597, and the word itself is first recorded in 1673. The growth in the use of self-service shops in the 1950s necessitated by the cost of shop labour led to a dramatic increase in shoplifting rates (cf. D.P.Walsh (1978), *Shoplifting: Controlling a Major Crime*). It is not the case that the female sex is over-represented among shoplifters (see H. Angenent (1981), 'Shoplifting: a review', *Criminology and Penology Abstracts*, 21 (3), 1). DPW

Shot-drill. See *Prison*.

Silent system A system of prison administration under which prisoners were compelled to be silent at all times. Men slept and ate alone in their cells, but worked together in association. This system was introduced to replace the *solitary system* (q.v.) in Auborn penitentiary in New York State and from 1830 was copied by many English prisons. Severe punishments were used to try to enforce silence, but prisoners countered this merely by developing non-verbal communication to a very high level. Up until about 1849, both the silent and the *separate system* (q.v.) were operating in parallel; from then on with the building of Pentonville prison the separate system gained unrivalled supremacy. For a discussion of the Auborn silent system see B. McKelvey (Chicago, 1936), *American Prisons*. DPW

Smuggling A crime of great antiquity and unclear frequency involving the unlawful importation of goods for sale from overseas, (now) contrary to the *Customs and Excise Act* (1952). Modern smuggling involves planes or boats and although items carried may vary, narcotics, gold and jewels, currency, alcohol or indecent publications are commonly smuggled. DPW

Social class The basic concern with social class is the inequality of income, wealth and access to opportunity (e.g. education) which it represents. Given that much identified crime is committed by the working class (but see *white-collar crime*), the central issue has been to what extent is this caused by class affiliation? Varying responses have emerged as follows:

(1) Positivist approaches have merely tried to specify which types of offence are linked to which social class.

(2) Marxist approaches have emphasised the inevitability of working-class crime given (a) the adverse economic position of the working class and (b) interpretation of the criminal law as an instrument constructed and used by the ruling group to

restrain the working class and punishing chiefly actions likely to be committed only by them.

(3) *Strain theory* (q.v.) regards the concentration of crime in the working class as reflecting blocked opportunities.

(4) *Radical criminology* (q.v.), on the other hand, sees social order as a pluralism of values and argues that value consensus is an illusion manipulated by the economically powerful in an attempt to imprint their values on widely diverse groups (classes). This is achieved by their control over both ideological and social control apparatus. Hence differences in crime committed by different classes are seen merely as the eruption of plural values through this patina.

(5) Recent studies (cf. *hidden crime, self-report studies*) have, however (while accepting working-class vulnerability to arrest and prosecution), anyway challenged the assertion that crime *is* concentrated in the working class, increasingly revealing a wide scatter of criminality across social classes, relatively little of which is reported.

See J. Braithwaite (1981), 'The myth of social class and criminality reconsidered', *ASR*, 46 (1), 36; D. Clelland *et al.* (1980), 'The new myth of class and crime', *Criminology*, 18 (3), 319.   DPW

Social control This term is usually applied to the range of institutions in society whose existence is designed to promote order and regulate behaviour, or to the means by which such institutions develop stability and predictability in society; the point being that all societies require some framework for regulating deviant behaviour. Principal control institutions are religion, education, law, family, and neighbourhood and community.   DPW

Social defence A programme or movement championed especially by the French jurist Marc Ancel in the late 1950s for the collaboration of criminologists with lawyers concerned in the administration of criminal justice. Fifty years earlier the term had been used by the Italian *positivists* (q.v.) as the rationale for measures to deal with criminals suggested by the biological, psychological and sociological factors thought to cause their behaviour. In 1949 an International Society of Social Defence was formed in Italy which organised international conferences, and in this arena a revised version of Social Defence emerged which emphasised the individual responsibility of the criminal and asserted that his social re-adaptation depended on individualised treatment. Now, with widespread scepticism as to what treatment can achieve, Social Defence appears to be rather a spent force. See M. Ancel (1965), *Social Defence: a Modern Approach to Criminal Problems.*   ARP

Social disorganisation A term expressing the belief that certain socially disorganised areas existed, peopled by immigrants, the unemployed, criminals, single-parent families, etc., which were fertile breeding-grounds for deviance. (See, for example, M. Elliott and F.E. Merrill (N.Y., 1961), *Social Disorganisation.*) From P. Wilmott and M. Young's *Family and Kinship in East London* (1957), it became clear that slum life, far from being disorganised, is in fact highly organised, and it is also now accepted that much crime and deviance is similarly anything but disorganised, hence the term has fallen into desuetude.

See also *Area studies*.   DPW

Social problems The dangers in a 'problems'-oriented approach are twofold. First, 'problems' may be generated by *moral panics* (q.v.) rather than possessing any absolute substance, and second, treating an issue as a discrete 'problem' ignores its context and relationship with the wider whole of which it is a part. The list of problems can of course be multiplied *ad nauseam* too. This term, now little used, was fashionable in the 1960s.   DPW

Social work From a criminological point of view, the importance of social work lies in its provision of an alternative framework for dealing with juvenile offenders from the rationale developed by the justice system. With the exception of *Probation* Orders (q.v.), the courts dispense decisions which either bind over the defendant or punish him. Since the nineteenth century, reformers have urged a distinction to be made in favour of juveniles, allowing for their immaturity, and permitting programmes of supervision, education or training. In nineteenth-century Britain, Mary Carpenter pioneered a system which allowed courts to send children below the age of criminal responsibility to 'industrial schools', and those under fourteen to 'reformatories'. In the USA, a more comprehensive Act in 1904 required courts to consider the welfare of juvenile offenders, and charged the public assistance authorities with providing for their training. Although an Act of 1908 set up *Juvenile Courts* (q.v.) in England and Wales, their jurisdiction was more traditional.

After the Second World War in England and Wales, the creation of local authority Children's Departments provided a national service for the care of children deprived of normal family life, which aimed to secure their best development. Certain Children's Departments pioneered attempts at diverting juvenile offenders from the approved schools (the successors of reformatories) into the local authority child care system. Interest in the experiments, carried out in Oxfordshire particularly, led the Labour Party to commit itself to reform of the juvenile justice system. The most thoroughgoing changes were in Scotland, where 'Children's Panels' replaced the courts, and parents and social workers negotiated with lay panels about difficult children. In England and Wales, the *Children and Young Persons Act* (1969) represented a compromise between the new ideas and traditional ones, and has never been fully implemented. Even so, it has been widely attacked as attempting to understand delinquency in terms of family maladjustment, and substituting open-ended 'Care Orders' for determinate sentences. The Act was implemented precisely at a time when American lawyers and criminologists were active in discrediting the 'welfare model' of juvenile justice in the USA, arguing that it caused injustice and was of unproved efficacy in reforming offenders. In England and Wales, the Act has not resulted in fewer juveniles being given custodial sentences; indeed, the numbers in juvenile detention centres and borstals have risen dramatically, while the proportion under Supervision Orders in the community have declined. Some criminologists have argued that this is an inevitable consequence of the imposition of a misguided 'welfare model'. Others suggest that it is rather an indication of the stronger 'law and order' lobby, since there is a parallel increase in orders of imprisonment for adults, and decline in the use of Probation Orders.

Labour Party (1964), *Crime a Challenge to Us All* (Longford Report); J. Carlebach (1970), *Caring for Children in Trouble*; J. Packman (1981), *The Child's Generation*; P. Parsloe (1978), *Juvenile Justice in Britain and the United States*; D. Thorpe, D. Smith, J. Paley and C. Green (1980), *Out of Care*.　　wjoj

Sociopath, the. See *Psychopath*.

Soliciting By a woman: see *prostitution*. By a man: it is an offence for a man persistently to solicit or importune in a public place for immoral purposes (*Sexual Offences Act* (1956), s. 32). Persistence implies a degree of repetition, of either more than one invitation to one person, or a series of invitations to different people, or simply a continuing activity. In practice the offence is used against men who solicit for homosexual purposes, but 'immoral' is not defined and remains a matter of fact. See M. Cohen (1982), 'Soliciting by men', *CLR*, 349.

ARP

Solitary confinement. See *Prison discipline*.

Solitary system This system of prison administration was used in Philadelphia, Pennsylvania from 1790 onwards (it was also tried and rejected at Auburn penitentiary). Under it, all prisoners spent the first part of their sentence in solitary confinement and serious offenders the entire sentence. Work was performed in the cells. The object of this Quaker-inspired conception was that in solitude a man could more easily meditate on his crimes and reform himself. It became the initial model for the English *separate system* (q.v.)

See H.E. Barnes (Indianapolis, 1927), *The Evolution of Penology in Pennsylvania*; N.K. Teeters (Philadelphia, 1955), *The Cradle of the Penitentiary: the Walnut Street Jail at Philadelphia 1773–1835*.

DPW

Somatotype W.H. Sheldon (1899–1977), in *The Varieties of Human Physique* (with S.S. Stevens and W.B. Tucker, N.Y., 1940), classified body type using three dimensions. Endomorphs had round, soft bodies, mesomorphs were hard and wide-shouldered and ectomorphs were thin and delicate. An individual was rated on a seven-point scale in respect of each dimension, his rating being known as his 'somatotype'. The same procedure of three dimensions and a seven-point scale for each was used for personality tendency, the result for an individual being his Index of Temperament (IT); cf. *The Varieties of Human Temperament* (with S.S. Stevens, N.Y., 1942). Sheldon sought to show that IT and somatotype were closely correlated (psychologically not proven). In his *Varieties of Delinquent Youth* (N.Y., 1949), he concluded that mesomorphy was the commonest criminal body-build.

See also *Constitutional theories*.

DPW

S

SPECIAL HOSPITALS

Special hospitals Hospitals provided and directly managed by the Secretary of State for Social Services for persons subject to detention under the *Mental Health Act* (1959), 'who in his opinion require treatment under conditions of special security on account of their dangerous, violent or criminal propensities' (*National Health Service Reorganisation Act* (1977), s. 40). There are four: Broadmoor, Rampton, Moss Side and Park Lane, taking 2,000 or so patients in all. They take only those subject to compulsory detention, though this may not necessarily be the outcome of criminal proceedings.   ARP

Stage system A system of prison administration in which a prisoner progresses during his sentence from one stage to another, each characterised by a different regimen, with each successive stage decreasing in severity and increasing in privileges. Based on the *marks system* (q.v.), the stage system was taken over as the basis for *penal servitude* (q.v.) when that was introduced in 1853. Staging had a profound effect on local prisons, where it was introduced from about 1878 onwards. There were four stages. Stage 1 lasted a month and during this a plank bed and bedding were provided but no mattress. Having earned enough marks, a man progressed to stage 2 where he was given a better diet and a mattress twice a week. At stage 3 (usually the end of the third month), further privileges were given as regards diet and bedding and with stage 4 a man got a mattress every night and the privilege of letters and visits. The sentence of *preventive detention* (q.v.) also used stages. In recent years, since the tendency with the system was for progress to be automatic, it has gradually given way to a policy of providing uniform conditions and withdrawing privileges only for abuse of them or for other misbehaviour.

See also *Separate system*.   DPW

Statistics. See *Official statistics*.

Status degradation Originally used by H. Garfinkel (1956), in 'Conditions of successful degradation ceremonies', *AJS*, 61, 421, to refer to the way in which in court and in custodial institutions an offender is exposed to a ritual role-stripping process, which is humiliating and drastically reduces self-esteem. What he stood for before the act which resulted in his court appearance is now of no consequence.

See also *Total institutions*.   DPW

Stereotype An unreal image of a person or group who is socially distant (but possibly physically close), formed in the absence of knowledge and used because of a periodic local need to have some view on such a person or group (or alleged means of identifying them) on which to base action or reaction. These condensed and distorted conceptions are used especially frequently where groups have low *visibility* (q.v.), such as criminals. See D. Chapman (1968), *Sociology and the Stereotype of the Criminal.* DPW

Stigma/Stigmatisation Suffering a degraded status and permanent hardship in social and economic relationships as a result of owning, permanently or temporarily, an attribute or condition considered by most people in the society to be wrong or bad in itself, or indicative of wrongness. The process of stigmatisation has been well described by E. Goffman (1968), *Stigma: Notes on the Management of Spoiled Identity.*
See also *Scapegoat.* DPW

S

Strain theory This theory emerged from the work of Merton (1964, 1966) and Cloward and Ohlin (1960) and a concise statement is to be found in Young (1981). Crime is seen as arising, not as the result of *pathology* (q.v.), but as the result of the occupancy of particular statuses in society. The Self is a product of social order and acquires through socialisation culturally defined means to achieve culturally defined goals. Crime and deviance are generated as a result of a disjunction between culturally induced aspirations of individuals (to achieve success goals) and the structurally determined opportunities to reach them. Constant emphasis on success in society and its possible attainment consistently contradicts the actual opportunities facing many people, and it is at the bottom of society that the strain of blocked opportunities to cultural goals is greatest and where the greatest amount of crime should (and does) occur. These strains are experienced by whole groups, and the concept of *sub-culture* (q.v.) is developed to describe jointly elaborated solutions to common problems. Crime and deviance are an attempt to solve the problems confronting groups in particular structural locations.
R. Cloward and L. Ohlin (Chicago, 1960), *Delinquency and Opportunity*; R.K. Merton (N.Y., 1964), 'Anomie, anomia and social interaction', in M. Clinard, ed., *Anomie and Deviant*

STRICT LIABILITY

Behaviour; R.K. Merton (N.Y. 1966), 'Social problems and
sociological theory', in R.K. Merton and R. Nisbet, eds.,
Contemporary Social Problems (2nd ed.); J. Young (1981),
'Thinking seriously about crime', in M. Fitzgerald, G. McLen-
nan and J. Pawson, eds, *Crime and Society*.   DPW

Strict liability   In some parts of the criminal law an offender
may be penalised even if he has not acted intentionally or
recklessly, that is to say without *mens rea* (q.v.). Such offences
have mostly come to be grouped together under the heading
'Regulatory Offences', since they regulate activities in which
the welfare of the general public is involved, e.g. the sale of
food and drugs. Liability is strict because an offender may
himself have taken reasonable care to avoid possible harm;
indeed it is often thought to be too strict. See G. Williams
(1978), *Textbook of Criminal Law*, c. 42.   ARP

Sub-culture   A group or groups inside the host culture with
different *values* (q.v.) from it, evident through their expression
in deviant behaviours. When A.K. Cohen first used the term in
Delinquent Boys: the Culture of the Gang (Chicago, 1955), he
was referring to structures previously dismissed as 'gangs' and
he used this concept to emphasise the underlying different
world view of such groups characterised and expressed in
'non-utilitarian, malicious, negativistic forms of delinquency'.
R. Cloward and L. Ohlin, in *Delinquency and Opportunity: a
Theory of Delinquent Gangs* (Chicago, 1960), saw the origin of
sub-cultures in a reaction to an ambiguous location in two
opportunity structures (working and middle class), and identified three specific forms of them, criminal (rationally using
crime to make money), conflict (concerned exclusively with
violence) and retreatist (withdrawing from society through the
use of alcohol or drugs). These latter were seen as 'double-
failures', failing to gain lodgement in either the legitimate world
or the criminal sub-culture. This is broadly the position taken in
strain theory (q.v.), which sees sub-cultural formation as a
(defensive) structural reaction to blocked opportunities. Good
descriptive studies of such groups are given by M. Brake (1980),
The Sociology of Youth Culture and Youth Sub-cultures and J.
Young (1971), *The Drugtakers*. D. Downes, however, in his
work on London gangs, *The Delinquent Solution* (1966),
suggested that any adjustment problems for the working-class
youngster were rapidly resolved not by sub-cultural mem-

bership but by the ultimate affirmation of traditional working-class values following a brief period of dissociation.

See also *Contra-culture*.   DPW

Subnormality.   See *Mental impairment*.

Summary offence   Those less serious crimes declared to be triable only in a *Magistrates' Court* (q.v.) and therefore by summary trial without a jury, as distinct from trial on indictment (see *Crown Court*). Many *indictable offences* (q.v.) may also be tried summarily; they are classified as 'offences triable either way'. See *Magistrates' Courts Act* (1980), ss. 17–28 & Sched. 1.   ARP

S

Supervision Order   *Juveniles* (q.v.) guilty of any offence may be ordered by the court to be supervised by the local authority or, sometimes, by a probation officer, for a maximum of three years. The court may vary or discharge the Order within such time. Requirements may be imposed, e.g. as to residence, or for *intermediate treatment* (q.v.), or simply 'to be of good behaviour'. On breach of any requirement the court may impose a fine or make an *attendance centre* order (q.v.) while continuing with the supervision; or it may be discontinued and the offender dealt with as if he had just committed the original offence (*Children and Young Persons Act* (1969), ss. 7, 11–19; *Criminal Law Act* (1977), ss. 37, 58). Supervision, whereby 'existing ties of family and community are left undisturbed' and are augmented 'by professional help, support and guidance', is so described in Home Office, *The Sentence of the Court* (1978), p. 161, but there is little research as yet to reveal what is actually achieved or indeed the circumstances in which orders are made in the first place. See Notes (1981), 'Research in progress on juveniles and young offenders', *BJC*, 21 (3), 271.

                                    ARP

'SUS' law   That part of s. 4 of the *Vagrancy Act* (1824) dealing with suspected persons and reputed thieves loitering with intent to commit an arrestable offence. There was much criticism of this provision as used by the police in recent years, especially in relation to young males thought to be 'up to no good' in city streets. It has now been repealed, but the specific offence of Interference with Vehicles has been created to deal with those who are out to commit a theft of or from a motor vehicle or to drive one away without consent (*Criminal Attempts Act* (1981), s. 9.) See I. Dennis (1981), 'The Criminal Attempts Act 1981', *CLR*, 5 and 14.   ARP

Suspended sentence This is a penal measure used in many countries. It is essentially a sentence of *imprisonment* (q.v.) which is held in abeyance (or 'suspense') during a so-called 'operational period' fixed by the court when imposing the sentence. The offender receiving a suspended sentence is initially set at liberty; if he then commits no offence during the operational period, he does not go to prison; if a further offence is committed, the suspended term is liable to be brought into effect *in addition to* any penalty the offender may receive for the new offence. The details of the sentence vary from country to country.

The first suspended sentence laws were passed in Belgium in 1888 and France in 1891; other Continental countries followed suit. England did not do so, turning instead to the measure of *probation* (q.v.). Continental countries subsequently used the framework of their suspended sentence laws to develop measures equivalent to probation.

After the Second World War there was pressure for the introduction of the suspended sentence, but this was rejected by the Home Secretary's Advisory Council on the Treatment of Offenders in 1952 and again in 1957. However, in the *Criminal Justice Act* (1967) a Labour administration anxious to reduce the prison population introduced the measure, making it available to the courts on a discretionary basis for any prison sentence of up to two years, and mandatorily (with specified exceptions) for sentences of six months or less. But the *mandatory suspended sentence* was unpopular with sentencers, and was repealed by the *Criminal Justice Act* (1972).

There is inferential evidence that courts have used the suspended sentence in place of the fine or probation, rather than imprisonment; also that the length of suspended imprisonment is in some courts longer than if an immediate sentence had been imposed. Neither of these effects was intended or anticipated by those introducing the suspended sentence in 1967. These unintended effects largely account for the failure of the suspended sentence to reduce the prison population significantly.

The *suspended sentence supervision order* was introduced in England in 1972; it combines a suspended sentence with compulsory supervision by a probation officer. Its availability is restricted to cases where suspended imprisonment of more than six months is imposed, and hence in practice it may be ordered only by the *Crown Court* (q.v.). Only a small minority of all suspended sentences carry supervision orders.

The English statutory provisions are now consolidated in the *Powers of Criminal Courts Act* (1973), ss. 22–27. There is no power to suspend a sentence of imprisonment in Scotland, but the courts there tend to rely upon the *deferred sentence* (q.v.) to fulfil a similar function. See further M. Ancel (1971), *Suspended Sentence*; R. Sparks (1970), *CLR*, 384; A.E. Bottoms (1981), *BJC*, 21, 1.

See also *Partly suspended sentence.*   AEB

Symbolic crusade   Studies of how criminal laws come to be enacted have, in the last decade or so, moved from the periphery of criminological research to a position of some significance. A view has emerged which asserts, *inter alia*, that those involved in the processes leading to legislation may not simply be concerned to see it achieve its ends (the 'instrumental orientation') but also, or instead, be concerned about the symbolic prestige they will acquire by its successful enactment. Gusfield's study of the American Temperance Movement is the best known for its use of this analysis.

J. Gusfield (Urbana, 1963), *Symbolic Crusade*; J. Gusfield (1968), '"Moral passage": the symbolic process in public designations of deviance', *Social Problems*, 15 (2), 175; W. Carson (1974), 'Symbolic and instrumental dimensions of early factory legislation: a case study in the social origins of criminal law', in R. Hood, ed., *Crime, Criminology and Public Policy*.

See also *Moral entrepreneur.*   ARP

T

Taking conveyances ('Taking and driving away') A motor vehicle taken, without authority, for joy-riding or even for use in a criminal enterprise, does not amount to *theft* (q.v.) if it is then abandoned and no intent to deprive the owner permanently can be proved. Since 1930, however, it has been a specific offence – 'Taking and Driving Away' – now dealt with by the *Theft Act* (1968), s. 12, which applies to 'any conveyance constructed or adapted for the carriage of a person or persons whether by land, water or air'. The provision also covers those who use a conveyance knowing it to have been taken. Pedal cycles are dealt with separately with a fine of up to £50. 'Theft or Unauthorised Taking of Motor Vehicles' is a joint category in the annual Home Office statistics, and one of the largest in the tables of serious offences recorded by the police.   ARP

Target hardening This is a term applied to a method of crime prevention, much supported by the police, for instance, which aims to increase the physical security of crime targets to make the offender's job more difficult. It is based on the premise that offenders will be deterred by less vulnerable targets which are now seen as presenting too many easy opportunities for crime. Target-hardening measures recommended for burglary, for instance, include alarms and better locks; for shoplifting, detector tags on goods for sale; for vandalism, unbreakable and paint-resistant materials; the protection of vulnerable objects by grilles or meshes; the use of fibreglass instead of upholstery on train and bus seats. Criticisms of target hardening are that it is a 'cosmetic' solution which leaves the underlying causes of crime untouched, and that it might lead to a 'fortress' society if widely pursued. Also, target hardening has been challenged on the grounds that it results in a 'displacement' of crime by causing offenders to shift to unprotected targets, or to use different and possibly more injurious methods. It is unclear to

218

date how much displacement follows from target hardening, but it is intuitively likely that different offenders will be affected in different ways, and that the amount of displacement will depend on the comprehensiveness of target-hardening coverage. The best preventive gains have come from measures which have been applied to all targets: steering-column locks were made compulsory on all cars in West Germany and reduced auto crime, while in this country introducing similar locks on new cars only resulted in higher risks for unprotected cars. A more successful example of total protection in this country has been the virtual elimination of thefts from telephone kiosks after the Post Office replaced aluminium coin-boxes with stronger steel ones.   PM

Tariff A sentence which merely reflects the nature and seriousness of the offence may be said to be based on 'the tariff' – a scale of penalties which may or may not be easily discernible in a given criminal justice system. In practice other factors are nearly always taken into account as well, so as to decrease or increase the sentence or otherwise alter its character to suit the offender rather than the offence. Analytically, however, the tariff concept is useful to reveal the nature of the sentencing process. See D. Thomas (2nd ed., 1979), *Principles of Sentencing*.   ARP

Tattooing A Polynesian word for any form of permanent skin decoration made by inserting colouring material (usually ink) into the skin, with display as its object. Tattooing has been popular with soldiers and sailors for several hundred years and the practice is almost entirely confined to manual workers. Frequently people regret having been tattooed and since removal is complex and expensive (there are several prisons which have facilities for removing unwanted tattoos) in 1969 the *Tattooing of Minors Act* was passed which makes it an offence to tattoo a person under eighteen. Periodically, criminologists have investigated the link between tattooing and crime, when it appeared that many convicted men were tattooed. The most famous study was by Lacassagne, *Les Tatouages* (1881), who found among 800 convicted French soldiers that 40 per cent were tattooed. Lombroso implied that atavistic criminal types disclosed their 'primitive' love of decoration through becoming tattooed, but it must be recalled that tattooed men are easier to identify and capture than non-tattooed and also that prison inmates often tattoo themselves to relieve boredom or attract attention.

See also *Self-mutilation*.   DPW

Television, effects of Most concern about television has centred on the possibility that frequent portrayals of *violence* on it encourage violent *modelling* (q.v.) and hence promote violence. Critics of this view argue that screen violence is only *one* influence out of many and frequently is of uncertain relevance. The literature is now vast, and two of the most important studies, H.T. Himmelweit, A.N. Oppenheim and P. Vince (1958), *Television and the Child*, and W.A. Belson (1978), *Television Violence and the Adolescent Boy*, have given a 'not proven' verdict on this. Belson established a significant difference in the level of violence reported by boys according to their degree of exposure to television violence which was quite clear. Although difficult to pin down it is highly likely that excessive exposure to screen violence *does* contribute to the level of *actual* violence, if only to a small degree.

See also *Media*.   DPW

Terrorism.   See *Political crime*.

Testimony, psychology of   Although it has long been known that accounts from witnesses of crime are frequently unreliable, only recently have attempts begun to be made to systematically document and analyse this, using experimentation and simulation. E.F. Loftus in *Eyewitness Testimony* (Cambridge, Mass., 1980), concludes that most witnesses are so fallible that any given account will be incorrect in some major detail. Error sources include poor viewing conditions, brief exposure, stress, expectations, biases, personal stereotypes and memory difficulties (condensing, distorting, rationalising and the 'implanting' of new 'memories' under interrogation).

See D.P. Farrington, K. Hawkins and S.M. Lloyd-Bostock (1979), *Psychology, Law and Legal Processes*, Pt IV; J.W. Shepherd, H.D. Ellis and G.M. Davies (1982), *Identification Evidence*.   DPW

Theft   'A person is guilty of theft if he dishonestly appropriates property belonging to another with the intention of permanently depriving the other of it; and "thief" and "steal" shall be construed accordingly.' So the *Theft Act* (1968), s. 1 (1), provides; and in its first six sections contains this basic definition and deals with its constituent terms. It takes into its scope what used to be the distinct offences of embezzlement (committed in certain circumstances by a 'clerk or servant') and fraudulent conversion (committed by one entrusted with property). The Act, coupled with the amending *Theft Act* (1978), also contains various offences of dishonestly getting something by deception, fraud and blackmail. Theft with violence to the person is dealt with as *robbery* (q.v.), and theft from premises unlawfully entered as *burglary* (q.v.). With a crime probably committed by almost everyone, a definition of theft has to contend with the ingenuity of the more articulate offenders and their lawyers to avoid its embrace, especially at the 'fringes of dishonesty'. This happened over the centuries, leading to the revisions of 1968 and 1978, and it is happening still. Sixty per cent or so of all serious offences recorded annually by the police fall within the Home Office categories of theft and *handling of stolen goods* (q.v.). Of these the specific offences most frequently committed appear to be Thefts and Unauthorised Takings of Motor Vehicles, Thefts from Vehicles, and *shoplifting* (q.v.)

T

Criminal Law Revision Committee (1966), *Report on Theft and Related Offences*, Cmnd 2977; W. Belson (1975), *Juvenile Theft: the causal factors*; D. Elliott (1982), 'Dishonesty in theft: a dispensable concept', *CLR*, 395; F. Quin (1982), 'Reforming the law of theft' (letter), *CLR*, 388; J. Smith (4th ed., 1979), *The Law of Theft*. ARP

Therapeutic community The aim of such communities is to treat long-term prisoners or the mentally ill in an atmosphere as far removed as possible from that of an *institution* (q.v.), hopefully avoiding either psychologically damaging consequences for inmates or the development of an *inmate culture* (q.v.) characterised by anti-social attitudes. A supportive, permissive atmosphere exists, and inmates are encouraged to talk about their own problems and those of others in group therapy sessions, where traditional barriers between staff and inmates are broken down and both social distance and fear reduced. Evidence as to the success of such establishments is contained in J. Gunn, G. Robertson, S. Dell and C. Way (1978), *Psychiatric Aspects of Imprisonment*; R.D. Hinshelwood and N. Manning, eds. (1979), *Therapeutic Communities: Reflections and Progress*. DPW

THERAPY

Therapy Strictly, therapy means curative medical treatment (treatment by transformation), although it has now also come to mean curative psycho-social treatment (treatment by communication). The range of treatment by transformation most likely to be used in prisons or mental hospitals to deal with behavioural problems includes anti-psychotic, anti-depressant, anti-anxiety and sedative and hypnotic drugs, electroconvulsive therapy, and so on. These forms of standard medical therapy are used in relation to specific problems where medication is indicated. On the other hand, treatment by communication, increasingly popular since the 1960s and based on learning or repair models, is commonly used for problems such as addictions, sexual or interpersonal difficulties, or absence of social skills. The two main forms (although many variants have been developed) are psychotherapy and group therapy. Psychotherapy is usually divided into supportive and interpretive therapy. Both forms rely on highly structured discussions between therapist and patient alone. Supportive psychotherapy consists of advice, explanation and sometimes intervention, in a situation devoid of stress, hostility or prejudice, based on the therapist's objective assessment of the patient's needs and what the patient can feasibly achieve. Interpretive psychotherapy presumes that insight and understanding are necessary to modify behaviour generated by emotional triggers, but accepts that the origin of much emotion is not accessible to introspection. Hence a structured discussion process which makes the patient conscious of the real significance of previously repressed emotional tensions should produce greater emotional control and stability. Group therapy, by contrast, consists of a series of therapeutic sessions held in small groups of people with similar problems who are led by a non-judgmental therapist. Sessions involve unstructured open discussion with the resources of the group developing a corpus of assessment and reaction to the area under consideration, and suggesting personal therapeutic directions and pointing out consequences of courses of action. The only demands made on members are those of honesty and participation. Unlike other forms of treatment, although some therapeutic groups are based in hospitals or other institutions, some (e.g. Alcoholics Anonymous) function autonomously. Numerous other forms of therapy are available, many being derived from one or other of these basic models.

See also *Aversion therapy*; *Behaviour modification*; *Conditionability*; *Therapeutic community*.   DPW

Thought reform. See *Attitude change*.

Ticket of leave. See *Penal servitude*.

Token economy. See *Behaviour modification*.

Total institution A concept first used by Goffman in the first essay in his *Asylums* (N.Y., 1961) to refer to a place where 'a large number of people cut off from society together lead a formally administered round of life'. Characteristics of such places are: absence of communication with the outside world, work and sleep occur in the same place, authority is total, there is a 'rational plan' for reaching one specific objective and there are two cultures, staff and inmates. In such institutions (examples of which are mental hospitals, 'homes' for the elderly, prisons, concentration camps, army camps, ships, public schools and closed religious organisations), inmates are divorced from their families and, unlike normal life where money derived from work is used to buy leisure, in such places there is only work without leisure. Total institutions exert extreme pressure on a personality leading to loss of Self through absence of privacy, substitution of numbers for names, harsh rules and physical humiliation. Survival then involves outward conformity to, and inward rejection of, official aims. *Inmate culture* (q.v.) and the inmate social system are best understood as a collective reaction to life in the institution and a means of reducing the impact of the very substantial pressure.   DPW

Traffic offences. See *Driving offences*.

Transportation Expulsion from the realm of those who were believed to have done it harm was the deepest purpose of the phenomenon known as transportation, which first appears as a disposal for criminal offenders reprieved from execution or the undeserving destitute in the late sixteenth century. In the seventeenth century the system expanded and became a main disposal for those convicted of felony and others, such as recalcitrant Quakers, defined as especially subversive. Apart however from the desire to be rid of such people there were other facets of this disposal which made it attractive. That offenders could so suddenly be shipped to another continent dramatically demonstrated the irresistible power of the state, while the threat of annihilation of membership of family and community was considered a singularly effective deterrent to those who might be considering adopting a criminal way of life. In addition the colonists of America, to which transportees were at first sent, had great need of manpower, and transportation initially satisfied their need for human beings whose labour would be compulsorily available to them or who could be assigned to work on public projects. Finally, transportation as a condition of reprieve from the death penalty was justified as a merciful opportunity for felons to build a new life in a vast, pure, natural world, freed from the contamination of gin-drenched slums and criminal associates.

Numbers of transportees were small by later standards – about four and a half thousand between 1655 and 1699 – and until the American Revolution, the eastern colonies of that continent were their main destination. After 1776, however, transportation lapsed for a short while but began again in the late eighteenth century, mainly to Australasia and later Bermuda and Gibraltar. Other places such as Sri Lanka and Cape Colony were considered, but the colonists there reacted most strongly against their lands being used for such a purpose.

By 1820 evangelical and medical men had begun to deplore the conditions which prevailed both before the voyages (cf. *hulks*) and during them, and they also felt that transportees ought to be subjected to the kinds of moral recasting and rational discipline which were proposed as bases of prison régimes by Howard and his successors. Consequently, new convict prisons were established in England to hold transportees often for lengthy periods prior to their voyage so that reformative, regenerative influences might be brought to bear (e.g. the *separate system*), and after 1840 on the Australasian continent itself more organised, regulated controls and systems such as labour gangs and convict prisons were established to continue such disciplines when the transportees arrived. By 1850 the prevailing approach was to induce good behaviour by offering staged improvement of conditions, and convicts might graduate from carceral internment to conditional freedom by docile, obedient, industrious behaviour. After expiry of the order of transportation, which was normally seven years, fourteen years or life, the transportee might return to England if he could pay his fare.

In time, certain of the Australian colonies began to oppose this use of their continent on the grounds that they were being overwhelmed by hordes of criminals from the mother country and that they were being forced to pay for costly penal systems. In addition, many in England felt that transportation had become a popular disposal among felons, thus eroding its deterrent value. Lastly, the theories of personal and moral reclamation within a prison which were thriving in the 1840s also played some part in calling into doubt the appropriateness of such banishment. At length, in the 1850s, the sentence of *penal servitude* (q.v.) replaced transportation and placed imprisonment at the heart of the systems of disposal for more than minor offenders by the state. In 1867 the last transport ship set sail for Australia; it and its predecessors had carried to that continent alone over 108,000 people since 1800, and even this figure excludes those transported from Ireland. See A.G.L. Shaw (1966), *Convicts and the Colonies*.   WJF

Treadmill. See *Prison*.

Treason   The law of treason is still basically that of the *Treason Act* (1351), though the Law Commission are proposing to replace it. It involves 'a breach of a duty of allegiance, but this may be either a breach of personal duty to the Sovereign or a breach of a duty to the constitutional system of the realm, which has its embodiment in the Sovereign' (Law Commission (1977), p. 8). More specifically, the *Treason Acts* of (1351) (1702) and (1795) penalise the following: (1) compassing or imagining the death of the Sovereign, his Queen or his eldest son and heir, (2) violating the Sovereign's wife, or his eldest daughter unmarried or the wife of his eldest son and heir, (3) levying war against the Sovereign in his realm, (4) being adherent to the Sovereign's enemies in his realm, (5) killing the Chancellor, Treasurer or the Sovereign's Justices, in their places doing their offices, (6) by overt act attempting to prevent the succession to the Crown of the person entitled thereto. (Sentence of death by hanging is mandatory.) In modern times prosecutions for treason have occurred only during war-time. See Law Commission (1977), *Treason, Sedition and Allied Offences* (Working Paper no. 72).
ARP

Truancy   A child's absence from school without excuse, with or without parental knowledge or connivance. Educational issues aside, truants have a substantial involvement with juvenile delinquency. See for example, D.P. Farrington (1980), 'Truancy, delinquency, the home and the school', in L. Hersov and I. Berg, eds, *Out of School*. In response to this, some police forces operate truancy patrols to collect up truants (P. Ekblom (1980), 'Police truancy patrols', in R.V.G. Clarke and P. Mayhew, eds, *Designing out Crime*. DPW

Twin studies. See *Heredity*.

Typology A system of classification of crimes or criminals which results in groups defined so as to be mutually exclusive. Empirically-based typologies may be distinguished from theoretically-based ones. A useful typology should be rich in types, each of which should be easily identifiable. It should include the greatest number of offenders or offences, and it should separate criminals or their behaviour into types, each of which has different theoretical explanations appropriate to it. Many early typologies (see *constitutional theories*) are no longer regarded as helpful and have been discarded. *Typologies of criminals* have been classified by age, sex, personality type, marital status, motive, social class, last known offence and previous convictions. For example Lindesmith and Dunham (1941) distinguished individual criminals from social (those whose activities are supported by the culture), and Rich (1956) classified by motivation into proving, comforting, marauding, secondary and other. Classifying by career, Roebuck (1965) isolated thirteen types, single, double or triple pattern (dedicated to one, two or three types of offence). Gibbons (1965) based a typology on the learning of criminal roles (see *career, criminal role*), and a classification of offender adaptation to prison has been produced by Schrag (1961). *Typologies of offences* have examined motive, circumstances of the act, type of norm violated, relationship with victim and frequency of behaviour. Clinard and Quinney (1967), for example, identified nine criminal behaviour systems in their typology.

M.B. Clinard and E.T. Quinney (N.Y., 1967), *Criminal Behaviour Systems: a Typology*; D. Gibbons (Englewood Cliffs, N.J., 1965), *Changing the Lawbreaker*; A.R. Lindesmith and H.W. Dunham (1941), 'Some principles of criminal typology', *Social Forces*, 19, 307; J. Rich (1956), 'Types of stealing', *Lancet*, 2, 496; J. Roebuck (Springfield, Ill., 1965), *Criminal Typology*; C. Schrag (1961), 'A preliminary criminal typology', *Pacific Sociological Review*, 4(1), 12.

See also *Extraversion*. DPW

U

Unemployment   Of course unemployment can lead via *poverty* (q.v.) to increased crime, and this is the standard way of regarding it (Glaser and Rice, 1959; Calvin, 1981). Phillips *et al.* (1972) found a strong relationship between rising arrest rates and lower rates of labour-force participation, and at times of high unemployment those who have previously been convicted are even less likely than usual to be able to find jobs (Martin, 1962). Carr-Hill and Stern (1979), however, draw attention to the relationship between legal and illegal job opportunities which may be either mutually exclusive or different but non-exclusive. Practically many criminals divide their time between legal and illegal job opportunities (Ehrlich, 1973; Block and Heineke, 1975), but the assumption of mutual exclusiveness is usually (and erroneously) often made in relation to unemployment. Feldman (1977, p. 193) points out that offenders are more frequently out of a job than controls, change jobs more often than controls and are more likely to commit an offence when unemployed than at other times. He regards unemployment as 'best seen as a potential instigator for the performance of an already acquired criminal behaviour' (1977, p. 193). But will law-abiding people suddenly facing unemployment begin to commit offences? The effects of unemployment are more likely to be apathy, mental stress, illness and drunkenness than crime *per se* and Feldman suggests that effects should be seen in relation to the probability of re-employment; i.e. when the chances of getting another job are low, unemployment will be an instigator to crime, but when the actor sees unemployment as only temporary, and the chances of re-employment as being diminished by detection, he may be more law-abiding than when employed. (It should not be forgotten that many employed people commit offences, especially in the course of their jobs in the form of *part-time crime* (q.v.).)

227

M.K. Block and J.M. Heineke (1975), 'A labour theoretical analysis of the criminal choice', *Am. Econ. Rev.*, 65, 314; A.D. Calvin (1981), 'Unemployment among black youths: demographics and crime', *Crime and Delinquency*, 27 (2), 234; R.A. Carr-Hill and N.H. Stern (1979), *Crime, the Police and Criminal Statistics*; I. Ehrlich (1973), 'Participation in illegitimate activities: a theoretical and empirical investigation', *J. Polit. Econ.*, 81 (3), 521; M.P. Feldman (1977), *Criminal Behaviour: a Psychological Analysis*; D. Glaser and A. Rice (1959), 'Crime, age and employment', *ASR*, 24 (5), 679; J.P. Martin (1962), *Offenders as Employees*; L. Phillips, H.L. Votey and D. Maxwell (1972), 'Crime, youth and the labour market', *J. Polit. Econ.*, 80 (3), 491.   DPW

Unlawful assembly   A common law offence, punishable at the court's discretion. The Law Commission (*Offences against Public Order*, Working Paper No. 82, 1982), after a review of the differing definitions of unlawful assembly offered by the authorities, describe the elements of the offence under the following headings: (1) three or more persons; (2) on public or private property; (3) being or coming together causing apprehension of a breach of the peace; (4) the mental element (*mens rea*), which is contentious: 'The question at issue is the extent to which the activities of persons seeking lawfully to exercise a right of assembly in public should be restricted because of the likelihood of opposition from others'. There is authority for the view that persons knowing of the likelihood of opposition themselves commit the offence when opposition occurs; and there is authority to the contrary. The Law Commission's view (in suggesting that there should be a new statutory definition of the whole offence) is that what must be proved here is a course of conduct purposively engaged in which is either itself violent or 'has by means of threatening, abusive or insulting words or behaviour the object of provoking the use of violence by others' (Working Paper, p. 150).

ARP

Unlawful sexual intercourse

(1) *With a girl under thirteen.* It is an offence for a man to have unlawful sexual intercourse with a girl under the age of thirteen (*Sexual Offences Act* (1956), s. 5). This amounts to little more than 1 per cent of all serious sexual offences recorded annually by the police.

(2) *With a girl under sixteen.*It is an offence for a man to have unlawful sexual intercourse with a girl under the age of sixteen unless he reasonably believes her to be his wife, or unless he reasonably believes her to be sixteen or over and he himself is under twenty-four and has not previously been charged with a like offence (*Sexual Offences Act* (1956), s. 6). This offence constitutes 15 to 20 per cent of all serious sexual offences recorded annually by the police, but far from all of them result in prosecution; 'the law . . . is intended to protect innocent girls from corruption by vicious men; it is not intended to make criminals out of respectable young couples who are courting, often with the approval of their parents, and fall to what is one of the strongest and most natural of temptations, or to punish otherwise decent young men who are picked up by girls who are acting in effect as prostitutes' (Sir Theobald Mathew, DPP, quoted by Steer (1970), p. 30).

In these two offences 'unlawful' means outside lawful marriage, for which sixteen is now the minimum age, though in some legal systems it is lower. D. Steer (1970), *Police Cautions: a Study in the Exercise of Police Discretion*.   ARP

U

V

Vagrancy Sections of the population who combine homelessness, intermittent and casual employment, marginal attachment to the conventional institutions of society, and survival through welfare benefits, begging and minor criminal activity have been identified as constituting the problem of vagrancy. The extent of the problem has varied considerably given specific socioeconomic and historical circumstances, although it has generally remained a minority problem. The earliest reference to vagrancy in the British Isles can be traced to AD 386. Traditionally the problem has periodically been redefined in terms of economic, social and legal criteria, with moral and medical considerations playing a more current role. In Tudor England poverty and an attendant threat to social and political order have informed society's attempt to control the problem of vagrancy. Up to the Industrial Revolution vagrancy was viewed as a product of economic and social oppression in which labourers were forced into nomadic life-styles through the need by landed and commercial interests for a cheap, mobile labour force. But the economic emphasis is replaced by a concern with the criminal dimensions of the problem when the control of felons (the crime of habitual vagrancy), as opposed to the movement of labourers, becomes the prime target of control. The consolidation of the vagrancy problem in terms of criminal activity was achieved during the eighteenth century through a series of statutes designed to protect the property of merchants in a society increasingly developing its commercial and industrial infrastructure.

Since the onset of industrialisation and urbanisation vagrancy has been regarded as an object of the criminal justice system. The *Vagrancy Acts* (1824) and (1935), particularly the former, remain actively on the statute books, seeking to control begging and sleeping rough. But a significant movement parallels the impact of criminal legislation, namely the attempt by philanthropy, medicine and social work to redefine vagrancy in the language of moral reform, disease and social inadequacy. Thus at present society simultaneously regards the problem as a domain for criminal law, moral reform, medical treatment and social work rehabilitation. It is however the socio-medical conceptualisation that is striving to become the dominant paradigm by which we understand and react to vagrancy.

A variety of responses has meant the establishment of a matrix of institutional provision ranging through police cells, courts and prison; soup kitchens, shelters, common lodging houses and government reception centres; and mental hospitals, alcoholism units, day centres and rehabilitation hostels. Such provision constitutes an institutional 'revolving door' through which vagrants repeatedly pass, punctuated by a life on the streets, begging, heavy public drinking and inevitable stigmatisation.

The current interest in the socio-medical aspects has underscored the elements of individual pathology and personal inadequacy as central to the vagrancy problem. Consequently our knowledge of the social organisation of vagrancy in Britain, viewed from the standpoint of vagrants, is relatively scant. However, some work has demonstrated a close symbiotic relationship between vagrancy and the institutions seeking to control the problem. Vagrancy, then, is as much made up of the incumbents using the institutions as it is of society's attempt to find solutions to the problem.

H.M. Bahr, ed. (Toronto, 1970), *Disaffiliated Man: Essays and Bibliography on Skid Row, Vagrancy and Outsiders*; T. Cook, ed. (1979), *Vagrancy: Some New Perspectives.*   PA

Vagrants   Government and voluntary welfare agencies have currently replaced the term 'vagrants' by the more neutral-sounding term 'single homeless persons'. But the concepts by which vagrants are identified are not value free; instead they reflect particular ways of thinking and acting towards the problem. Contemporary surveys aimed at establishing the dominant features of vagrancy, stressing demographic, socio-medical and criminal aspects, have uncovered a pattern of homelessness, habitual petty crime, chronic poverty, institutional dependence and poor physical and mental health. Generally speaking vagrants live in institutions such as common lodging houses and government reception centres, hostels, hospitals and prisons, and, to a lesser extent, in derelict buildings and public spaces. As an interconnected whole, these institutions may be viewed as a form of 'open asylum' on which vagrants depend for their survival and from which they rarely escape.

By far, vagrants in contemporary Britain are male, predominantly middle-aged and of working-class background. Unlike in previous ages, women and children are not normally found amongst today's vagrant population, although there is some evidence that women and young persons of both sexes are increasingly leading the life of urban nomads. It is against this background that contemporary policy has been formulated, directing attention to the social and medical pathology of the individual rather than the structural roots of the problem, and advocating improved treatment, rehabilitation and after-care services.

The depiction of vagrants as pathological and isolated has been countered to some extent by underlining the sub-cultural dimensions of the problem. The life-style of vagrants as viewed through their eyes has revealed a complex pattern of values and survival strategies in response to the iniquities of deprivation, oppression and poverty. Within this perspective the meaning that vagrants give to their life-style is heavily shaped by the kind of ideological and practical intervention of the state and social control agencies. In spite of industrialisation and welfare provision, the persistance of widespread poverty and high unemployment means that vagrants are still with us, although their values, attitudes and behaviour have adapted to the changing circumstances of social control.

See P. Archard (1979), *Vagrancy, Alcoholism and Social Control*; H.M. Bahr (1973), *Skid Row: an Introduction to Disaffiliation.* PA

Values To value something is to have a positive attitude towards it. Something valued is something worth maintaining or worth pursuing. Values provide reasons for action. Things (including actions themselves) may be valued *instrumentally*, as means to the attainment or preservation of other values, or *intrinsically*, as having value irrespective of their usefulness. To desire something is to value it; but to value something is not necessarily to desire it, it may be to believe that it ought to be desired even when it is not desired. Moral values have this latter feature. They express ideals. They also have two other features:

(a) what has moral value for someone belongs to a class of values which overrides all other classes of value.

(b) what has moral value for someone is regarded by that person as something which all other persons ought (rationally) to value.

Because values provide reasons for action they are important in explaining human action. Actions may be explained by citing the values which guide them or by explaining how values are acquired. Sub-cultural theories of deviance explain deviance as the expression of values which are different from those embodied in the law or in custom. Differential association theory explains deviance by giving an account of how 'non-normal' values are acquired. Anomie theory explains deviance by showing how strains in a system of 'normal' values can lead to expressions of 'non-normal' values.

Some theoretical orientations treat values as freely chosen by agents (e.g. phenomenology), whereas others treat them as deterministically acquired in socialisation processes. Those who adopt the latter view sometimes treat values as autonomous (e.g. structural-functionalism) or else as products of a biological or economic substructure (e.g. certain versions of Marxism).

Values also present methodological problems. One school of thought considers that social explanations can be value free, i.e. that explanations themselves are not necessarily dependent upon any specific adherence to (moral) values. This is denied by another school, of which 'Critical Sociology' and 'Critical Criminology' are prime examples.   DB

V

Vandalism. See *Criminal damage*.

Victim, the A person who has been wronged, harmed or injured by criminal action. In *The Criminal and his Victim* (New Haven, 1948), H. von Hentig was the first to draw attention to the potential significance of the link between criminal and victim and the need for closer examination of this.

See also *Victim precipitation*; *Victim surveys*.   DPW

Victim precipitation A term first used by M.E. Wolfgang in *Patterns in Criminal Homicide* (1958). He noted that in only 14 per cent of 588 cases of homicide occurring in Philadelphia were killer and victim unknown to each other. This led him to consider the phenomenon of victim precipitation which he defined as 'A situation in which the victim was the first to show and use a deadly weapon or strike a blow in altercation'; this he found applying in 26 per cent of cases. Subsequently the use of the term has been widened to include precipitation by victims of many other offences (e.g. *shoplifting* (q.v.)). Its importance is that it directly furthered *victim surveys* (q.v.).   DPW

Victim surveys   Surveys of usually representative groups of the general public who are asked about crimes they may have experienced during a specified reference period. They were first developed and utilised in the USA for the 1967 President's Commission on Law Enforcement and the Administration of Justice. Since then the Federal government, through the US Bureau of Census, has introduced the National Crime Survey – a continuous panel survey in which information is collected every six months from 60,000 households; further periodic surveys in selected cities have also been conducted. National surveys have now also been conducted in Scandinavia, Canada, Australia and The Netherlands, while particular localities in Germany and Switzerland, for instance, have also been surveyed. In this country, the best-known early victim survey was carried out in London in 1973 by Richard Sparks and his colleagues, *Surveying Victims*, (1977) although other local surveys, for instance in Sheffield and Manchester, have recently been completed. At a national level the *General Household Survey* included some limited victimisation questions in 1972, 1973, 1979 and 1980, while a much more comprehensive survey of crime, which centres on victimisation data, was conducted in 1982 by the Home Office Research and Planning Unit (M. Hough and P. Mayhew (1983), *The British Crime Survey*, HORS no. 76).

A chief purpose of victim surveys is to provide data on the incidence of crime which is independent of official statistics relating to crimes recorded by the police. Thus they provide some estimate of the 'dark figure' of crime and, if repeated, can yield information about crime trends independent of police figures. Victim surveys can also show what social groups are most at risk to different sorts of offences, and can allow further information to be obtained on the pattern of crime (e.g. the circumstances in which it is committed and the consequences for the victim). Typically, victim surveys have been used too as a vehicle for obtaining information on crime-related issues such as why crime is not always reported to the police, respondents' fear of crime, and the precautions they take to avoid victimisation.   PM

Victimless crimes E.M. Schur in *Crimes Without Victims* (Englewood Cliffs, N.J., 1965) was the first to draw attention to a number of crimes which had no actual victim as their common unifying factor. Abortion, homosexuality and drug-taking were among those identified where the harm that is adjudged to occur is to the perpetrator rather than to a separate victim.

DPW

Vigilantes, Vigilance committees These consist of self-constituted semi-judicial bodies (in their purest form) occasionally set up to protect life and property. Of American origin, they were common in the 'Wild West'; the first to be formed arose in San Francisco in June 1851 to deal with gold-rush criminals. Such committees shaded instantly into secret societies such as the Ku Klux Klan (see H.H. Bancroft, *Popular Tribunals* (1887, 2 vols; reprinted, N.Y., 1967), and T.J. Dimsdale, *The Vigilantes of Montana* (1866; reprinted, Norman, Okla., 1978)). When vigilante groups have arisen in recent times, the tendency is for them to be much more loosely organised and temporary. They tend to arise when fear of an individual or group of criminals is acute (after a series of incidents) and when the police are seen either to fail or to be inefficient in preventing the behaviour. Such extreme groups may engage in unregulated vengeance.

See also *Aggression*; *Modelling Victim surveys*.   DPW

Violence An imprecise term for mental, or more usually physical, harm or injury. Crimes of violence are only a part of a continuum of violence, most of which is legitimated and hence only rarely called violence (e.g. violent games and 'necessary' violence in the course of punishment). Society specifies the level of acceptable violence within it, the contexts for use and the rules. The less violence there is the greater the anxiety when it does occur (nobody reports a punch on the nose in war-time). Violence is meant to be frightening and offenders often find it is enough to frighten rather than injure, hence the efficiency of the display of lethal means. The reporting of violent crime (at present about 5 per cent of all) is suspect, only the most extreme cases with severe results being reported.

See R. Block (Lexington, 1977), *Violent Crime*; J. Gunn

(1973), *Violence in Human Society*; J.A. Inciardi and A.E. Pottieger (Beverly Hills, 1978), *Violent Crime.*
See also *Aggression*; *Modelling*; *Victim surveys*.   DPW

Visibility   Most crime is highly visible due to obvious depredations, the presence of witnesses, and so forth, but many illegal acts (e.g. illegal homosexuality, abortion, drug use) may have low visibility in that they take place in private locations which in turn affects their reporting and detection (see *victimless crimes*). Factors tending to increase visibility of crime include overcrowding and lack of privacy, bureaucratisation and surveillance equipment. Increases in levels of such factors disclose more forbidden behaviour which then has to be processed as crime, whereas previously its presence was undetected.   DPW

W

White-collar crime The first use of the term 'white-collar crime' is usually attributed to Edwin H. Sutherland (1940). It subsequently formed the title of a book by him (1949). Whether or not it denotes a specific form or category of conduct of criminological significance is debated. Sutherland regarded the term as covering crime committed by the 'upper, or white-collar class' initially, confining his description to 'the . . . merchant princes and captains of finance and industry' (1940). In business, the conduct involved took the form most frequently of misrepresentation and bribery in various contexts, manipulation on the stock exchange, embezzlement and misapplication of funds, short weights and measures and misgrading of commodities. In medicine, he referred to the illegal sale of drugs, abortion, illegal services of various types, and other forms of professional misconduct.

In business or the professions white-collar crimes 'consist principally of violation of delegated or implied trust, and many of them can be reduced to two categories: (1) misrepresentation of asset values and (2) duplicity in the manipulation of power' (Sutherland, 1940; see also Cressey, 1950). Quinney (1980) says that white-collar crime is a response within capitalism to new forms of labour exploitation, to which an increasing portion of the population is subject. Later, Sutherland extended the term to include the criminal activities of corporations, argued that it was *organised crime* (q.v.), and included within it activities which did not necessarily contravene the criminal law, strictly speaking, or, if they did, did not result in a conviction. In the latter case, the criterion was whether the act was punishable, not whether someone had actually been punished (Cressey, in Sutherland, 1949). This 'looseness' has been the basis of much of the criticism of Sutherland's work (*inter alia* Tappan, 1947; Caldwell, 1958; Hartung and Burgess, 1950). Vold (1958) says

WOUNDING

that there is an 'obvious and basic incongruity' in regarding a community's leaders and more responsible elements as its criminals also.

.G. Caldwell (1958), 'A re-examination of the concept of white-collar crime', *Federal Probation*, 22, 30; D.R. Cressey (1952) 'The criminal violation of financial trust', *ASR*, 15, 738; F.E. Hartung and F.W. Burgess (1950), 'White-collar offences in the wholesale meat industry in Detroit', *AJS*, 56, 25; R. Quinney (2nd ed., N.Y., 1980), *Class, State and Crime*; E.H. Sutherland (1940), 'White-collar criminality', *ASR*, 5, 1; E.H. Sutherland (N.Y., 1949, 1961), *White-Collar Crime*, Foreword by D.R. Cressey; E.H. Sutherland and D.R. Cressey (10th ed., Philadelphia 1978), *Criminology*; P.W. Tappan (1947), 'Who is the criminal?', *ASR*, 12, 96; G.B. Vold (1958), *Theoretical Criminology*.   MB

Wounding. See *Assaults*.

X

XYY chromosomes A chromosome is a rod-shaped structure in the nucleus of each cell in the human body. There are twenty-three pairs of chromosomes in the human body, of which in females one pair is XX and in males one pair is XY. Of various known chromosomal abnormalities that of an extra Y male chromosome in males first began to attract attention in the 1960s. Price and Whatmore (1967a, b) drew a profile of characteristics of XYY males drawn from a Scottish special hospital, linking their criminal activity with the presence of an extra Y chromosome. Reviews of the studies done to date (Hoffman, 1977; Owen, 1972) give a less certain picture than some of the early claims that the basis for aggressive psychopathy had been discovered, emphasising the role of subjective judgments in identification, an equal prevalence of XYY males in the normal population and the lack of a strikingly different clinical profile for these men from controls. Even when the issues are wholly clarified, at best chromosomal abnormality can have a bearing on only a minute fraction of the criminal population.

B. Hoffman (1977), 'Two new cases of XYY chromosome complement and a review of the literature', *Canad. Psychiatric Assoc.*, 22 (8), 447; D.R. Owen (1972), 'The 47, XYY male: a review', *Psychol. Bull.*, 18, 209; W.H. Price and P.B. Whatmore (1967a), 'Behaviour disorders and pattern of crime among XYY males identified at a maximum security hospital', *Brit. Med. J.*, 1, 533; W.H. Price and P.B. Whatmore (1967b), 'Criminal behaviour and the XYY male', *Nature*, 213, 815.

X

DPW

Y

Young adult offender, the The term was first used when the Advisory Council on the Penal System was asked in 1970 to examine sentencing arrangements with respect to persons aged seventeen and under twenty-one. See the Committee's Report under the chairmanship of Sir Kenneth Younger, *Young Adult Offenders* (1974). The Younger Report recommended a generic custodial sentence, the custody and control order, to replace imprisonment, borstal training and detention centre sentences, and a new non-custodial sentence, the supervision and control order. The central purpose of the Younger Committee was: 'the encouragement of treatment of an increasing proportion of young adults in the community, and the necessary switch of resources within the penal system in order to implement this change of policy to the benefit of public and offenders alike.' However, the thrust of the Younger Report was not acted upon and the Labour government's Green Paper *Youth Custody and Supervision: a New Sentence* (Cmnd 7406, 1978), dealt only with custodial arrangements. In the event it was the Conservative government's White Paper, *Young Offenders* (Cmnd 8045, 1980) which found legislative expression in the *Criminal Justice Act* (1982) with a new sentence of youth custody (replacing imprisonment and borstal) and modifications to the detention centre sentence.

Young adults have been recognised as a special category for sentencing purposes and within the penal system for most of this century. The Gladstone Report of 1895 recommended separation from adults in order to encourage special reformative efforts. The Prison Commission, impressed by work at the Elmira Reformatory in New York State with its indeterminate sentencing arrangements, set up the first Borstal facility at Borstal village in Kent in 1902. Borstal detention, as a sentence of the courts, received statutory form in the *Prevention of*

240

Crime Act (1908). During the inter-war years borstals received much international interest, given the innovatory approach to the paradox of 'training in conditions of captivity'. In the more sombre post-war years detention centres were introduced in the *Criminal Justice Act* (1948), and not the milder community-based 'Howard Houses' which were a feature of the Criminal Justice Bill (1938).

The distinction between young adults (seventeen- to twenty-year-olds) and young persons (fourteen- to sixteen-year-olds) by the 1980s had become blurred. *The Criminal Justice Act* (1982) repealed the intent contained in the *Children and Young Persons Act* (1969) to phase out use of custodial sentences for persons under the age of seventeen. The proportion of persons under the age of twenty-one received into Prison Department institutions on sentence increased between 1960 and 1980 (with reference to males received on sentence, including fine defaulters) from 18 to 39 per cent. In 1980 almost 30 per cent of the average daily sentenced prison population were under twenty-one. With reference to non-custodial provisions for young adult offenders the *Community Service Order* is an important penal sanction, and in 1980, of all orders imposed, 52 per cent involved young adults.

See, generally, Advisory Council on the Treatment of Offenders (1959), *The Treatment of Young Offenders* (1959); A.E. Bottoms and F.H. McClintock (1973), *Criminals Coming of Age.*   AR

Young person, the   One who has attained the age of fourteen years and is under seventeen.

See also *Child*; *Juvenile*.   ARP

Young prisoner, the   By the *Criminal Justice Act* (1982), young people under twenty-one can no longer be sentenced to imprisonment; instead they may be given a sentence of *youth custody* (q.v.) and placed in a youth custody centre. (Previously youngsters aged seventeen and under twenty-one were allocated to a special, separate, Young Prisoners' Wing in prison.)
                                                                  DPW

Youth custody   This sentence was introduced by the *Criminal Justice Act* (1982). It is available for persons aged fifteen and up to twenty-one convicted of an imprisonable offence. The minimum length of sentence for males, with certain exceptions

noted below, is for periods of over four months; maximum length is up to the period for which a person of twenty-one and over might be imprisoned. For persons under the age of seventeen the maximum sentence is twelve months. With respect to females (for whom detention centre sentences are not available) and for males where a detention centre sentence is precluded, youth custody sentences of four months or less may be imposed. Youth custody is a generic sentence which replaced borstal training and imprisonment. It does not encompass, as had been recommended by the Advisory Council on the Penal System (Younger Report, *Young Adult Offenders*, (1974)), detention centres, which remain a separate custodial option. Unlike borstal, the youth custody sentence is of a determinate nature, with allowance for remission and for time spent in custody on remand. Sentences of eighteen months or more are subject to parole release and supervision as applies to adult imprisonment. For sentences of less than eighteen months there is a period of compulsory supervision for three months or until the date on which their full sentence would have expired (whichever is the longer), subject to a maximum of twelve months. There are no powers to suspend a sentence of youth custody.

The Prison Department has considerable discretion as to where to place persons sentenced to youth custody; most are placed in youth custody centres, and those with sentences of eighteen months or less are guaranteed a place in an establishment with training facilities. This threshold period can be adjusted by means of an Order approved by Parliament. Persons with sentences in excess of the threshold or serving sentences of four months or less may be placed in adult prisons. The Home Secretary also has the power to reclassify young persons (who have reached the age of eighteen) to adult status. In June 1980 there were 769 reclassified persons in the prison system. See generally, the White Paper, *Young Offenders* (Cmnd 8045, 1980), and the *Criminal Justice Act* (1982).

AR